Mrs. Geoff

Duchess

Alpha Editions

This edition published in 2023

ISBN : 9789357959285

Design and Setting By
Alpha Editions
www.alphaedis.com
Email - info@alphaedis.com

Contents

CHAPTER I.

HOW GEOFFREY DECLARES HIS INTENTION OF SPENDING THE AUTUMN IN IRELAND.

"I don't see why I shouldn't put in a month there very comfortably," says Geoffrey, indolently, pulling the ears of a pretty, saucy little fat terrier that sits blinking at him, with brown eyes full of love, on a chair close by. "And it will be something new to go to Ireland, at all events. It is rather out of the running these times, so probably will prove interesting; and at least there is a chance that one won't meet every town acquaintance round every corner. That's the worry of going abroad, and I'm heartily sick of the whole thing."

"You will get murdered," says his mother, quite as indolently, half opening her eyes, which are gray as Geoffrey's own. "They always kill people, with things they call pikes, or burn them out of house and home, over there, without either rhyme or reason."

"They certainly must be a lively lot, if all one hears is true," says Geoffrey, with a suppressed yawn.

"You are not really going there, Geoff?"

"Yes, really."

"To what part of Ireland?"

"Somewhere beyond Bantry; you have heard of Bantry Bay?"

"Oh, I dare say! I am not sure," says Lady Rodney, pettishly, who is rather annoyed at the idea of his going to Ireland, having other plans in view for him.

"Ever heard of Botany Bay?" asks he, idly; but, this question being distinctly frivolous, she takes no notice of it. "Well, it's in Ireland," he goes on, after a slight but dignified pause. "You have heard of the Emerald Isle, I suppose? It's the country where they grow potatoes, and say 'bedad'; and Bantry is somewhere south, I think. I'm never very sure about anything: that's one of my charms."

"A very doubtful charm."

"The name of the place I mean to stay at—my own actual property—is called Coolnagurtheen," goes on Geoffrey, heedless of her censure.

"Eh?" says Lady Rodney.

"Coolnagurtheen."

"I always said you were clever," says his mother, languidly; "now I believe it. I don't think if I lived forever I should be able to pronounce such a sad word as that. Do—do the natives speak like that?"

"I'll tell you when I come back," says Geoffrey,—"if I ever do."

"So stupid of your uncle to leave you a property in such a country!" says Lady Rodney, discontentedly. "But very like him, certainly. He was never happy unless he was buying land in some uninhabitable place. There was that farm in Wallachia,—your cousin Jane nearly died of chagrin when she found it was left to her, and the lawyers told her she should take it, whether she liked it or not. Wallachia! I don't know where it is, but I am sure it is close to the Bulgarian atrocities!"

"Our 'pretty Jane,' on occasions, can talk as much nonsense as—as any woman I ever met," says Geoffrey,—the hesitation being full of filial reverence; "and that may be called, I think, unqualified praise."

"Better give up the Irish plan, dear, and come with Nichols and me to the Nugents. They are easy-going people, and will suit you."

"Free-and-easy-going would be a more appropriate term, from all I have heard."

"The shooting there is capital," says his mother, turning a deaf ear to his muttered interruption, "and I don't believe there is anything in Ireland, not even birds."

"There are landlords, at least; and very excellent shooting they are, if all accounts be true," says Geoffrey, with a grin,—"to say nothing of the partridge and grouse. Besides, it will be an experience; and a man should say 'how d'ye do?' to his tenants sometimes."

"If you are going to preach to me on that subject, of course I have nothing more to say. But I wish you would come with me to the Nugents."

"My dear mother, there is hardly anything I wouldn't do for you; but the Nugent scheme wouldn't suit at all. That girl of the Cheviots is sure to be there,—you know how fond Bessie Nugent is of her?—and I know she is bent on marrying me."

"Nonsense! Would you have me believe you are afraid of her?"

"I am afraid of her; I was never so afraid of any one before. I have made it the business of my life to avoid her ever since last New Year's Day, when some kind fellow told me it was leap-year. You know I never yet said 'No' to any one, and I shouldn't dare begin by saying it to Miss Cheviot. She has such a stony glare, and such a profusion of nose!"

"And a profusion of gold, too," says Lady Rodney, with a sigh.

"I hope she has, poor soul: she will want it," says Geoffrey, feelingly; and then he falls to whistling the "Two Obadiahs" softly, yet with a relish, beneath his breath.

"How long do you intend to banish yourself from civilized life?"

"A month, I dare say. Longer, if I like it; shorter, if I don't. By the by, you told me the other day it was the dream of your life to see me in Parliament, now that 'Old Dick' has decided on leading a sedentary existence,—a very stupid decision on his part, by the way, so clever as he is."

"He is not strong, you see: a little thing knocks him up, and he is too impressionable for a public career. But you are different."

"You think I am not impressionable? Well, time will tell. I shouldn't care about going into the House unless I went there primed and loaded with a real live grievance, Now, why should I not adopt the Irish? Consider the case as it stands: I go and see them; I come home, raving about them and their wretched condition, their cruel landlords, their noble endurance, magnificent physique, patient suffering, honest revenge, and so forth. By Jove! I feel as if I could do it already, even before I've seen them," says Mr. Rodney, with an irreverent laugh.

"Well don't go to Dublin, at all events," says her mother, plaintively. "It's wretched form."

"Is it? I always heard it was rather a jolly sort of little place, once you got into it—well."

"What a partisan you do make!" says Lady Rodney, with a faint laugh. "Perhaps after all we should consider Ireland the end and aim of all things. I dare say when you come back you will be more Irish than the Irish."

"It is a good thing to be in earnest over every matter, however trivial. As I am going to Ireland, you will advise me to study the people, would you not?"

"By all means study them, if you are really bent on this tiresome journey. It may do you good. You will at least be more ready to take my advice another time."

"What a dismal view you take of my trip! Perhaps, in spite of your forebodings, I shall enjoy myself down to the ground, and weep copiously on leaving Irish soil."

"Perhaps. I hope you won't get into a mess there, and make me more unhappy than I am. We are uncomfortable enough without that. You know you are always doing something bizarre,—something rash and uncommon!"

"How nice!" says Geoffrey, with a careless smile. "Your 'faint praise' fails 'to damn'! Why, one is nothing nowadays if not eccentric. Well," moving towards the door, with the fox-terrier at his heels, "I shall start on Monday. That will get me down in time for the 12th. Shall I send you up any birds?"

"Thanks, dear; you are always good," murmurs Lady Rodney, who has ever an eye to the main chance.

"If there are any," says Geoffrey, with a twinkle in his eye.

"If there are any," repeats she, unmoved.

CHAPTER II.

HOW GEOFFREY GOES TO IRELAND AND WHAT HE SEES THERE.

It is early morn. "The first low breath of waking day stirs the wide air." On bush and tree and opening flower the dew lies heavily, like diamonds glistening in the light of the round sun. Thin clouds of pearly haze float slowly o'er the sky to meet its rays; and

Envious streaksDo lace the severing clouds in yonder east.

Geoffrey, with his gun upon his shoulder, trudges steadily onward rejoicing in the freshness of the morning air.

To his right lies Bantry Bay, that now is spreading itself out in all its glory to catch the delicate hues of the sky above. They rush to greet it, and, sinking deep down into its watery embrace, lie there all day rocked to and fro by the restless ocean.

From the hills the scent of the heather is wafted towards him, filling him with a subtle keen sense of youth and gladness and the absolute joy of living. His good dog is at his heels; a boy—procured from some neighboring cabin, and warranted not to wear out, however long the journey to be undertaken or how many miles to travel—carries his bag beside him.

Game as yet is not exactly plentiful: neither yesterday nor the day before could it be said that birds flock to his gun; there is, indeed, a settled uncertainty as to whether one may or may not have a good day's sport. And yet perhaps this very uncertainty gives an additional excitement to the game.

Here and there a pack is discovered, so unexpectedly as to be doubly welcome. And sometimes a friendly native will tell him of some quiet corner where "his honor" will surely find some birds, "an be able in the evenin' to show raison for his blazin'." It is a somewhat wild life, but a pleasant one, and perhaps, on the whole, Mr. Rodney finds Ireland an agreeable take-in, and the inhabitants of it by no means as eccentric or as bloodthirsty as he has been led to believe. He has read innumerable works on the Irish peasantry, calculated to raise laughter in the breasts of those who claim the Emerald Isle as their own,—works written by people who have never seen Ireland, or, having seen it, have thought it a pity to destroy the glamour time has thrown over it, and so reduce it to commonplaceness.

He is, for instance, surprised, and indeed somewhat relieved, when he discovers that the drivers of the jaunting-cars that take him on his shooting-expeditions are not all modern Joe Millers, and do not let off witty remarks, like bombshells, every two minutes.

He is perhaps disappointed in that every Irish cloak does not conceal a face beautiful as a houri's. And he learns by degrees that only one in ten says "bedad," and that "och murther?" is an expression almost extinct.

They appear a kindly, gentle, good-humored people,—easily led, no doubt (which is their undoing), but generous to the heart's core; a people who can speak English fluently (though with a rich brogue) and more grammatically than the Sassenachs themselves (of their own class), inasmuch as they respect their aspirates and never put an *h* in or leave one out in the wrong place.

The typical Irishman, in whom Lever delighted, with his knee-breeches and long-tailed coat, his pig under one arm and his shillalah under the other, is literally nowhere! The caubeen and the dhudheen which we are always hearing about may indeed be seen, but they are very usual objects in all lands, if one just alters the names, and scarcely create astonishment in the eyes of the on-looker.

The dhudheen is an institution, no doubt, but the owner of it, as a rule, is not to be found seated on a five-barred gate, with a shamrock pinned in his hat and a straw in his mouth, singing "Rory O'More" or "Paddy O'Rafferty," as the case may be. On the contrary, poor soul, he is found by Geoffrey either digging up his potatoes or stocking his turf for winter use.

Altogether, things are very disappointing; though perhaps there is comfort in the thought that no one is waiting round a corner, or lying *perdu* in a ditch, ready to smash the first comer with a blackthorn stick, or reduce him to submission with a pike, irrespective of cause or reason.

Rodney, with the boy at his side, is covering ground in a state of blissful uncertainty. He may be a mile from home, or ten miles, for all he knows, and the boy seems none the wiser.

"Where are we now?" says Geoffrey, suddenly, stopping and facing "the boy."

"I don't know, sir."

"But you said you knew the entire locality,—couldn't be puzzled within a radius of thirty miles. How far are we from home?"

"I don't know, sir. I never was abroad before, an' I'm dead bate now, an' the bag's like lead."

"You're a nice boy, you are!" says Mr. Rodney; "Here, give me the bag! Perhaps you would like me to carry you too; but I shan't, so you needn't ask me. Are you hungry?"

"No," says the boy valiantly; but he looks hungry, and Geoffrey's heart smites him, the more in that he himself is starving likewise.

"Come a little farther," he says, gently, slinging the heavy bag across his own shoulders. "There must be a farmhouse somewhere."

There is. In the distance, imbedded in trees, lies an extensive farmstead, larger and more home-like than any he has yet seen.

"Now, then, cheer up, Paddy!" he says to the boy: "yonder lies an oasis in our howling wilderness."

Whereat the boy smiles and grins consumedly, as though charmed with his companion's metaphor, though in reality he understands it not at all.

As they draw still nearer, Geoffrey becomes aware that the farmyard before him is rich with life. Cocks are crowing, geese are cackling, and in the midst of all this life stands a girl with her back turned to the weary travellers.

"Wait here," says Geoffrey to his squire, and, going forward, rests the bag upon a low wall, and waits until the girl in question shall turn her head. When she does move he is still silent, for, behold, *she* has turned *his* head!

She is country bred, and clothed in country garments, yet her beauty is too great to be deniable. She is not "divinely tall," but rather of medium height, with an oval face, and eyes of "heaven's own blue." Their color changes too, and deepens, and darkens, and grows black and purple, as doth the dome above us. Her mouth is large, but gracious, and full of laughter mixed with truth and firmness. There is no feature that can so truly express character as the mouth. The eyes can shift and change, but the mouth retains its expression always.

She is clad in a snowy gown of simple cotton, that sits loosely to her lissom figure yet fails to disguise the beauty of it. A white kerchief lies softly on her neck. She has pulled up her sleeves, so that her arms are bare,—her round, soft, naked arms that in themselves are a perfect picture. She is standing with her head well thrown back, and her hands—full of corn—lifted high in the air, as she cries aloud, "Cooee! Cooee!" in a clear musical voice.

Presently her cry is answered. A thick cloud of pigeons—brown and white and bronze and gray—come wheeling into sight from behind the old house, and tumble down upon her in a reckless fashion. They perch upon her head, her shoulders, her white soft arms, even her hands, and one, more adventurous than the rest, has even tried to find a slippery resting-place upon her bosom.

"What greedy little things!" cries she aloud, with the merriest laugh in the world. "Sure you can't eat more than enough, can you? an' do your best! Oh, Brownie," reproachfully, "what a selfish bird you are!"

Here Geoffrey comes forward quietly, and lifts his hat to her with all the air of a man who is doing homage to a princess. It has occurred to him that perhaps this peerless being in the cotton gown will feel some natural chagrin on being discovered by one of the other sex with her sleeves tucked up. But in this instance his knowledge of human nature receives a severe shock.

Far from being disconcerted, this farmyard goddess is not even ashamed (as indeed how could she be?) of her naked arms, and, coming up to him, rests them upon the upper rung of the entrance-gate and surveys him calmly if kindly.

"What can I do for you?" she asks, gently.

"I think," says Geoffrey, slightly disconcerted by the sweet leisure of her gaze, "I have lost my way. I have been walking since sunrise, and I want you to tell me where I am."

"You are at Mangle Farm," returns she. Then, judging by the blank expression on his face that her words bring him no comfort, she continues with a smile, "That doesn't seem to help you much, does it?"

He returns her smile in full,—*very* full. "I confess it doesn't help me at all," he says. "Mangle Farm, I am sure, is the most attractive spot on earth, but it tells me nothing about latitude or longitude. Give me some further help."

"Then tell me where you come from, and perhaps I may be able." She speaks softly, but quickly, as do all the Irish, and with a brogue musical but unmistakable.

"I am staying at a shooting-lodge called Coolnagurtheen. Do you know where that is."

"Oh, of course," returns she, with a sudden accession of animation. "I have often seen it. That is where the young English gentleman is staying for the shooting."

"Quite right. And I am the young English gentleman," says Geoffrey, lifting his hat again by way of introduction.

"Indeed, are you?" asks she, raising her pretty brows. Then she smiles involuntarily, and the pink flush in her rounded cheeks grows a shade deeper. Yet she does not lower her eyes, or show the slightest touch of confusion. "I might have guessed it," she says, after a minute's survey of the tall gray-coated young man before her. "You are not a bit like the others down here."

"Am I not?" says he, humbly, putting on his carefully crestfallen air that has generally been found so highly successful. "Tell me my fault."

"I will—when I find it," returns she, with an irrepressible glance, full of native but innocent coquetry, from her beautiful eyes.

At this moment one of the pigeons—a small, pretty thing, bronze-tinged—flies to her, and, resting on her shoulder, makes a tender cooing sound, and picks at her cheek reproachfully, as though imploring more corn.

"Would you bite me?" murmurs she, fondly, as the bird flies off again alarmed at the presence of the tall stranger, who already is busy comparing most favorably the face of its mistress with the faces of all the fashionable beauties London has been raving about for eighteen months. "Every morning they torment me like this," she says, turning to Geoffrey, with a little pleasant confidential nod.

"He looked as if he wanted to eat you; and I'm sure I don't wonder at it," says Geoffrey, making the addition to his speech in a lower key.

"And have you walked from Coolnagurtheen this morning? Why, it is eight miles from this," says she, taking no notice of his last speech. "You could have had no breakfast!"

"Not yet; but I suppose there must be a village near here, and an inn, and I want you to direct me how to get to it. I am giving you a great deal of trouble," remorsefully, "but my boy knows nothing."

He points as he speaks to the ignorant Paddy, who is sitting on the ground with his knees between his hands, crooning a melancholy ditty.

"The village is two miles farther on. I think you had better come in and breakfast here. Uncle will be very glad to see you," she says, hospitably. "And you must be tired."

He hesitates. He *is* tired, and hungry too; there is no denying. Even as he hesitates, a girl coming out to the door-step puts her hand over her eyes, and shouts pleasantly from afar to her mistress,—

"Miss Mona, come in; the tay will be cold, an' the rashers all spoiled, an' the masther's callin' for ye."

"Come, hurry," says Mona, turning to Geoffrey, with a light laugh that seems to spring from her very heart. "Would you have the 'tay' get cold while you are making up your mind? I at least must go."

She moves from him.

"Then thank you, and I shall go with you, if you will allow me," says Geoffrey, hurriedly, as he sees her disappearing.

"Tell your boy to go to the kitchen," says Mona, thoughtfully, and, Paddy being disposed of, she and Geoffrey go on to the house.

They walk up a little gravelled path, on either side of which trim beds of flowers are cut, bordered with stiff box. All sorts of pretty, sweetly-smelling old wild blossoms are blooming in them, as gayly as though they have forgotten the fact that autumn is rejoicing in all its matured beauty. Crimson and white and purple asters stand calmly gazing towards the sky; here a flaming fuchsia droops its head, and there, apart from all the rest, smiles an enchanting rose.

"That like a virgin queen salutes the sunDew-diadem'd."

Behind the house rises a thick wood,—a "solemn wood," such as Dickens loved to write of, with its lights and shades and every-varying tints. A gentle wind is rushing through it now; the faint murmur of some "hidden brook," singing its "quiet tune," fall upon the ear; some happy birds are warbling in the thickets. It is a day whose beauty may be felt.

"I have no card but my name is Geoffrey Rodney," says the young man, turning to his companion.

"And mine is Mona Scully," returns she, with the smile that seems part of her lips, and which already has engraven itself on Mr. Rodney's heart. "Now, I suppose, we know each other."

They walk up two steps, and enter a small hall, and then he follows her into a room opening off it, in which breakfast lies prepared.

It is in Geoffrey's eyes a very curious room, unlike anything he has ever seen before; yet it possesses for him (perhaps for that very reason) a certain charm. It is uncarpeted, but the boards are white as snow, and on them lies a fine sprinkling of dry sand. In one of the windows—whose panes are diamond-shaped—two geraniums are in full flower; upon the deep seat belonging to the other lie some books and a stocking half knitted.

An old man, rugged but kindly-featured, rises on his entrance, and gazes at him expectantly. Mona, going up to him, rests her hand upon his arm, and, indicating Geoffrey by a gesture, says, in a low tone,—

"He has lost his way. He is tired, and I have asked him to have some breakfast. He is the English gentleman who is living at Coolnagurtheen."

"You're kindly welcome, sir," says the old man, bowing with the slow and heavy movement that belongs to the aged. There is dignity and warmth, however, in the salute, and Geoffrey accepts with pleasure the toil-worn hand his host presents to him a moment later. The breakfast is good, and, though composed of only country fare, is delicious to the young man, who has been walking since dawn, and whose appetite just now would have astonished those dwelling in crowded towns and living only on their excitements.

The house, is home-like, sweet, and one which might perhaps day by day grow dearer to the heart; and this girl, this pretty creature who every now and then turns her eyes on Geoffrey, as though glad in a kindly fashion to see him there, seems a necessary part of the whole,—her gracious presence rendering it each moment sweeter and more desirable. "My precept to all who build is," says Cicero, "that the owner should be an ornament to the house, and not the house to the owner."

Mona pours out the tea—which is excellent—and puts in the cream—which is a thing to dream of—with a liberal hand. She smiles at Geoffrey across the sugar-bowl, and chatters to him over the big bowl of flowers that lies in the centre of the table. Not a hothouse bouquet faultlessly arranged, by any means, but a great, tender, happy, straggling bunch of flowers that seem to have fallen into their places of their own accord, regardless of coloring, and fill the room with their perfume.

His host going to the window when breakfast is at an end, Geoffrey follows him; and both look out upon the little garden before them that is so carefully and lovingly tended.

"It is all her doing," says the old man,—"Mona's, I mean. She loves those flowers more than anything on earth, I think. Her mother was the same; but she wasn't half the lass that Mona is. Never a mornin' in the cowld winter but she goes out there to see if the frost hasn't killed some of 'em the night before."

"There is hardly any taste so charming or so engrossing as that for flowers," says Geoffrey, making this trite little speech, that sounds like a copy-book, in his most engaging style. "My mother and cousin do a great deal of that sort of thing when at home."

"Ay, it looks pretty and gives the child something to do." There is a regretful ring in his tone that induces Geoffrey to ask the next question.

"Does she—does Miss Scully find country life unsatisfying? Has she not lived here always?"

"Law, no, sir," says the old man, with a loud and hearty laugh. "I think if ye could see the counthry girls round here, an' compare 'em with my Mona, you'd see that for yerself. She's as fine as the queen to them. Her mother, you see, was the parson's daughter down here; tiptop she was, and purty as a fairy, but mighty delicate; looked as if a march wind would blow her into heaven.

Dan—he was a brother of mine, an' a solicitor in Dublin. You've been there, belike?"

"Yes; I stopped there for two or three days on my way down here. Well— and—your brother?" He cannot to himself explain the interest he feels in this story.

"Dan? He was a fine man, surely; six feet in his stockin', he was, an' eyes like a woman's. He come down here an' met her, an' she married him. Nothing would stop her, though the parson was fit to be tied about it. An' of course he was no match for her,—father bein' only a bricklayer when he began life,—but still I will say Dan was a fine man, an' one to think about; an' no two ways in him, an' *that* soft about the heart. He worshipped the ground she walked on; an' four years after their marriage she told me herself she never had an ache in her heart since she married him. That was fine tellin', sir, wasn't it? Four years, mind ye. Why, when Mary was alive (my wife, sir) we had a shindy twice a week, reg'lar as clockwork. We wouldn't have known ourselves without it; but, however, that's nayther here nor there," says Mr. Scully, pulling himself up short. "An' I ask yer pardon, sir, for pushing private matters on ye like this."

"But you have interested me," says Geoffrey, seating himself on the broad sill of the window, as though preparing for a long dissertation on matters still unknown. "Pray tell me how your brother and his lovely wife—who evidently was as wise and true as she was lovely—got on."

Mr. Rodney's face being of that rare kind that is as tender as it is manly, and by right of its beauty demands confidence, the old man (who dearly loves his own voice) is encouraged to proceed.

"They didn't get on for long," he says, mournfully,—and what voice is so full of melancholy as the Irish voice when it sinks into sadness? "When the little one—Mona—was barely five years old, they went to ground; Mount Jerome got them. Fever it was; and it carried 'em both off just while ye'd have time to look round ye. Poor souls, they went to the blessed land together. Perhaps the Holy Virgin knew they would have got on badly without each other anywhere."

"And the child,—Miss Mona?" asks Geoffrey.

"She went to live in Anthrim with her mother's sister. Later she got to Dublin, to her aunt there,—another of the parson's daughters,—who married the Provost in Thrinity; a proud sort he was, an' awful tiresome with his Greeks an' his Romans, an' not the height of yer thumb," says Mr. Scully, with ineffable contempt. "I went to Dublin one day about cattle, and called to see me niece; an' she took to me, bless her, an' I brought her down with me for change of air, for her cheeks were whiter than a fleece of wool, an' she has stayed ever since. Dear soul! I hope she'll stay forever. She is welcome."

"She must be a great comfort to you," says Geoffrey from his heart.

"She is that. More than I can say. An' keeps things together, too. She is clever like her father, an' he was on the fair way to make a fortune. Ay, I always say it, law is the thing that pays in Ireland. A good sound fight sets them up. But I'm keeping you, sir, and your gun is waitin' for ye. If you haven't had enough of me company by this," with another jolly laugh, "I'll take ye down to a field hard by, an' show ye where I saw a fine young covey only yesternight."

"I—I should like to say good-by to Miss Mona, and thank her for all her goodness to me, before going," says the young man, rising somewhat slowly.

"Nay, you can say all that on your way back, an' get a half-shot into the bargain," says old Scully, heartily. "You'll hardly beat the potheen I can give ye." He winks knowingly, pats Rodney kindly on the shoulder, and leads the way out of the house. Yet I think Geoffrey would willingly have bartered potheen, partridge, and a good deal more, for just one last glance at Mona's beautiful face before parting. Cheered, however, by the prospect that he may see her before night falls, he follows the farmer into the open air.

CHAPTER III.

HOW GEOFFREY'S HEART IS CLAIMED BY CUPID AS A TARGET, AND HOW MONA STOOPS TO CONQUER.

It is ten days later. The air is growing brisker, the flowers bear no new buds. More leaves are falling on the woodland paths, and the trees are throwing out their last bright autumn tints of red and brown and richest orange, that tell all too plainly of the death that lies before them.

Great cascades of water are rushing from the high hills, tumbling, hurrying, with their own melodious music, into the rocky basins that kind nature has built to receive them. The soothing voices of the air are growing louder, more full of strength; the branches of the elms bow down before them; the gentle wind, "a sweet and passionate wooer," kisses the blushing leaf with perhaps a fiercer warmth than it did a month agone.

It is in the spring—so we have been told—that "a young man's fancy lightly turns to thoughts of love;" yet it is in the autumn that *our* young man takes to this pleasing if somewhat unsatisfactory amusement.

Not that he himself is at all aware of the evil case into which he has fallen. He feels not the arrow in his heart, or the tender bands that slowly but surely are winding themselves around him,—steel bands, decked out and hidden by perfumed flowers. As yet he feels no pang; and, indeed, were any one to even hint at such a thing, he would have laughed aloud at the idea of his being what is commonly termed "in love."

That he—who has known so many seasons, and passed through the practised hands of some of the prettiest women this world can afford, heart-whole, and without a scratch—should fall a victim to the innocent wiles of a little merry Irish girl of no family whatever, seems too improbable even of belief, however lovely beyond description this girl may be (and is), with her wistful, laughing, mischievous Irish eyes, and her mobile lips, and her disposition half angelic, half full of fire and natural coquetry.

Beauty, according to Ovid, is "a favor bestowed by the gods;" Theophrastus says it is "a silent cheat;" and Shakspeare tells us it

"Is but a vain and doubtful good,A shining gloss that fadeth suddenly,A flower that dieth when first it 'gins to bud,A brittle glass that's broken presently,A doubtful good, a gloss, a glass, a flower,Lost, faded, broken, dead within an hour."

Mere beauty of form and feature will fade indeed, but Mona's beauty lies not altogether in nose or eyes or mouth, but rather in her soul, which compels her face to express its lightest meaning. It is in her expression, which varies with each passing thought, changing from "grave to gay, from lively to severe," as the soul within speaks to it, that her chief charm dwells. She is never quite the same for two minutes running,—which is the surest safeguard against satiety. And as her soul is pure and clean, and her face is truly the index to her mind, all it betrays but endears her to and makes richer him who reads it.

"Age cannot wither her, nor custom staleHer infinite variety."

Whenever these lines come to me I think of Mona.

It is midday, and Geoffrey, gun in hand, is idly stalking through the sloping wood that rises behind Mangle Farm. The shooting he has had since his arrival in Ireland, though desultory,—perhaps because of it,—has proved delightful in his sight. Here coveys come upon one unawares, rising out of fields when least expected, and therefore when discovered possess all the novelty of a gigantic surprise. Now and then he receives kindly warning of birds seen "over night" in some particular corner, and an offer to escort him to the scene of action without beat of drum.

As for instance, in the morning his man assails him with the news that Micky Brian or Dinny Collins (he has grown quite familiar with the gentry around) "is without, an' would like to spake wid him." Need I remark that he has widely hired his own particular attendant from among the gay and festive youths of Bantry?

Whereupon he goes "without," which means to his own hall-door that always stands wide open, and there acknowledges the presence of Mickey or Dinny, as the case may be, with a gracious nod. Mickey instantly removes his caubeen and tells "his honor" (regardless of the fact that his honor can tell this for himself) that "it is a gran' fine day," which as a rule is the first thing an Irish person will always say on greeting you, as though full of thankfulness to the powers above, in that sweet weather has been given.

Then follows a long-winded speech on the part of Mickey about birds in general and grouse in particular, finishing up with the announcement that he can tell where the finest covey seen this season lies hidden.

"An' the biggest birds, an' as full o' corn as iver ye see, the rogues!"

At this his honor requests Mickey to step into the hall, and with his own hands administers to him a glass of whiskey, which mightily pleases the son of Erin, though he plainly feels it his duty to make a face at it as he swallows it off neat. And then Geoffrey sallies forth and goes for the promised covey, followed closely by the excited Mickey, and, having made account of most of them, presses backsheesh into the hands of his informant, and sends him home rejoicing.

For the most part these bonnie brown birds have found their way into Miss Mona's pantry, and are eaten by that little gourmand with the rarer pleasure that in her secret heart she knows that the giver of them is not blind to the fact that her eyes are faultless and her nose pure Greek.

Just at this moment he is coming down through brake and furze, past tangling blackberry-bushes that are throwing out leaves of brilliant crimson and softest yellow, and over rustling leaves, towards the farm that holds his divinity.

Ill luck has attended his efforts to-day, or else his thoughts have been wandering in the land where love holds sway, because he is empty-handed. The bonnie brown bird has escaped him, and no gift is near to lay at Mona's shrine.

As he reaches the broad stream that divides him from the land he would reach, he pauses and tries to think of any decent excuse that may enable him to walk with a bold front up to the cottage door. But no such excuse presents itself. Memory proves false. It refuses to assist him. He is almost in despair.

He tries to persuade himself that there is nothing strange or uncommon in calling upon Wednesday to inquire with anxious solicitude about the health of a young woman whom he had seen happy and robust on Tuesday. But the trial is not successful, and he is almost on the point of flinging up the argument and going home again, when his eye lights upon a fern small but rare, and very beautiful, that growing on a high rock far above him, overhangs the stream.

It is a fern for which Mona has long been wishing. Oh! happy thought! She has expressed for it the keenest admiration. Oh! blissful remembrance! She has not one like it in all her collection. Oh! certainty full of rapture.

Now will he seize this blessed opportunity, and, laden with the spoils of war, approach her dwelling (already she is "she"), and triumphantly, albeit humbly, lay the fern at her feet, and so perchance gain the right to bask for a few minutes in the sunshine of her presence.

No sooner thought than done! Laying his gun carefully upon the ground, he looks around him to see by what means he shall gain possession of this lucky fern which is growing, deeply rooted in its native soil, far above him.

A branch of a tree overspreading the water catches his attention. It is not strong, but it suggests itself as a means to the desired end. It is indeed slim to a fault, and unsatisfactory to an alarming degree, but it must do, and

Geoffrey, swinging himself up to it, tries it first, and then standing boldly upon it, leans over towards the spot where the fern can be seen.

It is rather beyond his reach, but he is determined not to be outdone. Of course by stepping into the water and climbing the slimy rock that holds the desired treasure, it can be gained; but with a lazy desire to keep his boots dry, he clings to his present position, regardless of the fact that bruised flesh (if nothing worse) will probably be the result of his daring.

He has stooped very much over indeed. His hand is on the fern; he has safely carefully extracted it, roots and all (one would think I was speaking of a tooth! but this is by the way), from its native home, when cr-r-k goes something; the branch on which he rests betrays him, and smashing hurls him head downwards into the swift but shallow stream below.

A very charming vision clad in Oxford shirting, and with a great white hat tied beneath her rounded chin with blue ribbons,—something in the style of a Sir Joshua Reynolds,—emerges from among the low-lying firs at this moment. Having watched the (seemingly) light catastrophe from afar, and being apparently amused by it, she now gives way to unmistakable mirth and laughs aloud. When Mona laughs, she does it with all her heart, the correct method of suppressing all emotion, be it of joy or sorrow,—regarding it as a recreation permitted only to the vulgar,—being as yet unlearned by her. Therefore her expression of merriment rings gayly and unchecked through the old wood.

But presently, seeing the author of her mirth does not rise from his watery resting-place, her smile fades, a little frightened look creeps into her eyes, and, hastening forward, she reaches the bank of the stream and gazes into it. Rodney is lying face downwards in the water, his head having come with some force against the sharp edge of a stone against which it is now resting.

Mona turns deadly pale, and then instinctively loosening the strings of her hat flings it from her. A touch of determination settles upon her lips, so prone to laughter at other times. Sitting on the bank, she draws off her shoes and stockings, and with the help of an alder that droops to the river's brim lowers herself into the water.

The stream, though insignificant, is swift. Placing her strong young arms, that are rounded and fair as those of any court dame, beneath Rodney, she lifts him, and, by a supreme effort, and by right of her fresh youth and perfect health, draws him herself to land.

In a minute or two the whole affair proves itself a very small thing indeed, with little that can be termed tragical about it. Geoffrey comes slowly back to life, and in the coming breathes her name. Once again he is trying to reach the distant fern; once again it eludes his grasp. He has it; no, he hasn't; yet, he has. Then at last he wakes to the fact that he has indeed *got it* in earnest, and that the blood is flowing from a slight wound in the back of his head, which is being staunched by tender fingers, and that he himself is lying in Mona's arms.

He sighs, and looks straight into the lovely frightened eyes bending over him. Then the color comes with a sudden rush back into his cheeks as he tells himself she will look upon him as nothing less than a "poor creature" to lose consciousness and behave like a silly girl for so slight a cause. And something else he feels. Above and beyond everything is a sense of utter happiness, such as he has never known before, a thrill of rapture that has in it something of peace, and that comes from the touch of the little brown hand that rests so lightly on his head.

"Do not stir. Your head is badly cut, an' it bleeds still," says Mona, with a shoulder. "I cannot stop it. Oh, what shall I do?"

"Who got me out of the water?" asks he, lazily, pretending (hypocrite that he is) to be still overpowered with weakness. "And when did you come?"

"Just now," returns she, with some hesitation, and a rich accession of coloring, that renders her even prettier than she was a moment since. Because

"From every blush that kindles in her cheeks,Ten thousand little loves and graces spring."

Her confusion, however, and the fact that no one else is near, betrays the secret she fain would hide.

"Was it you?" asks he, raising himself on his elbow to regard her earnestly, though very loath to quit the spot where late he has been tenant. "You? Oh, Mona!"

It is the first time he has ever called her by her Christian name without a prefix. The tears rise to her eyes. Feeling herself discovered, she makes her confession slowly, without looking at him, and with an air of indifference so badly assumed as to kill the idea of her ever attaining prominence upon the stage.

"Yes, it was I," she says. "And why shouldn't I? Is it to see you drown I would? I—I didn't want you to find out; but"—quickly—"I would do the same for *any one* at *any* time. You know that."

"I am sure you would," says Geoffrey, who has risen to his feet and has taken her hand. "Nevertheless, though, as you say, I am but one in the crowd,— and, of course, nothing to you,—I am very glad you did it for me."

With a little touch of wilfulness, perhaps pride, she withdraws her hand.

"I dare say," she says, carelessly, purposely mistaking his meaning: "it must have been cold lying there."

"There are things that chill one more than water," returns he, slightly offended by her tone.

"You are all wet. Do go home and change your clothes," says Mona, who is still sitting on the grass with her gown spread carefully around her. "Or perhaps"-reluctantly—"it will be better for you to go to the farm, where Bridget will look after you."

"Thank you; so I shall, if you will come with me."

"Don't mind me," says Miss Scully, hastily. "I shall follow you by and by."

"By and by will suit me down to the ground," declares he, easily. "The day is fortunately warm: damp clothes are an advantage rather than otherwise."

Silence. Mona taps the mound beside her with impatient fingers, her mind being evidently great with thought.

"I really wish," she says, presently, "you would do what I say. Go to the farm, and—stay there."

"Well, come with me, and I'll stay till you turn me out.'

"I can't," faintly.

"Why not?" in a surprised tone.

"Because—I prefer staying here."

"Oh! if you mean by that you want to get rid of me, you might have said so long ago, without all this hinting," says Mr. Rodney, huffily, preparing to beat an indignant retreat.

"I didn't mean that, and I never hint," exclaims Mona, angrily; "and if you insist on the truth, if I must explain to you what I particularly desire to keep secret, you——"

"You are hurt!" interrupts he, with passionate remorse. "I see it all now. Stepping into that hateful stream to save me, you injured yourself severely. You are in pain,—you suffer; whilst I——"

"I am in no pain," says Mona, crimson with shame and mortification. "You mistake everything. I have not even a scratch on me; and—I have no shoes or stockings on me either, if you must know all!"

She turns from him wrathfully; and Geoffrey, disgusted with himself, steps back and makes no reply. With any other woman of his acquaintance he might perhaps at this juncture have made a mild request that he might be allowed to assist in the lacing or buttoning of her shoes; but with this strange little Irish girl all is different. To make such a remark would be, he feels, to offer her a deliberate insult.

"There, do go away!" says this woodland goddess. "I am sick of you and your stupidity."

"I'm sure I don't wonder," says Geoffrey, very humbly. "I beg your pardon a thousand times; and—good-by, Miss Mona."

She turns involuntarily, through the innate courtesy that belongs to her race, to return his parting salutation, and, looking at him, sees a tiny spot of blood trickling down his forehead from the wound received awhile since.

On the instant all is forgotten,—chagrin, shame, shoes and stockings, everything! Springing to her little naked feet, she goes to him, and, raising her hand, presses her handkerchief against the ugly stain.

"It has broken out again!" she says, nervously. "I am sure—I am certain—it is a worst wound than you imagine. Ah! do go home, and get it dressed."

"But I shouldn't like any one to touch it except you," says Mr. Rodney, truthfully. "Even now, as your fingers press it, I feel relief."

"Do you really?" asks Mona, earnestly.

"Honestly, I do."

"Then just turn your back for one moment," says Mona simply, "and when my shoes and stockings are on I'll go home with you an' bathe it. Now, don't turn round, for your life!"

"'Is thy servant a dog, that he should do this thing?'" quotes Mr. Rodney; and, Mona having got into her shoes, she tells him he is at liberty to follow her across the rustic bridge lower down, that leads from the wood into Mangle Farm.

"You have spoiled your gown on my account," says Geoffrey, surveying her remorsefully; "and such a pretty gown, too. I don't think I ever saw you looking sweeter than you look to-day. And now your dress is ruined, and it is all my fault!"

"How dare you find a defect in my appearance?" says Mona, with her old gay laugh. "You compel me to retaliate. Just look at yourself. Did you ever see such a regular pickle as you are?"

In truth he is. So when he has acknowledged the melancholy fact, they both laugh, with the happy enjoyment of youth, at their own discomfiture, and go back to the cottage good friends once more.

On the middle of the rustic bridge before mentioned he stops her, to say, unexpectedly,—

"Do you know by what name I shall always call you in my thoughts?"

To which she answers, "No. How should I? But tell me."

"'Bonnie Lesley:' the poet says of her what I think of you."

"And what do you think of me?" She has grown a little pale, but her eyes have not left his.

"To see her is to love her,And love but her forever;For nature made her what she is,And ne'er made sie anither,"

quotes Geoffrey, in a low tone, that has something in it almost startling, so full is it of deep and earnest feeling.

Mona is the first to recover herself.

"That is a pretty verse," she says, quietly. "But I do not know the poem. I should like to read it."

Her tone, gentle but dignified, steadies him.

"I have the book that contains it at Coolnagurtheen," he says, somewhat subdued. "Shall I bring it to you?"

"Yes. You may bring it to me—to-morrow," returns she, with the faintest hesitation, which but enhances the value of the permission, whereon his heart once more knows hope and content.

CHAPTER IV.

HOW GEOFFREY AND MONA ENTER A CABIN AND SEE ONE OF THE RESULTS OF PARNELL'S ELOQUENCE.

But when to-morrow comes it brings to him a very different Mona from the one he saw yesterday. A pale girl, with great large sombrous eyes and compressed lips, meets him, and places her hand in his without a word.

"What is it?" asks he, quick to notice any change in her.

"Oh! haven't you heard?" cries she. "Sure the country is ringing with it. Don't you know that they tried to shoot Mr. Moore last night?"

Mr. Moore is her landlord, and the owner of the lovely wood behind Mangle Farm where Geoffrey came to grief yesterday.

"Yes, of course; but I heard, too, how he escaped his would-be assassin."

"He did, yes; but poor Tim Maloney, the driver of the car on which he was, he was shot through the heart, instead of him! Oh, Mr. Rodney," cries the girl, passionate emotion both in her face and voice, "what can be said of those men who come down to quiet places such as this was, to inflame the minds of poor ignorant wretches, until they are driven to bring down murder on their souls! It is cruel! It is unjust! And there seems no help for us. But surely in the land where justice reigns supreme, retribution will fall upon the right heads."

"I quite forgot about the driver," says Geoffrey, beneath his breath. This remark is unfortunate. Mona turns upon him wrathfully.

"No doubt," she says scornfully. "The gentleman escaped, the man doesn't count! Perhaps, indeed, he has fulfilled his mission now he has shed his ignoble blood for his superior! Do you know it is partly such thoughts as these that have driven our people to desperation! One law for the poor, another for the rich! Friendship for the great, contempt for the needy."

She pauses, catching her breath with a little sob.

"Who is uttering seditious language now?" asks he, reproachfully. "No, you wrong me. I had, indeed, forgotten for the moment all about that unfortunate driver. You must remember I am a stranger here. The peasants are unknown to me. I cannot be expected to feel a keen interest in each one individually. In fact, had Mr. Moore been killed instead of poor Maloney, I shouldn't have felt it a bit the more, though he was the master and the other the man. I can only suffer with those I know and love."

The "poor Maloney" has done it. She forgives him; perhaps because—sweet soul—harshness is always far from her.

"It is true," she says, sadly. "I spoke in haste because my heart is sore for my country, and I fear for what we may yet live to see. But of course I could not expect you to feel with me."

This cuts him to the heart.

"I do feel with you," he says, hastily. "Do not believe otherwise." Then, as though impelled to it, he says in a low tone, though very distinctly, "I would gladly make your griefs mine, if you would make my joys yours."

This is a handsome offer, all things considered, but Mona turns a deaf ear to it. She is standing on her door-step at this moment, and now descends until she reaches the tiny gravelled path.

"Where are you going?" asks Rodney, afraid lest his last speech has offended her. She has her hat on,—a big Gainsborough hat, round which soft Indian muslin is clinging, and in which she looks nothing less than adorable.

"To see poor Kitty Maloney, his widow. Last year she was my servant. This year she married; and now—here is the end of everything—for her."

"May I go with you?" asks he, anxiously. "These are lawless times, and I dare say Maloney's cabin will be full of roughs. You will feel happier with some man beside you whom you can trust."

At the word "trust" she lifts her eyes and regards him somewhat steadfastly. It is a short look, yet a very long one, and tells more than she knows. Even while it lasts he swears to himself an oath that he never to his life's end breaks.

"Come, then," she says, slowly, "if you will. Though I am not afraid. Why should I be? Do you forget that I am one of themselves? My father and I belong to the people."

She says this steadily, and very proudly, with her head held high, but without looking at him; which permits Geoffrey to gaze at her exhaustively. There is an unconscious meaning in her words, quite clear to him. She is of "the people," he of a class that looks but coldly upon hers. A mighty river, called Caste, rolls between them, dividing him from her. But shall it? Some hazy thought like this floats through his brain. They walk on silently, scarcely exchanging a syllable one with the other, until they come within sight of a small thatched house built at the side of the road. It has a manure-heap just in front of it, and a filthy pool to its left, in which an ancient sow is wallowing, whilst grunting harmoniously.

Two people, a man and a woman, are standing together some yards from the cabin, whispering and gesticulating violently, as is "their nature to."

The man, seeing Mona, breaks from the woman, and comes up to her.

"Go back again, miss," he says, with much excitement. "They've brought him home, an' he's bad to look at. I've seed him, an' it's given me a turn I won't forget in a hurry. Go home, I tell ye. 'Tis a sight not fit for the eyes of the likes of you."

"Is he there?" asks Mona, pointing with trembling fingers to the house.

"Ay, where else?" answers the woman, sullenly who has joined them. "They brought him back to the home he will never rouse again with step or voice. 'Tis cold he is, an' silent this day."

"Is—is he covered?" murmurs Mona, with difficulty, growing pale, and shrinking backwards. Instinctively she lays her hand on Rodney's arm, as though desirous of support. He, laying his own hand upon hers, holds it in a warm and comforting clasp.

"He's covered, safe enough. They've throwed an ould sheet over him,—over what remains of him this cruel day. Och, wirra-wirra!" cries the woman, suddenly, throwing her hands high above her head, and giving way to a peculiar long, low, moaning sound, so eerie, so full of wild despair and grief past all consolation, as to make the blood in Rodney's veins run cold.

"Go back the way ye came," says the man again, with growing excitement. "This is no place for ye. There is ill luck in yonder house. His soul won't rest in peace, sent out of him like that. If ye go in now, ye'll be sorry for it. 'Tis a thing ye'll be thinkin' an' dhramin' of till you'll be wishin' the life out of yer cursed body!"

A little foam has gathered round his lips, and his eyes are wild. Geoffrey, by a slight movement, puts himself between Mona and this man, who is evidently besides himself with some inward fear and horror.

"What are ye talkin' about? Get out, ye spalpeen," says the woman, with an outward show of anger, but a warning frown meant for the man alone. "Let her do as she likes. Is it spakin' of fear ye are to Dan Scully's daughter?"

"Come home, Mona; be advised by me," says Geoffrey, gently, as the man skulks away, walking in a shambling, uncertain fashion, and with a curious trick of looking every now and then over his shoulder, as though expecting to see an unwelcome follower.

"No, no; this is not a time to forsake one in trouble," says Mona, faithfully, but with a long, shivering sigh. "I need see nothing, but I *must* speak to Kitty."

She walks deliberately forward and enters the cabin, Geoffrey closely following her.

A strange scene presents itself to their expectant gaze. Before them is a large room (if so it can be called), possessed of no flooring but the bare brown earth that Mother Nature has supplied. To their right is a huge fireplace, where, upon the hearthstone, turf lies burning dimly, emitting the strong aromatic perfume that belongs to it. Near it crouches an old woman with her blue-checked apron thrown above her head, who rocks herself to and fro in silent grief, and with every long-drawn breath—that seems to break from her breast like a stormy wave upon a desert shore—brings her old withered palms together with a gesture indicative of despair.

Opposite to her is a pig, sitting quite erect, and staring at her blankly, without the slightest regard to etiquette or nice feeling. He is plainly full of anxiety, yet without power to express it, except in so far as his tail may aid him, which is limp and prostrate, its very curl being a thing of the past. If any man has impugned the sagacity of pigs, that man has erred!

In the background partly hidden by the gathering gloom, some fifteen men, and one or two women, are all huddled together, whispering eagerly, with their faces almost touching. The women, though in a great minority, are plainly having the best of it.

But Mona's eyes see nothing but one object only.

On the right side of the fireplace, lying along the wall, is a rude stretcher,—or what appears to be such,—on which, shrouded decently in a white cloth, lies something that chills with mortal fear the heart, as it reminds it of that to which we all some day must come. Beneath the shroud the murdered man lies calmly sleeping, his face smitten into the marble smile of death.

Quite near to the poor corpse, a woman sits, young, apparently, and with a handsome figure, though now it is bent and bowed with grief. She is dressed in the ordinary garb of the Irish peasant, with a short gown well tucked up, naked feet, and the sleeves of her dress pushed upwards until they almost reach the shoulder, showing the shapely arm and the small hand that, as a rule, belong to the daughters of Erin and betray the existence of the Spanish blood that in days gone by mingled with theirs.

Her face is hidden; it is lying on her arms, and they are cast, in the utter recklessness and abandonment of her grief, across the feet of him who, only yesterday, had been her "man,"—her pride and her delight.

Just as Mona crosses the threshold, a man, stepping from among the group that lies in shadow, approaching the stretcher, puts forth his hand, as though he would lift the sheet and look upon what it so carefully conceals. But the woman, springing like a tigress to her feet, turns upon him, and waves him back with an imperious gesture.

"Lave him alone!" cries she; "take yer hands off him! He's dead, as ye well know, the whole of ye. There's no more ye can do to him. Then lave his poor body to the woman whose heart is broke for the want of him!"

The man draws back hurriedly, and the woman once more sinks back into her forlorn position.

"Kitty, can I do anything for you?" asks Mona, in a gentle whisper, bending over her and taking the hand that lies in her lap between both her own, with a pressure full of gentle sympathy. "I know there is nothing I can *say* but can I *do* nothing to comfort you?"

"Thank ye, miss. Ye mane it kindly, I know," says the woman, wearily. "But the big world is too small to hold one dhrop of comfort for me. He's dead, ye see!"

The inference is full of saddest meaning. Even Geoffrey feels the tears rise unbidden to his eyes.

"Poor soul! poor soul!" says Mona, brokenly; then she drops her hand, and the woman, turning again to the lifeless body, as though in the poor cold clay lies her only solace, lets her head fall forward upon it.

Mona, turning, confronts the frightened group in the corner, both men and women, with a face changed and aged by grief and indignation.

Her eyes have grown darker; her mouth is stern. To Rodney, who is watching her anxiously, she seems positively transformed. What a terrible power lies within her slight frame to feel both good and evil! What sad days may rest in store for this girl, whose face can whiten at a passing grievance, and whose hands can tremble at a woe in which only a dependant is concerned! Both sorrow and joy must be to her as giants, strong to raise or lower her to highest elevations or lowest depths.

"Oh, what a day is this!" cries she, with quivering lips. "See the ruin you have brought upon this home, that only yestermorn was full of life and gladness! Is this what has come of your Land League, and your Home Rulers, and your riotous meetings? Where is the soul of this poor man, who was hurried to his last account without his priest, and without a prayer for pardon on his lips? And how shall the man who slew him dare to think on his own soul?"

No one answers; the very moanings of the old crone in the chimney-corner are hushed as the clear young voice rings through the house, and then stops abruptly, as though its owner is overcome with emotion. The men move back a little, and glance uneasily and with some fear at her from under their brows.

"Oh, the shameful thought that all the world should be looking at us with horror and disgust, as a people too foul for anything but annihilation! And what is it you hope to gain by all this madness? Do you believe peace, or a blessing from the holy heavens, could fall and rest on a soil soaked in blood and red with crime? I tell you no; but rather a curse will descend, and stay with you, that even Time itself will be powerless to lift."

Again she pauses, and one of the men, shuffling his feet nervously, and with his eyes bent upon the floor, says, in a husky tone,—

"Sure, now, you're too hard on us, Miss Mona. We're innocent of it. Our hands are clean as yer own. We nivir laid eyes on him since yesterday till this blessed minit. Ye should remember that, miss."

"I know what you would say; and yet I do denounce you all, both men and boys,—yes, and the women too,—because, though your own actual hands may be free of blood, yet knowing the vile assassin who did this deed, there is not one of you but would extend to him the clasp of good-fellowship and shield him to the last,—a man who, fearing to meet another face to face, must needs lie in ambush for him behind a wall, and shoot his victim without giving him one chance of escape! Mr. Moore walks through his lands day by day, unprotected and without arms: why did this man not meet him there, and fight him fairly, to the death, if, indeed, he felt that for the good of his country he should die! No! there was danger in that thought," says Mona, scornfully: "it is a safer thing to crouch out of sight and murder at one's will."

"Then why does he prosecute the poor? We can't live; yet he won't lower the rints," says a sullen voice from the background.

"He did lower them. He, too, must live; and, at all events, no persecution can excuse murder," says Mona, undaunted. "And who was so good to you as Mr. Moore last winter, when the famine raged round here? Was not his house open to you all? Were not many of your children fed by him? But that is all forgotten now; the words of a few incendiaries have blotted out the remembrance of years of steady friendship. Gratitude lies not with you. I, who am one of you, waste my time in speaking. For a very little matter you would shoot me too, no doubt!"

This last remark, being in a degree ungenerous, causes a sensation. A young man, stepping out from the confusion, says, very earnestly,—

"I don't think ye have any call to say that to us, Miss Mona. 'Tisn't fair like, when ye know in yer own heart that we love the very sight of ye, and the laste sound of yer voice!"

Mona, though still angered, is yet somewhat softened by this speech, as might any woman. Her color fades again, and heavy tears, rising rapidly, quench the fire that only a moment since made her large eyes dark and passionate.

"Perhaps you do," she says, sadly. "And I, too,—you know how dear you all are to me; and it is just that that makes my heart so sore. But it is too late to warn. The time is past when words might have availed."

Turning sorrowfully away, she drops some silver into the poor widow's lap; whereon Geoffrey, who has been standing close to her all the time, covers it with two sovereigns.

"Send down to the Farm, and I will give you some brandy," says Mona to a woman standing by, after a lengthened gaze at the prostrate form of Kitty, who makes no sign of life. "She wants it." Laying her hand on Kitty's shoulder, she shakes her gently. "Rouse yourself," she says, kindly, yet with energy. "Try to think of something,—anything except your cruel misfortune."

"I have only one thought," says the woman, sullenly, "I can't betther it. An' that is, that it was a bitther day when first I saw the light."

Mona, not attempting to reason with her again, shakes her head despondingly, and leaves the cabin with Geoffrey at her side.

For a little while they are silent. He is thinking of Mona; she is wrapped in remembrance of all that has just passed. Presently, looking at her, he discovers she is crying,—bitterly, though quietly. The reaction has set in, and the tears are running quickly down her cheeks.

"Mona, it has all been too much for you," exclaims he, with deep concern.

"Yes, yes; that poor, poor woman! I cannot get her face out of my head. How forlorn! how hopeless! She has lost all she cared for; there is nothing to fall back upon. She loved him; and to have him so cruelly murdered for no crime, and to know that he will never again come in the door, or sit by her hearth, or light his pipe by her fire,—oh, it is horrible! It is enough to kill her!" says Mona, somewhat disconnectedly.

"Time will soften her grief," says Rodney, with an attempt at soothing. "And she is young; she will marry again, and form new ties."

"Indeed she will not;" says Mona indignantly. "Irish peasants very seldom do that. She will, I am sure, be faithful forever to the memory of the man she loved."

"Is that the fashion here? If—if you loved a man, would you be faithful to him forever?"

"But how could I help it?" says Mona, simply. "Oh, what a wretched state this country is in! turmoil and strife from morning till night. And yet to talk to those very people, to mix with them, they seem such courteous, honest, lovable creatures!"

"I don't think the gentleman in the flannel jacket, who spoke about the reduction of 'rints,' looked very lovable," says Mr. Rodney, without a suspicion of a smile; "and—I suppose my sight is failing—but I confess I didn't see much courtesy in his eye or his upper lip. I don't think I ever saw so much upper lip before, and now that I have seen it I don't admire it. I shouldn't single him out as a companion for a lonely road. But no doubt I wrong him."

"Larry Doolin is not a very pleasant person, I acknowledge that," says Mona, regretfully; "but he is only one among a number. And for the most part, I maintain, they are both kind and civil. Do you know," with energy, "after all I believe England is most to blame for all this evil work? We are at heart loyal: you must agree with me in this, when you remember how enthusiastically they received the queen when, years ago, she condescended to pay us a flying visit, never to be repeated. And how gladly we welcomed the Prince of Wales, and how the other day all Ireland petted and made much of the Duke of Connaught! I was in Dublin when he was there; and I know there was no feeling towards him but loyalty and affection. I am sure," earnestly, "if you asked him he would tell the same story."

"I'll ask him the very moment I see him," says Geoffrey, with *empressement*. "Nothing shall prevent me. And I'll telegraph his answer to you."

"We should be all good subjects enough, if things were on a friendlier footing," says Mona, too absorbed in her own grievance to notice Mr. Rodney's suppressed but evident enjoyment of her conversation. "But when you despise us, you lead us to hate you."

"I never heard such awful language," says Rodney. "To tell me to my face that you hate me. Oh, Miss Mona! How have I merited such a speech?"

"You know what I mean," says Mona, reproachfully. "You needn't pretend you don't. And it is quite true that England does despise us."

"What a serious accusation! and one I think slightly unfounded. We don't despise this beautiful island or its people. We even admit that you possess a charm to which we can lay no claim. The wit, the verve, the pure gayety that springs direct from the heart that belongs to you, we lack. We are a terrible prosy, heavy lot capable of only one idea at a time. How can you say we despise you?"

"Yes, you do," says Mona, with a little obstinate shake of her head. "You call us dirty, for one thing."

"Well, but is that altogether a falsehood? Pigs and smoke and live fowls and babies are, I am convinced, good things in their own way and when well at a distance. But, under the roof with one and in an apartment a few feet square,

I don't think I seem to care about them, and I'm sure they can't tend towards cleanliness."

"I admit all that. But how can they help it, when they have no money and when there are always the dear children? I dare say we are dirty, but so are other nations, and no one sneers at them as they sneer at us. Are we dirtier than the canny Scots on whom your queen bestows so much of her society? Tell me that!"

There is triumph in her eye, and a malicious sparkle, and just a touch of rebellion.

"What a little patriot!" says Rodney, pretending fear and stepping back from her. "Into what dangerous company have I fallen! And with what an accent you say '*your* queen'! Do you then repudiate her? Is she not yours as well? Do you refuse to acknowledge her?"

"Why should I? She never comes near us, never takes the least notice of us. She treats us as though we were a detested branch grafted on, and causing more trouble than we are worth, yet she will not let us go."

"I don't wonder at that. If I were the queen I should not let you go either. And so you throw her over? Unhappy queen! I do not envy her, although she sits upon so great a throne. I would not be cast off by you for the wealth of all the Indies."

"Oh, you are my friend," says Mona, sweetly. Then, returning to the charge, "Perhaps after all it is not so much her fault as that of others. Evil counsellors work mischief in all ages."

"'A Daniel come to judgment!' So sage a speech is wonderful from one so young. In my opinion, you ought to go into Parliament yourself, and advocate the great cause. Is it with the present government that you find fault?

"A government which, knowing not true wisdom,Is scorned abroad, and lives on tricks at home?"

says Mr. Rodney, airing his bit of Dryden with conscious pride, in that it fits in so nicely. "At all events, you can't call it,

'A council made of such as dare not speak,And could not if they durst,'

because your part of it takes care to make itself heard."

"How I wish it didn't!" says Mona, with a sigh.

The tears are still lingering on her lashes; her mouth is sad. Yet at this instant, even as Geoffrey is gazing at her and wondering how he shall help to dispel the cloud of sorrow that sits upon her brow, her whole expression changes. A merry gleam comes into her wet eyes, her lips widen and lose their lachrymose look, and then suddenly she throws up her head and breaks into a gay little laugh.

"Did you see the pig," she says, "sitting up by the fireplace? All through I couldn't take my eyes off him. He struck me as so comical. There he sat blinking his small eyes and trying to look sympathetic. I am convinced he knew all about it. I never saw so solemn a pig."

She laughs again with fresh delight at her own thought. That pig in the cabin has come back to her, filling her with amusement. Geoffrey regards her with puzzled eyes. What a strange temperament is this, where smiles and tears can mingle!

"What a curious child you are!" he says, at length. "You are never the same for two minutes together."

"Perhaps that is what makes me so nice," retorts Miss Mona, saucily, the sense of fun still full upon her, making him a small grimace, and bestowing upon him a bewitching glance from under her long dark lashes, that lie like shadows on her cheeks.

CHAPTER V.

HOW MONA BETRAYS WHAT MAKES GEOFFREY JEALOUS, AND HOW AN APPOINTMENT IS MADE THAT IS ALL MOON-SHINE.

"Yes, it certainly is a charm," says Geoffrey slowly "but it puzzles me. I cannot be gay one moment and sad the next. Tell me how you manage it."

"I can't, because I don't know myself. It is my nature. However depressed I may feel at one instant, the next a passing thought may change my tears into a laugh. Perhaps that is why we are called fickle; yet it has nothing to do with it: it is a mere peculiarity of temperament, and a rather merciful gift, for which we should be grateful, because, though we return again to our troubles, still the moment or two of forgetfulness soothes us and nerves us for the conflict. I speak, of course, of only minor sorrows; such a grief as poor Kitty's admits of no alleviation. It will last for her lifetime."

"Will it?" says Geoffrey, oddly.

"Yes. One can understand that," replies she, gravely, not heeding the closeness of his regard. "Many things affect me curiously," she goes on, dreamily,—"sad pictures and poetry and the sound of sweet music."

"Do you sing?" asks he, through mere force of habit, as she pauses.

"Yes."

The answer is so downright, so unlike the usual "a little," or "oh, nothing to signify," or "just when there is nobody else," and so on, that Geoffrey is rather taken back.

"I am not a musician," she goes on, evenly, "but some people admire my singing very much. In Dublin they liked to hear me, when I was with Aunt Anastasia; and you know a Dublin audience is very critical."

"But you have no piano?"

"Yes I have: aunty gave me hers when I was leaving town. It was no use to her and I loved it. I was at school in Portarlington for nearly three years, and when I came back from it I didn't care for Anastasia's friends, and found my only comfort in my music. I am telling you everything am I not," with a wistful smile, "and perhaps I weary you?"

"Weary me! no, indeed. That is one of the very few unkind things you have ever said to me. How could I weary of your voice? Go on; tell me where you keep this magical piano."

"In my own room. You have not seen that yet. But it belongs to myself alone, and I call it my den, because in it I keep everything that I hold most precious. Some time I will show it to you."

"Show it to me to-day," says he, with interest.

"Very well, if you wish."

"And you will sing me something?"

"If you like. Are you fond of singing!"

"Very. But for myself I have no voice worth hearing. I sing, you know, a little, which is my misfortune, not my fault; don't you think so?"

"Oh, no; because if you can sing at all—that is correctly, and without false notes—you must feel music and love it."

"Well for my part I hate people who sing a little. I always wish it was even less. I hold that they are a social nuisance, and ought to be put down by law. My eldest brother Nick sings really very well,—a charming tenor, you know, good enough to coax the birds off the bushes. He does all that sort of *dilettante* business,—paints, and reads tremendously about things dead and gone, that can't possibly advantage anybody. Understands old china as well as most people (which isn't saying much), and I think—but as yet this statement is unsupported—I think he writes poetry."

"Does he really?" asks Mona, with eyes wide open. "I am sure if I ever meet your brother Nick I shall be dreadfully afraid of him."

"Don't betray me, at all events. He is a touchy sort of fellow, and mightn't like to think I knew that about him. Jack, my second brother, sings too. He is coming home from India directly, and is an awfully good sort, though I think I should rather have old Nick after all."

"You have two brothers older than you?" asks Mona, meditatively.

"Yes; I am that most despicable of all things, a third son."

"I have heard of it. A third son would be poor, of course, and—and worldly people would not think so much of him as of others. Is that so?"

She pauses. But for the absurdity of the thing, Mr. Rodney would swear there is hope in her tone.

"Your description is graphic," he answers, lightly, "if faintly unkind; but when is the truth civil? You are right. Younger sons, as a rule, are not run after. Mammas do not hanker after them, or give them their reserve smiles, or pull their skirts aside to make room for them upon small ottomans."

"That betrays the meanness of the world," says Mona, slowly and with indignation. "Has not Geoffrey just declared himself to be a younger son?"

"Does it? I was bred in a different belief. In my world the mighty do no wrong; and a third son is nowhere. He is shunted; handed on; if possible, scotched. The sun is not made for *him*, or the first waltz, or caviare, or the 'sweet shady side' of anything. In fact, he 'is the man of no account' with a vengeance!"

"What a shame!" says Mona, angrily. Then she changes her note, and says, with a soft, low, mocking laugh, "How I pity you!"

"Thanks. I shall try to believe you, though your mirth is somewhat out of place, and has a tendency towards heartlessness." (He is laughing too.) "Yet there have been instances," goes on Mr. Rodney, still smiling, while watching her intently, "when maiden aunts have taken a fancy to third sons, and have died leaving them lots of tin."

"Eh?" says Mona.

"Tin,—money," explains he.

"Oh, I dare say. Yes, sometimes: but—" she hesitates, and this time the expression of her face cannot be misunderstood: dejection betrays itself in every line—"but it is not so with you, is it? No aunt has left you anything?"

"No,—no aunt," returns Rodney, speaking the solemn truth, yet conveying a lie: "I have not been blessed with maiden aunts wallowing in coin."

"So I thought," exclaims Mona, with a cheerful nod, that under other circumstances should be aggravating, so full of content it is. "At first I fea— I thought you were rich, but afterwards I guessed it was your brothers' ground you were shooting over. And Bridget told me, too. She said you could not be well off, you had so many brothers. But I like you all the better for that," says Mona, in a tone that actually savors of protection, slipping her little brown hand through his arm in a kindly, friendly, lovable fashion.

"Do you?" says Rodney. He is strangely moved; he speaks quietly, but his heart is beating quickly, and Cupid's dart sinks deeper in its wound.

"Is your brother, Mr. Rodney, like you?" asks Mona presently.

He has never told her that his eldest brother is a baronet. Why he hardly knows, yet now he does not contradict her when she alludes to him as Mr. Rodney. Some inward feeling prevents him. Perhaps he understands instinctively that such knowledge will but widen the breach that already exists between him and the girl who now walks beside him with a happy smile upon her flower-like face.

"No; he is not like me," he says, abruptly: "he is a much better fellow. He is, besides, tall and rather lanky, with dark eyes and hair. He is like my father, they tell me; I am like my mother."

At this Mona turns her gaze secretly upon him. She studies his hair, his gray eyes, his irregular nose,—that ought to have known better,—and his handsome mouth, so resolute, yet so tender, that his fair moustache only half conceals. The world in general acknowledges Mr. Rodney to be a well-looking young man of ordinary merits, but in Mona's eyes he is something more than all this; and I believe the word "ordinary," as applied to him, would sound offensive in her ears.

"I think I should like your mother," she says, naively and very sweetly, lifting her eyes steadily to his. "She is handsome, of course; and is she good as she is beautiful?"

Flattery goes a long way with most men, but in this instance the subtle poison touches Mr. Rodney even more than it pleases him. He presses the hand that rests upon his arm an eighth of an inch nearer to his heart than it was before, if that be possible.

"My mother is a real good sort when you know her," he says, evasively; "but she's rather rough on strangers. However, she is always all there, you know, so far as manners go, and that."

Miss Mona looks puzzled.

"I don't think I understand you," she says, at length, gravely. "Where would the rest of her be, if she wasn't all in the same place?"

She says this in such perfect good faith that Mr. Rodney roars with laughter.

"Perhaps you may not know it," says he, "but you are simply perfection!"

"So Mr. Moore says," returns she, smiling.

Had she put out all her powers of invention with a view to routing him with slaughter, she could not have been more successful than she is with this small unpremeditated speech. Had a thunderbolt fallen at his feet, he could not have betrayed more thorough and complete discomfiture.

He drops her arm, and looks as though he is prepared to drop her acquaintance also, at a moment's notice.

"What has Mr. Moore to do with you?" he asks, haughtily. "Who is he, that he should so speak to you?"

"He is our landlord," says Mona, calmly, but with uplifted brows, stopping short in the middle of the road to regard him with astonishment.

"And thinks you perfection?" in an impossible tone, losing both his head and his temper completely. "He is rich, I suppose; why don't you marry him?"

Mona turns pale.

"To ask the question is a rudeness," she says, steadily, though her heart is cold and hurt. "Yet I will answer you. In our country, and in our class," with an amount of inborn pride impossible to translate, "we do not marry a man because he is 'rich,' or in other words, sell ourselves for gold."

Having said this, she turns her back upon him contemptuously, and walks towards her home.

He follows her, full of remorse and contrition. Her glance, even more than her words, has covered him with shame, and cured him of his want of generosity.

"Forgive me, Mona," he says, with deep entreaty. "I confess my fault. How could I speak to you as I did! I implore your pardon. Great sinner as I am, surely I shall not knock for forgiveness at your sweet heart in vain!"

"Do not ever speak to me like that again," says Mona, turning upon him eyes humid with disappointment, yet free from wrath of any kind. "As for Mr. Moore," with a curl of her short upper lip that it does him good to see, and a quick frown, "why, he is as old as the hills, and as fat as Tichborne, and he hasn't got a single hair on his head!"

But that Mr. Rodney is still oppressed with the fear that he has mortally offended her, he could have laughed out loud at this childish speech; but anxiety helps him to restrain his mirth. Nevertheless he feels an unholy joy as he thinks on Mr. Moore's bald pate, his "too, too solid flesh," and his "many days."

"Yet he dares to admire you?" is what he does say, after a decided pause.

"Sure they all admire me," says Miss Mona, with an exasperating smile, meant to wither.

But Mr. Rodney is determined to "have it out with her," as he himself would say, before consenting to fade away out of her sight.

"But he wants to marry you. I know he does. Tell me the truth about that," he says, with flattering vehemence.

"Certainly I shall not. It would be very mean, and I wonder at you to ask the question," says Mona, with a great show of virtuous indignation. "Besides," mischievously, "if you know, there is no necessity to tell you anything."

"Yet answer me," persists he, very earnestly.

"I can't," says Mona; "it would be very unfair; and besides," petulantly, "it is all too absurd. Why, if Mr. Moore were to ask me to marry him ten thousand times again, I should never say anything but 'no.'"

Unconsciously she has betrayed herself. He hears the word "again" with a strange sinking of the heart. Others, then, are desirous of claiming this wild flower for their own.

"Oh, Mona, do you mean that?" he says. But Mona, who is very justly incensed, declines to answer him with civility.

"I begin to think our English cousins are not famous for their veracity," she says, with some scorn. "You seem to doubt every one's word; or is it mine in particular? Yet I spoke the truth. I do not want to marry any one."

Here she turns and looks him full in the face; and something—it may be in the melancholy of his expression—so amuses her that (laughter being as natural to her lips as perfume to a flower) she breaks into a sunny smile, and holds out to him her hand in token of amity.

"How could you be so absurd about that old Moore?" she says, lightly. "Why he has got nothing to recommend him except his money; and what good," with a sigh, "does that do him, unless to get him murdered!"

"If he is as fat as you say, he will be a good mark for a bullet," says Mr. Rodney, genially, almost—I am ashamed to say—hopefully. "I should think they would easily pot him one of these dark night that are coming. By this time I suppose he feels more like a grouse than a man, eh?—'I'll die game' should be his motto."

"I wish you wouldn't talk like that," says Mona, with a shudder. "It isn't at all nice of you; and especially when you know how miserable I am about my poor country."

"It is a pity anything should be said against Ireland," says Rodney, cleverly; "it is such a lovely little spot."

"Do you really like it?" asks she, plainly delighted.

"I should rather think so. Who wouldn't? I went to Glengariffe the other day, and can hardly fancy anything more lovely than its pure waters, and its purple hills that lie continued in the depths beneath."

"I have been there. And at Killarney, but only once, though we live so near."

"That has nothing to do with it," says Rodney. "The easier one can get to a place the more one puts off going. I knew a fellow once, and he lived all his time in London, and I give you my word he had never seen the Crystal Palace. With whom did you go to Killarney?"

"With Lady Mary. She was staying at the castle there; it was last year, and she asked me to go with her. I was delighted. And it was so pleasant, and everything so—so like heaven. The lakes are delicious, so calm, so solitary, so full of thought. Lady Mary is old, but young in manner, and has read and travelled so much, and she likes me," says Mona, naively. "And I like her. Do you know her?"

"Lady Mary Crighton? Yes, I have met her. An old lady with corkscrew ringlets, patches, and hoops? She is quite *grande dame*, and witty, like all you Irish people."

"She is very seldom at home, but I think I like her better than any one I ever met."

"Do you?" says Geoffrey, in a tone that means much.

"Yes,—better than all the women I ever met," corrects Mona, but without placing the faintest emphasis upon the word "women," which omission somehow possesses its charm in Rodney's eyes.

"Well, I shall go and judge of Killarney myself some day," he says, idly.

"Oh, yes, you must indeed," says the little enthusiast, brightening. "It is more than lovely. How I wish I could go with you!"

She looks at him as she says this, fearlessly, honestly, and without a suspicion of coquetry.

"I wish you could!" says Geoffrey from his heart.

"Well, I can't, you know," with a sigh. "But no matter: you will enjoy the scenery even more by yourself."

"I don't think I shall," says Geoffrey, in a low tone.

"Well, we have both seen the bay," says Mona, cheerfully,—"Bantry Bay I mean: so we can talk about that. Yet indeed"—seriously—"you cannot be said to have seen it properly, as it is only by moonlight its full beauty can be appreciated. Then, with its light waves sparkling beneath the gleam of the stars, and the moon throwing a path across it that seems to go on and on, until it reaches heaven, it is more satisfying than a happy dream. Do you see that hill up yonder?" pointing to an elevation about a mile distant: "there I sometimes sit when the moon is full, and watch the bay below. There is a lovely view from that spot."

"I wish I could see it!" says Geoffrey, longingly.

"Well so you can," returns she, kindly. "Any night when there is a good moon come to me and I will go with you to Carrickdhuve—that is the name of the hill—and show you the bay."

She looks at him quite calmly, as one might who sees nothing in the fact of accompanying a young man to the top of a high mountain after nightfall. And in truth she does see nothing in it. If he wishes to see the bay she loves so well, of course he must see it; and who so competent to point out to him all its beauties as herself?

"I wonder when the moon will be full," says Geoffrey, making this ordinary remark in an everyday tone that does him credit, and speaks well for his kindliness and delicacy of feeling, as well as for his power of discerning character. He makes no well-turned speeches about the bay being even more enchanting under such circumstances, or any orthodox compliment that might have pleased a woman versed in the world's ways.

"We must see," says Mona, thoughtfully.

They have reached the farm again by this time, and Geoffrey, taking up the guns he had left behind the hall door,—or what old Scully is pleased to call the front door in contradistinction to the back door, through which he is in the habit of making his exits and entrances,—holds out his hand to bid her good-by.

"Come in for a little while and rest yourself," says Mona, hospitably, "while I get the brandy and send it up to poor Kitty."

It strikes Geoffrey as part of the innate sweetness and genuineness of her disposition that, after all the many changes of thought that have passed through her brain on their return journey, her first concern on entering her own doors is for the poor unhappy creature in the cabin up yonder.

"Don't be long," he says, impulsively, as she disappears down a passage.

"I won't, then. Sure you can live alone with yourself for one minute," returns she, in very fine Irish; and, with a parting smile, sweet as nectar and far more dangerous, she goes.

When she is gone, Geoffrey walks impatiently up and down the small hall, conflicting emotions robbing him of the serenity that usually attends his footsteps. He is happy, yet full of a secret gnawing uneasiness that weighs upon him daily, hourly. Near Mona—when in her presence—a gladness that amounts almost to perfect happiness is his; apart from her is unrest. Love, although he is but just awakening to the fact, has laid his chubby hands upon him, and now holds him in thrall; so that no longer for him is that most desirable thing content,—which means indifference. Rather is he melancholy now and then, and inclined to look on life apart from Mona as a doubtful good.

For what, after all, is love, but

"A madness most discreet,A choking gall, and a preserving sweet?"

There are, too, dispassionate periods, when he questions the wisdom of giving his heart to a girl lowly born as Mona undoubtedly is, at least on her father's side. And, indeed, the little drop of blue blood inherited from her mother is so faint in hue as to be scarcely recognizable by those inclined to cavil.

And these he knows will be many: there would be first his mother, and then Nick, with a silent tongue but brows uplifted, and after them Violet, who in the home circle is regarded as Geoffrey's "affinerty," and who last year was asked to Rodney Towers for the express purpose (though she knew it not) of laying siege to his heart and bestowing upon him in return her hand and— fortune. To do Lady Rodney justice, she was never blind to the fortune!

Yet Violet, with her pretty, slow, *trainante* voice and perfect manner, and small pale attractive face, and great eyes that seem too earnest for the fragile body to which they belong, is as naught before Mona, whose beauty is strong and undeniable, and whose charm lies as much in inward grace as in outward loveliness.

Though uncertain that she regards him with any feeling stronger than that of friendliness (because of the strange coldness that she at times affects, dreading perhaps lest he shall see too quickly into her tender heart), yet instinctively he knows that he is welcome in her sight, and that "the day grows brighter for his coming." Still, at times this strange coldness puzzles him, not understanding that

"No lesse was she in secret heart affected,But that she masked it in modestie,For feare she should of lightnesse be detected."

For many days he had not known "that his heart was darkened with her shadow." Only yesterday he might perhaps have denied his love for her, so strange, so uncertain, so undreamt of, is the dawning of a first great attachment. One looks upon the object that attracts, and finds the deepest joy in looking, yet hardly realizes the great truth that she has become part of one's being, not to be eradicated until death or change come to the rescue.

Perhaps Longfellow has more cleverly—and certainly more tenderly—than any other poet described the earlier approaches of the god of Love, when he says,—

"The first sound in the song of loveScarce more than silence is, and yet a sound.Hands of invisible spirits touch the stringsOf that mysterious instrument, the soul,And play the prelude of our fate."

For Geoffrey the prelude has been played, and now at last he knows it. Up and down the little hall he paces, his hands behind his back, as his wont when deep in day-dreams, and asks himself many a question hitherto unthought of. Can he—shall he—go farther in this matter? Then this thought presses to the front beyond all others:—"Does she—will she—ever love me?"

"Now, hurry, Bridget," says Mona's low soft voice,—that "excellent thing in woman." "Don't be any time. Just give that to Kitty, and say one prayer, and be back in ten minutes."

"Law, Miss Mona, ye needn't tell me; sure I'm flyin' I'll be there an' back before ye'll know I'm gone." This from the agile Biddy, as (exhilarated with the knowledge that she is going to see a corpse) she rushes up the road.

"Now come and see my own room," says Mona, going up to Rodney, and, slipping her hand into his in a little trustful fashion that is one of her many, loving ways, she leads him along the hall to a door opposite the kitchen. This she opens, and with conscious pride draws him after her across its threshold. So holding him, she might at this moment have drawn him to the world's end,—wherever that may be!

It is a very curious little room they enter,—yet pretty, withal, and suggestive of care and affection, and certainly not one to be laughed at. Each object that meets the view seems replete with pleasurable memory,—seems part of its gentle mistress. There are two windows, small, and with diamond panes like the parlor, and in the far end is a piano. There are books, and some ornaments, and a huge bowl of sweetly-smelling flowers on the centre-table, and a bracket or two against the walls. Some loose music is lying on a chair.

"Now I am here, you will sing me something," says Geoffrey, presently.

"I wonder what kind of songs you like best," says Mona, dreamily, letting her fingers run noiselessly over the keys of the Collard. "If you are like me, you like sad ones."

"Then I am like you?" returns he, quickly.

"Then I will sing you a song I was sent last week," says Mona, and forthwith sings him "Years Ago," mournfully, pathetically, and with all her soul, as it should be sung. Then she gives him "London Bridge," and then "Rose-Marie," and then she takes her fingers from the piano and looks at him with a fond hope that he will see fit to praise her work.

"You are an artiste," says Geoffrey, with a deep sigh when she has finished. "Who taught you, child? But there is no use in such a question. Nobody could teach it to you: you must feel it as you sing. And yet you are scarcely to be envied. Your singing has betrayed to me one thing: if ever you suffer any great trouble it will kill you."

"I am not going to suffer," says Mona, lightly. "Sorrow only falls on every second generation; and you know poor mother was very unhappy at one time: therefore I am free. You will call that superstition, but," with a grave shake of her head, "it is quite true."

"I hope it is," says Geoffrey; "though, taking your words for gospel, it rather puts me out in the cold. My mother seems to have had rather a good time all through, devoid of anything that might be termed trouble."

"But she lost her husband," says Mona, gently.

"Well, she did. I don't remember about that, you know. I was quite a little chap, and hustled out of sight if I said 'boo.' But of course she's got over all that, and is as jolly as a sand-boy now," says Geoffrey, gayly. (If only Lady Rodney could have heard him comparing her to a "sand-boy"!)

"Poor thing!" says Mona, sympathetically, which sympathy, by the by, is utterly misplaced, as Lady Rodney thought her husband, if anything, an old bore, and three months after his death confessed to herself that she was very glad he was no more.

"Where do you get your music?" asks Geoffrey, idly, wondering how "London Bridge" has found its way to this isolated spot, as he thinks of the shops in the pretty village near, where Molloy and Adams, and their attendant sprite called Weatherley, are unknown.

"The boys send it to me. Anything new that comes out, or anything they think will suit my voice, they post to me at once."

"The boys!" repeats he, mystified.

"Yes, the students, I mean. When with aunty in Dublin I knew ever so many of them, and they were very fond of me."

"I dare say," says Mr. Rodney, with rising ire.

"Jack Foster and Terry O'Brien write to me very often," goes on Mona, unconsciously. "And indeed they all do occasionally, at Christmas, you know, and Easter and Midsummer, just to ask me how I am, and to tell me how they have got through their exams. But it is Jack and Terry, for the most part, who send me the music."

"It is very kind of them, I'm sure," says Geoffrey, unreasonably jealous, as, could he only have seen the said Terry's shock head of red hair, his fears of rivalry would forever have been laid at rest. "But they are favored friends. You can take presents from them, and yet the other day when I asked you if you would like a little gold chain to hang to your mother's watch, you answered me 'that you did not require it' in such a tone as actually froze me and made me feel I had said something unpardonably impertinent."

"Oh, no," says Mona, shocked at this interpretation of her manner. "I did not mean all that; only I really did not require it; at least"—truthfully—"not *much*. And, besides, a song is not like a gold chain; and you are quite different from them; and besides, again,"—growing slightly confused, yet with a last remnant of courage,—"there is no reason why you should give me anything. Shall I"—hurriedly—"sing something else for you?"

And then she sings again, some old-world song of love and chivalry that awakes within one a quick longing for a worthier life. Her sweet voice rings through the room, now glad with triumph, now sad with a "lovely melancholy," as the words and music sway her. Her voice is clear and pure and full of pathos! She seems to follow no rule; an "f" here or a "p" there, on the page before her, she heeds not, but sings only as her heart dictates.

When she has finished, Geoffrey says "thank you" in a low tone. He is thinking of the last time when some one else sang to him, and of how different the whole scene was from this. It was at the Towers, and the hour with its dying daylight, rises before him. The subdued light of the summer eve, the open window, the perfume of the drowsy flowers, the girl at the piano with her small drooping head and her perfectly trained and very pretty voice, the room, the soft silence, his mother leaning back in her crimson velvet chair, beating time to the music with her long jewelled, fingers,—all is remembered.

It was in the boudoir they were sitting, and Violet was dressed in some soft gray dress that shone and turned into palest pearl as she moved. It was his mother's boudoir, the room she most affects, with its crimson and gray coloring and its artistic arrangements, that blend so harmoniously, and are so tremendously becoming to the complexion when the blinds are lowered. How pretty Mona would look in a gray and crimson room? how——

"What are you thinking of?" asks Mona, softly, breaking in upon his soliloquy.

"Of the last time I heard any one sing," returns he, slowly. "I was comparing that singer very unfavorably with you. Your voice is so unlike what one usually hears in drawing-rooms."

He means highest praise. She accepts his words as a kind rebuke.

"Is that a compliment?" she says, wistfully. "Is it well to be unlike all the world? Yet what you say is true, no doubt. I suppose I am different from— from all the other people you know."

This is half a question; and Geoffrey, answering it from his heart, sinks even deeper into the mire.

"You are indeed," he says, in a tone so grateful that it ought to have betrayed to her his meaning. But grief and disappointment have seized upon her.

"Yes, of course," she says, dejectedly. A cloud seems to have fallen upon her happy hour. "When did you hear that—that last singer?" she asks, in a subdued voice.

"At home," returns he. He is gazing out of the window, with his hands clasped behind his back, and does not pay so much attention to her words as is his wont.

"Is your home very beautiful?" asks she, timidly, looking at him the more earnestly in that he seems rapt in contemplation of the valley that spreads itself before him.

"Yes, very beautiful," he answers, thinking of the stately oaks and aged elms and branching beeches that go so far to make up the glory of the ivied Towers.

"How paltry this country must appear in comparison with your own!" goes on the girl, longing for a contradiction, and staring at her little brown hands, the fingers of which are twining and intertwining nervously with one another, "How glad you will be to get back to your own home!"

"Yes, very glad," returns he, hardly knowing what he says. He has gone back again to his first thoughts,—his mother's boudoir, with its old china, and its choice water-colors that line the walls, and its delicate Italian statuettes. In his own home—which is situated about fourteen miles from the Towers, and which is rather out of repair through years of disuse—there are many rooms. He is busy now trying to remember them, and to decide which of them would look best decked out in crimson and gray, or blue and silver: he hardly knows which would suit her best. Perhaps, after all——

"How strange it is!" says Mona's voice, that has now a faint shade of sadness in it. "How people come and go in one's lives, like the waves of the restless sea, now breaking at one's feet, now receding, now——"

"Only to return," interrupts he, quickly. "And—to break at your feet? to break one's heart, do you mean? I do not like your simile."

"You jest," says Mona, full of calm reproach. "I mean how strangely people fall into one's lives and then out again!" She hesitates. Perhaps something in his face warns her, perhaps it is the weariness of her own voice that frightens her, but at this moment her whole expression changes, and a laugh, forced but apparently full of gayety, comes from her lips. It is very well done indeed, yet to any one but a jealous lover her eyes would betray her. The usual softness is gone from them, and only a well-suppressed grief and a pride that cannot be suppressed take its place.

"Why should they fall out again?" says Rodney, a little angrily, hearing only her careless laugh, and—man-like—ignoring stupidly the pain in her lovely eyes. "Unless people choose to forget."

"One may choose to forget, but one may not be able to accomplish it. To forget or to remember is not in one's own power."

"That is what fickle people say. But what one feels one remembers."

"That is true, for a time, with some. *Forever* with others."

"Are you one of the others?"

She makes him no answer.

"Are *you?*" she says, at length, after a long silence.

"I think so, Mona. There is one thing I shall never get."

"Many things, I dare say," she says, nervously, turning from him.

"Why do you speak of people dropping out of your life?"

"Because, of course, you will, you must. Your world is not mine."

"You could make it yours."

"I do not understand," she says, very proudly, throwing up her head with a charming gesture. "And, talking of forgetfulness, do you know what hour it is?"

"You evidently want to get rid of me," says Rodney, discouraged, taking up his hat. He takes up her hand, too, and holds it warmly, and looks long and earnestly into her face.

"By the by," he says, once more restored to something like hope, as he notes her drooping lids and changing color and how she hides from his searching gaze her dark, blue, Irish eyes, that, as somebody has so cleverly expressed it, seem "rubbed into her head with a dirty finger," so marked lie the shadows beneath them, that enhance and heighten their beauty,—"by the by, you told me you had a miniature of your mother in your desk, and you promised to show it to me." He merely says this with a view to gaining more time, and not from any overwhelming desire to see the late Mrs. Scully.

"It is here," says Mona, rather pleased at his remembering this promise of hers, and, going to a desk, proceeds to open a secret drawer, in which lies the picture in question.

It is a very handsome picture, and Geoffrey duly admires it; then it is returned to its place, and Mona, opening the drawer next to it, shows him some exquisite ferns dried and gummed on paper.

"What a clever child you are!" says Geoffrey, with genuine admiration. "And what is here?" laying his hand on the third drawer.

"Oh, do not open that—do not!" says Mona, hastily, in an agony of fear, to judge by her eyes, laying a deterring hand upon his arm.

"And why not this or any other drawer?" says Rodney, growing pale. Again jealousy, which is a demon, rises in his breast, and thrusts out all gentler feelings. Her allusion to Mr. Moore, most innocently spoken, and, later on, her reference to the students, have served to heighten within him angry suspicion.

"Do not!" says Mona, again, as though fresh words are impossible to her, drawing her breath quickly. Her evident agitation incenses him to the last degree. Opening the drawer impulsively, he gazes at its contents.

Only a little withered bunch of heather, tied by a blade of grass! Nothing more!

Rodney's heart throbs with passionate relief, yet shame covers him; for he himself, one day, had given her that heather, tied, as he remembers, with that selfsame grass; and she, poor child, had kept it ever since. She had treasured it, and laid it aside, apart from all other objects, among her most sacred possessions, as a thing beloved and full of tender memories; and his had been the hand to ruthlessly lay bare this hidden secret of her soul.

He is overcome with contrition, and would perhaps have said something betraying his scorn of himself, but she prevents him.

"Yes," she says, with cheeks colored to a rich carmine, and flashing eyes, and lips that quiver in spite of all her efforts at control, "that is the bit of heather you gave me, and that is the grass that tied it. I kept it because it reminded me of a day when I was happy. Now," bitterly, "I no longer care for it: for the future it can only bring back to me an hour when I was grieved and wounded."

Taking up the hapless heather, she throws it on the ground, and, in a fit of childish spleen, lays her foot upon it and tramples it out of all recognition. Yet, even as she does so, the tears gather in her eyes, and, resting there unshed, transfigure her into a lovely picture that might well be termed "Beauty in Distress." For this faded flower she grieves, as though it were, indeed, a living thing that she has lost.

"Go!" she says, in a choked voice, and with a little passionate sob, pointing to the door. "You have done mischief enough." Her gesture is at once imperious and dignified. Then in a softer voice, that tells of sorrow, and with a deep sigh, "At least," she says, "I believed in your honor!"

The reproach is terrible, and cuts him to the heart. He picks up the poor little bruised flower, and holds it tenderly in his hand.

"How can I go," he says, without daring to look at her, "until, at least, I *ask* for forgiveness?" He feels more nervous, more crushed in the presence of this little wounded Irish girl with her pride and her grief, than he has ever felt in the presence of an offended fashionable beauty full of airs and caprices. "Mona, love makes one cruel: I ask you to remember that, because it is my only excuse," he says, warmly. "Don't condemn me altogether; but forgive me once more."

"I am always forgiving you, it seems to me," says Mona, coldly, turning from him with a frown. "And as for that heather," facing him again, with eyes shamed but wrathful, "I just kept it because—because—oh, because I didn't like to throw it away! That was all!"

Her meaning, in spite of her, is clear; but Geoffrey doesn't dare so much as to think about it. Yet in his heart he knows that he is glad because of her words.

"You mustn't think I supposed you kept it for any other purpose," he says, quite solemnly, and in such a depressed tone that Mona almost feels sorry for him.

He has so far recovered his courage that he has taken her hand, and is now holding it in a close grasp; and Mona, though a little frown still lingers on her low, broad forehead, lets her hand so lie without a censure.

"Mona, *do* be friends with me," he says at last, desperately, driven to simplicity of language through his very misery. There is a humility in this speech that pleases her.

"It is really hardly worth talking about," she says, grandly. "I was foolish to lay so great a stress on such a trifling matter. It doesn't signify, not in the least. But—but," the blood mounting to her brow, "if ever you speak of it again,—if ever you even *mention* the word 'heather,'—I shall *hate you!*"

"That word shall never pass my lips again in your company,—never, I swear!" says he, "until you give me leave. My darling," in a low tone, "if you could only know how vexed I am about the whole affair, and my unpardonable conduct! Yet, Mona, I will not hide from you that this little bit of senseless heather has made me happier than I have ever been before."

Stooping, he presses his lips to her hand for the first time. The caress is long and fervent.

"Say I am quite forgiven," he pleads, earnestly, his eyes on hers.

"Yes. I forgive you," she says, almost in a whisper, with a seriousness that amounts to solemnity.

Still holding her hand, as though loath to quit it, he moves towards the door; but before reaching it she slips away from him, and says "Good-by" rather coldly.

"When am I to see you again?" says Rodney, anxiously.

"Oh not for ever so long," returns she, with much and heartless unconcern. (His spirits sink to zero.) "Certainly not until Friday," she goes on, carelessly. (As this is Wednesday, his spirits once more rise into the seventh heaven.) "Or Saturday, or Sunday, or perhaps some day next week," she says, unkindly.

"If on Friday night there is a good moon," says Rodney, boldly, "will you take me, as you promised, to see the Bay?"

"Yes, if it is fine," says Mona, after a faint hesitation.

Then she accompanies him to the door, but gravely, and not with her accustomed gayety. Standing on the door-step he looks at her, and, as though impelled to ask the question because of her extreme stillness, he says, "Of what are you thinking?"

"I am thinking that the man we saw before going into Kitty's cabin is the murderer!" she says, with a strong shudder.

"I thought so all along," says Geoffrey, gravely.

CHAPTER VI.

HOW THE MYSTIC MOONBEAMS THROW THEIR RAYS ON MONA; AND HOW GEOFFREY, JEALOUS OF THEIR ADMIRATION, DESIRES TO CLAIM HER AS HIS OWN.

Friday is fine, and towards nightfall grows still milder, until it seems that even in the dawn of October a summer's night may be born.

The stars are coming out one by one,—slowly, tranquilly, as though haste has got no part with them. The heavens are clothed in azure. A single star, that sits apart from all the rest, is twinkling and gleaming in its blue nest, now throwing out a pale emerald ray, now a blood-red fire, and anon a touch of opal, faint and shadowy, yet more lovely in its vagueness than all the rest, until verily it resembles "a diamond in the sky."

Geoffrey coming to the farm somewhat early in the evening, Mona takes him round to the yard, where two dogs, hitherto unseen by Geoffrey, lie chained. They are two splendid bloodhounds, that, as she approaches, rise to their feet, and, lifting their massive heads, throw out into the night-air a deep hollow bay that bespeaks welcome.

"What lovely creatures!" says Geoffrey, who has a passion for animals: they seem to acknowledge him as a friend. As Mona looses them from their den, they go to him, and, sniffing round him, at last open their great jaws into a satisfied yawn, and, raising themselves, rest their paws upon his breast and rub their faces contentedly against his.

"Now you are their friend forever," says Mona, in a pleased tone. "Once they do that, they mean to tell you they have adopted you. And they like very few people: so it is a compliment."

"I feel it keenly," says Rodney, caressing the handsome creatures as they crouch at his feet. "Where did you get them?"

"From Mr. Moore." A mischievous light comes into her face as she says this, and she laughs aloud. "But, I assure you, not as a love-token. He gave them to me when they were quite babies, and I reared them myself. Are they not lovely? I call them? 'Spice' and 'Allspice,' because one has a quicker temper than the other."

"The names are original, at all events," says Geoffrey,—"which is a great charm. One gets so tired of 'Rags and Tatters,' 'Beer and Skittles,' 'Cakes and Ale,' and so forth, where pairs are in question, whether they be dogs or ponies."

"Shall we set out now?" says Mona; and she calls "Mickey, Mickey," at the top of her strong young lungs.

The man who manages the farm generally—and is a plague and a blessing at the same time to his master—appears round a corner, and declares, respectfully, that he will be ready in a "jiffy" to accompany Miss Mona, if she will just give him time to "clane himself up a bit."

And in truth the "claning" occupies a very short period,—or else Mona and Geoffrey heed not the parting moments. For sometimes

"Time, as he passes us, has a dove's wing,Unsoiled and swift, and of a silken sound."

"I'm ready now, miss, if you are," says Mickey from the background, with the utmost *bonhommie*, and in a tone that implies he is quite willing not to be ready, if it so pleases her, for another five minutes or so, or even, if necessary, to efface himself altogether. He is a stalwart young Hibernian, with rough hair and an honest face, and gray eyes, merry and cunning, and so many freckles that he looks like a turkey-egg.

"Oh, yes, I am quite ready," says Mona, starting somewhat guiltily. And then they pass out through the big yard-gate, with the two dogs at their heels, and their attendant squire, who brings up the rear with a soft whistle that rings through the cool night-air and tells the listening stars that the "girl he loves is his dear," and his "own, his artless Nora Creana."

Geoffrey and Mona go up the road with the serenader behind them, and, turning aside, she guiding, mount a stile, and, striking across a field, make straight for the high hill that conceals the ocean from the farm. Over many fields they travel, until at length they reach the mountain's summit and gaze down upon the beauteous scene below.

The very air is still. There is no sound, no motion, save the coming and going of their own breath as it rises quickly from their hearts, filled full of passionate admiration for the loveliness before them.

From the high hill on which they stand, steep rocks descend until they touch the water's edge, which lies sleeping beneath them, lulled into slumber by the tranquil moon as she comes forth "from the slow opening curtains of the clouds."

Far down below lies the bay, calm and placid. Not a ripple, not a sigh comes to disturb its serenity or mar the perfect beauty of the silver pathway thrown so lightly upon it by the queen of heaven. It falls there so clear, so unbroken, that almost one might deem it possible to step upon it, and so walk onwards to the sky that melts into it on the far horizon.

The whole firmament is of a soft azure, flecked here and there with snowy clouds tipped with palest gray. A little cloud—the tenderest veil of mist—hangs between earth and sky.

"The moon is up; it is the dawn of night;Stands by her side one bold, bright, steady star,Star of her heart.Mother of stars! the heavens look up to thee."

Mona is looking up to it now, with a rapt, pensive gaze, her great blue eyes gleaming beneath its light. She is sitting upon the side of the hill, with her hands clasped about her knees, a thoughtful expression on her lovely face. At each side of her, sitting bolt upright on their huge haunches, are the dogs, as though bent on guarding her against all evil.

Geoffrey, although in reality deeply impressed by the grandeur of all the surroundings, yet cannot keep his eyes from Mona's face, her pretty attitude, her two mighty defenders. She reminds him in some wise of Una and the lion, though the idea is rather far-fetched; and he hardly dares speak to her, lest he shall break the spell that seems to lie upon her.

She herself destroys it presently.

"Do you like it?" she asks, gently, bringing her gaze back from the glowing heavens, to the earth, which is even more beautiful.

"The praise I heard of it, though great, was too faint," he answers her, with such extreme sincerity in his tone as touches and gladdens the heart of the little patriot at his feet. She smiles contentedly, and turns her eyes once more with lazy delight upon the sea, where each little point and rock is warmed with heavenly light. She nods softly to herself, but says nothing.

To her there is nothing strange or new, either in the hour or the place. Often does she come here in the moonlight with her faithful attendant and her two dogs, to sit and dream away a long sweet hour brimful of purest joy, whilst drinking in the plaintive charm that Nature as a rule flings over her choicest paintings.

To him, however, all is different; and the hour is fraught with a tremulous joy, and with a vague sweet longing that means love as yet untold.

"This spot always brings to my mind the thoughts of other people," says Mona, softly. "I am very fond of poetry: are you?"

"Very," returns he, surprised. He has not thought of her as one versed in lore of any kind. "What poets do you prefer?"

"I have read so few," she says, wistfully, and with hesitation. Then, shyly, "I have so few to read. I have a Longfellow, and a Shakspeare, and a Byron: that is all."

"Byron?"

"Yes. And after Shakspeare, I like him best, and then Longfellow. Why do you speak in that tone? Don't you like him?"

"I think I like no poet half so well. You mistake me," replies he, ashamed of his own surprise at her preference for his lordship beneath the calm purity of her eyes. "But—only—it seemed to me Longfellow would be more suited to you."

"Well, so I do love him. And just then it was of him I was thinking: when I looked up to the sky his words came back to me. You remember what he says about the moon rising 'over the pallid sea and the silvery mist of the meadows,' and how,—

'Silently, one by one, in the infinite meadows of heaven,Blossomed the lovely stars, the forget-me-nots of the angels,

That is so sweet, I think."

"I remember it; and I remember, too, who watched all that: do you?" he asks, his eyes fixed upon hers.

"Yes; Gabriel—poor Gabriel and Evangeline," returns she, too wrapped up in recollections of that sad and touching tale to take to heart his meaning:—

'Meanwhile, apart, in the twilight gloom of a window's embrasureSat the lovers, and whispered together.'

That is the part you mean, is it not? I know all that poem very nearly by heart."

He is a little disappointed by the calmness of her answer.

"Yes; it was of them I thought," he says, turning his head away,—"of the—lovers. I wonder if *their* evening was as lovely as *ours*?"

Mona makes no reply.

"Have you ever read Shelley?" asks he, presently, puzzled by the extreme serenity of her manner.

She shakes her head.

"Some of his ideas are lovely. You would like his poetry, I think."

"What does he say about the moon?" asks Mona, still with her knees in her embrace, and without lifting her eyes from the quiet waters down below.

"About the moon? Oh, many things. I was not thinking of the moon," with faint impatience; "yet, as you ask me, I can remember one thing he says about it."

"Then tell it to me," says Mona.

So at her bidding he repeats the lines slowly, and in his best manner, which is very good:—

"The cold chaste moon, the queen of heaven's bright isles,Who makes all beautiful on which she smiles!That wandering shrine of soft yet icy flame,Which ever is transformed, yet still the same,And warms, but not illumines."

He finishes; but, to his amazement, and a good deal to his chagrin, on looking at Mona he finds she is wreathed in smiles,—nay, is in fact convulsed with silent laughter.

"What is amusing you?" asks he, a trifle stiffly.—To give way to recitation, and then find your listener in agonies of suppressed mirth, isn't exactly a situation one would hanker after.

"It was the last line," says Mona, in explanation, clearly ashamed of herself, yet unable wholly to subdue her merriment. "It reminded me so much of that speech about tea, that they always use at temperance meetings; they call it the beverage 'that cheers but not inebriates.' You said 'that warms but not illumines,' and it sounded exactly like it. Don't you see!"

He doesn't see.

"You aren't angry, are you?" says Mona, now really contrite. "I couldn't help it, and it *was* like it, you know."

"Angry? no!" he says, recovering himself, as he notices the penitence on the face upraised to his.

"And do say it is like it," says Mona, entreatingly.

"It is, the image of it," returns he, prepared to swear to anything she may propose And then he laughs too, which pleases her, as it proves he no longer bears in mind her evil deed; after which, feeling she still owes him something, she suddenly intimates to him that he may sit down on the grass close beside her. He seems to find no difficulty in swiftly following up this hint, and is soon seated as near to her as circumstances will allow.

But on this picture, the beauty of which is undeniable, Mickey (the barbarian) looks with disfavor.

"If he's goin' to squat there for the night,—an' I see ivery prospect of it," says Mickey to himself,—"what on airth's goin' to become of me?"

Now, Mickey's idea of "raal grand" scenery is the kitchen fire. Bays and rocks and moonlight, and such like comfortless stuff, would be designated by him as "all my eye an' Betty Martin." He would consider the bluest water that ever rolled a poor thing if compared to the water that boiled in the big kettle, and sadly inferior to such cold water as might contain a "dhrop of the crather." So no wonder he views with dismay Mr. Rodney's evident intention of spending another half hour or so on the top of Carrick dhuve.

Patience has its limits. Mickey's limit comes quickly When five more minutes have passed, and the two in his charge still make no sign, he coughs respectfully but very loudly behind his hand. He waits in anxious hope for the result of this telling man[oe]uvre, but not the faintest notice is taken of it. Both Mona and Geoffrey are deaf to the pathetic appeal sent straight from his bronchial tubes.

Mickey, as he grows desperate, grows bolder. He rises to speech.

"Av ye plaze, miss, will ye soon be comin'?"

"Very soon, Mickey," says Mona, without turning her head. But, though her words are satisfactory, her tone is not. There is a lazy ring in it that speaks of anything but immediate action. Mickey disbelieves in it.

"I didn't make up the mare, miss, before comin' out wid ye," he says, mildly, telling this lie without a blush.

"But it is early yet, Mickey, isn't it?" says Mona.

"Awfully early," puts in Geoffrey.

"It is, miss; I know it, sir; but if the old man comes out an' finds the mare widout her bed, there'll be all the world to pay, an' he'll be screechin' mad."

"He won't go into the stable to-night," says Mona, comfortably.

"He might, miss. It's the very time you'd wish him aisy in his mind that he gets raal troublesome. An' I feel just as if he was in the stable this blessid minit lookin' at the poor baste, an' swearin' he'll have the life uv me."

"And I feel just as if he had gone quietly to bed," says

Mona, pleasantly, turning away.

But Mickey is not to be outdone. "An' there's the pigs, miss," he begins again, presently.

"What's the matter with them?" says Mona, with some pardonable impatience.

"I didn't give them their supper yet, miss; an' it's very bad for the young ones to be left starvin'. It's on me mind, miss, so that I can't even enjoy me pipe, and it's fresh baccy I have an' all, an' it might as well be dust for what comfort I get from it. Them pigs is callin' for me now like Christians: I can a'most hear them."

"I shouldn't think deafness is in your family," says Geoffrey, genially.

"No, sir; it isn't, sir. We're none of us hard of hearin' glory be to——. Miss Mona," coaxingly, "sure, it's only a step to the house: wouldn't Misther Rodney see ye home now, just for wanst?"

"Why, yes, of course he can," says Mona, without the smallest hesitation. She says it quite naturally, and as though it was the most usual thing in the world for a young man to see a young woman home, through dewy fields and beneath "mellow moons," at half-past ten at night. It is now fully nine, and she cannot yet bear to turn her back upon the enchanting scene before her. Surely in another hour or so it will be time enough to think of home and all other such prosaic facts.

"Thin I may go, miss?" says Mickey.

"Oh, yes, you may go," says Mona. Geoffrey says nothing. He is looking at her with curiosity, in which deep love is mingled. She is so utterly unlike all other women he has ever met, with their petty affectations and mock modesties, their would-be hesitations and their final yieldings. She has no idea she is doing anything that all the world of women might not do, and can see no reason why she should distrust her friend just because he is a man.

Even as Geoffrey is looking at her, full of tender thought, one of the dogs, as though divining the fact that she is being left somewhat alone, lays its big head upon her shoulder, and looks at her with large loving eyes. Turning to him in response, she rubs her soft cheek slowly up and down against his. Geoffrey with all his heart envies the dog. How she seems to love it! how it seems to love her!

"Mickey, if you are going, I think you may as well take the dogs with you," says Mona: "they, too, will want their suppers. Go, Spice, when I desire you. Good-night, Allspice; dear darling,—see how he clings to me."

Finally the dogs are called off, and reluctantly accompany the jubilant Mickey down the hill.

"Perhaps you are tired of staying here," says Mona, with compunction, turning to Geoffrey, "and would like to go home? I suppose every one cannot love this spot as I do. Yes," rising, "I am selfish. Do come home."

"Tired!" says Geoffrey, hastily. "No, indeed. What could tire of anything so divine? If it is your wish, it is mine also, that we should stay here for a little while longer." Then, struck by the intense relief in her face, he goes on: "How you do enjoy the beauties of Nature! Do you know I have been studying you since you came here, and I could see how your whole soul was wrapped in the glory of the surrounding prospect? You had no thoughts left for other objects,—not even one for me. For the first time," softly, "I learned to be jealous of inanimate things."

"Yet I was not so wholly engrossed as you imagine," she says, seriously. "I thought of you many times. For one thing, I felt glad that you could see this place with my eyes. But I have been silent, I know; and—and——"

"How Rome and Spain would enchant you," he says watching her face intently, "and Switzerland, with its lakes and mountains!"

"Yes. But I shall never see them."

"Why not? You will go there, perhaps when you are married."

"No," with a little flickering smile, that has pain and sorrow in it; "for the simple reason that I shall never marry."

"But why?" persists he.

"Because"—the smile has died away now, and she is looking down upon him, as he lies stretched at her feet in the uncertain moonlight, with an expression sad but earnest,—"because, though I am only a farmer's niece, I cannot bear farmers, and, of course, other people would not care for me."

"That is absurd," says Rodney; "and your own words refute you. That man called Moore cared for you, and very great impertinence it was on his part."

"Why, you never even saw him," says Mona, opening her eyes.

"No; but I can fancy him, with his horrid bald head. Now, you know," holding up his hand to stop her as she is about to speak, "you know you said he hadn't a hair left on it."

"Well, he was different," says Mona, giving in ignominiously. "I couldn't care for him either; but what I said is true all the same. Other people would not like me."

"Wouldn't they?" says Rodney, leaning on his elbow as the argument waxes warmer; "then all I can say is, I never met any 'other people.'"

"You have met only them, I suppose, as you belong to them."

"Do you mean to tell me that *I* don't care for you?" says Rodney, quickly.

Mona evades a reply.

"How cold it is!" she says, rising, with a little shiver. "Let us go home."

If she had been nurtured all her life in the fashionable world, she could scarcely have made a more correct speech. Geoffrey is puzzled, nay more, discomfited. Just in this wise would a woman in his own set answer him, did she mean to repel his advances for the moment. He forgets that no tinge of worldliness lurks in Mona's nature, and feels a certain amount of chagrin that she should so reply to him.

"If you wish," he says, in a courteous tone, but one full of coldness; and so they commence their homeward journey.

"I am glad you have been pleased to-night," says Mona, shyly, abashed by his studied silence. "But," nervously, "Killarney is even more beautiful. You must go there."

"Yes; I mean to,—before I return to England."

She starts perceptibly, which is balm to his heart.

"To England!" she repeats, with a most mournful attempt at unconcern, "Will—will that be soon?"

"Not very soon. But some time, of course, I must go."

"I suppose so," she says, in a voice from which all joy has flown. "And it is only natural; you will be happier there." She is looking straight before her. There is no quiver in her tone; her lips do not tremble; yet he can see how pale she has grown beneath the vivid moonlight.

"Is that what you think?" he says, earnestly. "Then for once you are wrong. I have never been—I shall hardly be again—happier than I have been in Ireland."

There is a pause. Mona says nothing, but taking out the flower that has lain upon her bosom all night, pulls it to pieces petal by petal. And this is unlike Mona, because flowers are dear to her as sunshine is to them.

At this moment they come to a high bank, and Geoffrey, having helped Mona to mount it, jumps down at the other side, and holds out his arms to assist her to descend. As she reaches the ground, and while his arms are still round her, she says, with a sudden effort, and without lifting her eyes, "There is very good snipe-shooting here at Christmas."

The little pathetic insinuation is as perfect as it is touching.

"Is there? Then I shall certainly return for it," says Geoffrey, who is too much of a gentleman to pretend to understand all her words seem to imply. "It is really no journey from this to England."

"I should think it a long journey," says Mona, shaking her head.

"Oh, no, you won't," says Rodney, absently. In truth, his mind is wandering to that last little speech of hers, and is trying to unravel it.

Mona looks at him. How oddly he has expressed himself! "You won't," he said, instead of "you wouldn't." Does he then deem it possible she will ever be able to cross to that land that calls him son? She sighs, and, looking down at her little lean sinewy hands, clasps and unclasps them nervously.

"Why need you go until after Christmas?" she says, in a tone so low that he can barely hear her.

"Mona! Do you want me to stay?" asks he, suddenly, taking her hands in his. "Tell me the truth."

"I do," returns she, tremulously.

"But why?—why? Is it because you love me? Oh, Mona! If it is that! At times I have thought so, and yet again I have feared you do not love me as—as I love you."

"You love me?" repeats she, faintly.

"With all my heart," says Rodney, fervently. And, indeed, if this be so, she may well count herself in luck, because it is a very good and true heart of which he speaks.

"Don't say anything more," says the girl, almost passionately, drawing back from him as though afraid of herself. "Do not. The more you say now, the worse it will be for me by and by, when I have to think. And—and—it is all quite impossible."

"But why, darling? Could you not be happy as my wife?"

"Your wife?" repeats she, in soft, lingering tones, and a little tender seraphic smile creeps into her eyes and lies lightly on her lips. "But I am not fit to be that, and——"

"Look here," says Geoffrey, with decision, "I will have no 'buts,' and I prefer taking my answer from your eyes than from your lips. They are kinder. You are going to marry me, you know, and that is all about it. *I* shall marry *you*, whether you like it or not, so you may as well give in with a good grace. And I'll take you to see Rome and all the places we have been talking about, and we shall have a real good old time. Why don't you look up and speak to me, Mona?"

"Because I have nothing to say," murmurs the girl, in a frozen tone,— "nothing." Then passionately, "I will not be selfish. I will not do this thing."

"Do you mean you will not marry me?" asks he, letting her go, and moving back a step or two, a frown upon his forehead. "I confess I do not understand you."

"Try, *try* to understand me," entreats she, desperately, following him and laying her hand upon his arm. "It is only this. It would not make you happy,—not *afterwards*, when you could see the difference between me and the other women you have known. You are a gentleman; I am only a farmer's niece." She says this bravely, though it is agony to her proud nature to have to confess it.

"If that is all," says Geoffrey, with a light laugh, laying his hand over the small brown one that still rests upon his arm, "I think it need hardly separate us. You are, indeed, different from all the other women I have met in my life,— which makes me sorry for all the other women. You are dearer and sweeter in my eyes than any one I have ever known! Is not this enough? Mona, are you sure no other reason prevents your accepting me? Why do you hesitate?" He has grown a little pale in his turn, and is regarding her with intense and jealous earnestness. Why does she not answer him? Why does she keep her eyes—those honest telltales—so obstinately fixed upon the ground? Why does she show no smallest sign of yielding?

"Give me my answer," he says, sternly.

"I have given it," returns she, in a low tone,—so low that he has to bend to hear it. "Do not be angry with me, do not—I——"

"'Who excuses himself, accuses himself,'" quotes Geoffrey. "I want no reasons for your rejection. It is enough that I know you do not care for me."

"Oh, no! it is not that! you must know it is not that," says Mona, in deep grief. "It is that I *cannot* marry you!"

"Will not, you mean!"

"Well, then, I *will* not," returns she, with a last effort at determination, and the most miserable face in the world.

"Oh, if you *will* not," says Mr. Rodney, wrathfully.

"I—will—not," says Mona, brokenly.

"Then I don't believe you!" breaks out Geoffrey, angrily. "I am positive you want to marry me; and just because of some wretched fad you have got into your head you are determined to make us both wretched."

"I have nothing in my head," says Mona, tearfully.

"I don't think you can have much, certainly," says Mr. Rodney, with the grossest rudeness, "when you can let a few ridiculous scruples interfere with both our happiness." Then, resentfully, "Do you hate me?"

No answer.

"Say so, if you do: it will be honester. If you don't," threateningly, "I shall of course think the contrary."

Still no answer.

She has turned away from him, grieved and frightened by his vehemence, and, having plucked a leaf from the hedge near her, is trifling absently with it as it lies upon her little trembling palm.

It is a drooping blackberry-leaf from a bush near where she is standing, that has turned from green into a warm and vivid crimson. She examines it minutely, as though lost in wonder at its excessive beauty, for beautiful exceedingly it is, clothed in the rich cloak that Autumn's generosity has flung upon it; yet I think, she for once is blind to its charms.

"I think you had better come home," says Geoffrey, deeply angered with her. "You must not stay here catching cold."

A little soft woollen shawl of plain white has slipped from her throat and fallen to the ground, unheeded by her in her great distress. Lifting it almost unwillingly, he comes close to her, and places it round her once again. In so doing he discovers that tears are running down her cheeks.

"Why, Mona, what is this?" exclaims he, his manner changing on the instant from indignation and coldness to warmth and tenderness. "You are crying? My darling girl! There, lay your head on my shoulder, and let us forget we have ever quarrelled. It is our first dispute; let it be our last. And, after all," comfortably, "it is much better to have our quarrels before marriage than after."

This last insinuation, he flatters himself, is rather cleverly introduced.

"Oh, if I could be quite, *quite* sure you would never regret it!" says Mona, wistfully.

"I shall never regret anything, as long as I have you!" says Rodney. "Be assured of that."

"I am so glad you are poor," says Mona. "If you were rich or even well off, I should never consent,—never!"

"No, of course not," says Mr. Rodney, unblushingly! "as a rule, girls nowadays can't endure men with money."

This is "sarkassum;" but Mona comprehends it not.

Presently, seeing she is again smiling and looking inexpressibly happy, for laughter comes readily to her lips, and tears, as a rule, make no long stay with her,—ashamed, perhaps, to disfigure the fair "windows of her soul," that are so "darkly, deeply, beautifully blue,"—"So you will come to England with me, after all?" he says, quite gayly.

"I would go to the world's end with you," returns she, gently. "Ah! I think you knew that all along."

"Well, I didn't," says Rodney. "There were moments, indeed, when I believed in you; but five minutes ago, when you flung me over so decidedly, and refused to have anything to do with me, I lost faith in you, and began to think you a thorough-going coquette like all the rest. How I wronged you, my *dear* love! I should have known that under no circumstances could you be untruthful."

At his words, a glad light springs to life within her wonderful eyes. She is so pleased and proud that he should so speak of her.

"Do you know, Mona," says the young man, sorrowfully, "you are too good for me,—a fellow who has gone racketing all over the world for years. I'm not half worthy of you."

"Aren't you?" says Mona, in her tender fashion, that implies so kind a doubt. Raising one hand (the other is imprisoned), she draws his face down to her own. "I wouldn't have you altered in any way," she says; "not in the smallest matter. As you are, you are so dear to me you could not be dearer; and I love you now, and I shall always love you, with all my heart and soul."

"My sweet angel!" says her lover, pressing her to his heart. And when he says this he is not so far from the truth, for her tender simplicity and perfect faith and trust bring her very near to heaven!

CHAPTER VII.

HOW GEOFFREY AND MONA FALL INTO STRANGE COMPANY AND HOW THEY PROFIT BY IT; AND HOW MONA, OUTSTRIPPING WICKED VENGEANCE, SAVES A LIFE.

"Is it very late?" says Mona, awaking from her happy dreams with a start.

"Not very," says Geoffrey. "It seems only just now that Mickey and the dogs left us." Together they examine his watch, by the light of the moon, and see that it is quite ten o'clock.

"Oh, it is dreadfully late!" says Mona, with much compunction. "Come, let us hurry."

"Well, just one moment," says Geoffrey, detaining her, "let us finish what we were saying. Would you rather go to the East or to Rome?"

"To Rome," says Mona. "But do you mean it? Can you afford it? Italy seems so far away." Then, after a thoughtful silence, "Mr. Rodney——"

"Who on earth are you speaking to?" says Geoffrey.

"To you!" with surprise.

"I am not Mr. Rodney: Jack is that. Can't you call me anything else?"

"What else?" says Mona, shyly.

"Call me Geoffrey."

"I always think of you as Geoffrey," whispers she, with a swift, sweet, upward glance; "but to say it is so different. Well," bravely, "I'll try. Dear, dear, *dear* Geoffrey, I want to tell you I would be as happy with you in Wicklow as in Rome."

"I know that," says Geoffrey, "and the knowledge makes me more happy than I can say. But to Rome you shall go, whatever it may cost. And then we shall return to England to our own home. And then—little rebel that you are—you must begin to look upon yourself as an English subject, and accept the queen as your gracious sovereign."

"I need no queen when I have got a king," says the girl, with ready wit and great tenderness.

Geoffrey raises her hand to his lips. "*Your* king is also your slave," he says, with a fond smile.

Then they move on once more, and go down the road that leads towards the farm.

Again she has grown silent, as though oppressed with thought; and he too is mute, but all his mind is crowded with glad anticipations of what the near future is to give him. He has no regrets, no fears. At length, struck by her persistent taciturnity, he says, "What is it, Mona?"

"If ever you should be sorry afterwards," she says, miserably, still tormenting herself with unseen evils,—"if ever I should see discontent in your eyes, how would it be with me then?"

"Don't talk like a penny illustrated," says Mr. Rodney in a very superior tone. "If ever you do see all you seem to anticipate, just tell yourself I am a cur, and despise me accordingly. But I think you are paying both yourself and me very bad compliments when you talk like that. Do try to understand that you are very beautiful, and far superior to the general run of women, and that I am only pretty well so far as men go."

At this they both laugh heartily, and Mona returns no more to the lachrymose mood that has possessed her for the last five minutes.

The moon has gone behind a cloud, the road is almost wrapped in complete gloom, when a voice, coming from apparently nowhere, startles them, and brings them back from visions of impossible bliss to the present very possible world.

"Hist, Miss Mona! hist!" says this voice close at Mona's ear. She starts violently.

"Oh! Paddy," she says, as a small figure, unkempt, and only half clad, creeps through the hedge and stops short in her path.

"Don't go on, miss," says the boy, with much excitement. "Don't ye. I see ye comin', an', no matter what they do to me, I says to myself, I'll warn her surely. They're waitin' for the agint below, an' maybe they might mistake ye for some one else in the dark, an' do ye some harm."

"Who are they waiting for?" says Mona, anxiously.

"For the agint, miss. Oh, if ye tell on me now they'll kill me. Maxil, ye know; me lord's agint."

"Waiting—for what? Is it to shoot him?" asks the girl, breathlessly.

"Yes, miss. Oh, Miss Mona, if ye bethray me now 'twill be all up wid me. Fegs an' intirely, miss, they'll murdher me out uv hand."

"I won't betray you," she says. "You may trust me. Where are they stationed?"

"Down below in the hollow, miss,—jist behind the hawthorn-bush. Go home some other way, Miss Mona: they're bint on blood."

"And, if so, what are you doing here?" says Mona, reprovingly.

"On'y watchin', miss, to see what they'd do," confesses he, shifting from one foot to the other, and growing palpably confused beneath her searching gaze.

"Is it murder you want to see?" asks she slowly, in a horrified tone. "Go home, Paddy. Go home to your mother." Then, changing her censuring manner to one of entreaty, she says, softly, "Go, because I ask you."

"I'm off, miss," says the miscreant, and, true to his word, darts through the hedge again like a shaft from a bow, and, scurrying through the fields, is soon lost to sight.

"Come with me," says Mona to Rodney; and with an air of settled determination, and a hard look on her usually mobile lips, she moves deliberately towards the hawthorn-bush, that is about a quarter of a mile distant.

"Mona," says Rodney, divining her intent, "stay you here while I go and expostulate with these men. It is late, darling, and their blood is up, and they may not listen to you. Let me speak to them."

"You do not understand them," returns she, sadly. "And I do. Besides, they will not harm me. There is no fear of that. I am not at all afraid of them. And—I *must* speak to them."

He knows her sufficiently well to refrain from further expostulation, and just accompanies her silently along the lonely road.

"It is I,—Mona Scully," she calls aloud, when she is within a hundred yards of the hiding-place. "Tim Ryan, come here: I want you."

It is a mere guess on her part,—supported certainly by many tales she has heard of this Ryan of late, but a guess nevertheless. It proves, however, to be a correct one. A man, indistinct, but unmistakable, shows himself on the top of the wall, and pulls his forelock through force of habit.

"What are you doing here, Tim?" says Mona, bravely, calmly, "at this hour, and with—yes, do not seek to hide it from me—a gun! And you too, Carthy," peering into the darkness to where another man, less plucky than Ryan lies concealed. "Ah! you may well wish to shade your face, since it is evil you have in your heart this night."

"Do ye mane to inform on us?" says Ryan, slowly, who is "a man of a villanous countenance," laying his hand impulsively upon his gun, and glancing at her and Rodney alternately with murder in his eyes. It is a critical moment. Rodney, putting out his hand, tries to draw her behind him.

"No, I am not afraid," says the girl, resisting his effort to put himself before her; and when he would have spoken she puts up her hands, and warns him to keep silence.

"You should know better than to apply the word 'informer' to one of my blood," she says, coldly, speaking to Ryan, without a tremor in her voice.

"I know that," says the man, sullenly. "But what of him?" pointing to Rodney, the ruffianly look still on his face. "The Englishman, I mane. Is he sure? It's a life, for a life afther all, when everything is towld."

He handles the gun again menacingly. Mona, though still apparently calm, whitens perceptibly beneath the cold penetrating rays of the "pale-faced moon" that up above in "heaven's ebon vault, studded with stars unutterably bright," looks down upon her perhaps with love and pity.

"Tim," she says, "what have I ever done to you that you should seek to make me unhappy?"

"I have nothing to do with you. Go your ways. It is with him I have to settle," says the man, morosely.

"But *I* have to do with him," says Mona, distinctly.

At this, in spite of everything, Rodney laughs lightly, and, taking her hand in his, draws it through his arm. There is love and trust and great content in his laugh.

"Eh!" says Ryan; while the other man whom she has called Carthy—and who up to this has appeared desirous of concealing himself from view—now presses forward and regards the two with lingering scrutiny.

"Why, what have you to do with her?" says Ryan, addressing Rodney, a gleam of something that savors of amusement showing itself even in his ill-favored face. For an Irishman, under all circumstances, dearly loves "a courting, a *bon-mot*, and a broil."

"This much," says Rodney, laughing again: "I am going to marry her, with her leave."

"If that be so, she'll make you keep from splittin' on us," says the man. "So now go; we've work in hand to-night not fit for her eyes."

Mona shudders.

"Tim," she says, distractedly, "do not bring murder on your soul. Oh, Tim, think it over while there is yet time. I have heard all about it; and I would ask you to remember that it is not Mr. Maxwell's fault that Peggy Madden was evicted, but the fault of his master. If any one must be shot, it ought to be

Lord Crighton" (as his lordship is at this moment safe in Constantinople, she says this boldly), "and not his paid servant."

"I dare say we'll get at the lord by an' by" says Ryan, untouched. "Go yer ways, will ye? an' quick too. Maybe if ye thry me too far, ye'll learn to rue this night."

Seeing further talk is useless, Mona slips her hand into Rodney's and leads him down the road.

But when they have turned a corner and are quite out of sight and hearing, Rodney stops short and says, hurriedly,—

"Mona, can you manage to get home by some short way by yourself? Because I must return. I must stand by this man they are going to murder. I must indeed, darling. Forgive me that I desert you here and at such an hour, but I see you are safe in the country, and five minutes will take you to the farm, and I cannot let his life be taken without striking a blow for him."

"And did you think I was content to let him die" says Mona, reproachfully. "No! There is a chance for him still, and I will explain it to you. It is early yet. He seldom passes here before eleven, and it is but a little after ten. I know the hour he usually returns, because he always goes by our gate, and often I bid him good-night in the summer-time. Come with me," excitedly. "I can lead you by a cross-path to the Ballavacky road, by which he must come, and, if we overtake him before he reaches that spot, we can save his life. Come; do not delay!"

She turns through a broken gap into a ploughed field, and breaks into a quick run.

"If we hurry we must meet his car there, and can send him back into Bantry, and so save him."

All this she breathes forth in disjointed sentences as she rushes, like a light-footed deer, across the ploughed land into the wet grass beyond.

Over one high bank, across a stile, through another broken gap, on to a wall, straight and broad, up which Rodney pulls her, carefully taking her down in his arms at the other side.

Still onward,—lightly, swiftly: now in sight of the boundless sea, now diving down into the plain, without faintness or despondency, or any other feeling but a passionate determination to save a man's life.

Rodney's breath is coming more quickly, and he is conscious of a desire to stop and pull himself together—if only for a minute—before bracing himself for a second effort. But to Mona, with her fresh and perfect health, and lithe and lissom body, and all the rich young blood that surges upward in her veins, excitement serves but to make her more elastic; and with her mind strung to its highest pitch, and her hot Irish blood aflame, she runs easily onward, until at length the road is reached that is her goal.

Springing upon the bank that skirts the road on one side, she raises her hands to her head, and listens with all her might for the sound of wheels in the distance.

But all is still.

Oh, if they should be too late! If Maxwell has passed and gone down the other road, and is perhaps now already "done to death" by the cruel treacherous enemy that lieth in wait for him!

Her blood heated by her swift run grows cold again as this thought comes to her,—forced to the front by the fact that "all the air a solemn stillness holds," and that no sound makes itself heard save the faint sighing of the night-wind in the woods up yonder, and the "lone and melancholy voice" of the sea, a mile away, as it breaks upon the silent shore.

These sounds, vague and harmonious as they are, yet full of mystery and unexplained sadness, but serve to heighten the fear that chills her heart.

Rodney, standing beside her, watches her anxiously. She throws up her head, and pushes back her hair, and strains her eyes eagerly into the darkness, that not all the moonbeams can make less than night.

Alas! alas! what foul deed may even now be doing while she stands here powerless to avert it,—her efforts all in vain! How richly shines the sweet heaven, studded with its stars! how cool, how fragrant, is the breeze! How the tiny wavelets move and sparkle in the glorious bay below. How fair a world it is to hold such depths of sin! Why should not rain and storms and howling tempest mark a night so——

But hark! What is this that greets her ear? The ring of horse's feet upon the quiet road!

The girl clasps her hands passionately, and turns her eyes on Rodney.

"Mona, it is—it must be!" says Geoffrey, taking her hand; and so they both stand, almost breathless, on the high bank, listening intently.

Now they can hear the sound of wheels; and presently a light tax-cart swings round the corner, drawn by a large, bony, bay mare, and in which sits a heavy-looking, elderly man, in a light overcoat.

"Mr. Maxwell! Mr. Maxwell!" cries Mona, as he approaches them; and the heavy man, drawing up, looks round at her with keen surprise, bending his head a little forward, as though the better to pierce the gloom.

"Miss Scully, is it you?" he says, at length; "and here at this hour?"

"Go back to Bantry," says Mona, not heeding his evident surprise, "at once,—*now*. Do not delay. There are those waiting for you on the Tullymore road who will take your life. I have run all this way to warn you. Oh, go back, while there is yet time!"

"Do you mean they want to shoot me?" says Maxwell, in a hurried tone.

"Yes; I know it! Oh, do not wait to ask questions, but go. Even now they may have suspected my purpose, and may be coming here to prevent your ever returning."

Each moment of delay only helps to increase her nervous excitement.

"But who are they? and where?" demands the agent, completely taken aback.

"I can tell you no more; I will not; and you must never ask me. It is enough that I speak the truth, and that I have been able to save your life."

"How can I thank you?" says Maxwell, "for all——"

"Some other day you can do that. Now go," says Mona, imperiously, waving her hand.

But Maxwell still lingers, looking first at her and then very intently at her companion.

"It is late," he says. "You should be at home, child. Who am I, that you should do me so great a service?" Then, turning quietly to Rodney, "I have not the pleasure of your acquaintance, sir," he says, gravely; "but I entreat you to take Miss Scully safely back to the Farm without delay."

"You may depend upon me," says Rodney, lifting his hat, and respecting the elder man's care for the well-being of his beloved, even in the midst of his own immediate danger. Then, in another moment, Maxwell has turned his horse's head, and is soon out of sight.

The whole scene is at an end. A life has been saved. And they two, Mona and Geoffrey, are once more alone beneath the "earnest stars."

"Take me down," says Mona, wearily, turning to her lover, as the last faint ring of the horse's feet dies out on the breeze.

"You are tired," says he, tenderly.

"A little, now it is all over. Yet I must make great haste homeward. Uncle Brian will be uneasy about me if he discovers my absence, though he knew I was going to the Bay. Come, we must hurry."

So in silence, but hand in hand, they move back through the dewy meads, meeting no one until they reach the little wooden gate that leads to her home.

Here they behold the faithful Biddy, craning her long neck up and down the road, and filled with wildest anxiety.

"Oh, may I niver agin see the light," cries this excitable damsel, rushing out to Mona, "if I iver hoped to lay eyes on yer face again! Where were ye at all, darlin'? An' I breakin' me heart wid fear for ye. Did ye know Tim Ryan was out to-night? When I heerd tell of that from that boy of the Cantys', I thought I'd have dhropped. 'Tis no good he's up to. Come in, asthore: you must be near kilt with the cowld."

"No; I am quite warm," says Mona, in a low, sad tone.

"'Tis I've bin prayin' for ye," says Biddy, taking her mistress's hand and kissing it fondly. "On me bended knees I was with the blessid beads for the last two hours. An' shure I've had me reward, now I see ye safe home agin. But indeed, Miss Mona, 'tis a sore time I've had uv it."

"And Uncle Brian?" asks Mona, fearfully.

"Oh, I got the ould man to bed hours ago; for I knew if he stayed up that he'd get mortial wearin', an' be the death of us if he knew ye were out so late. An' truth to say, Miss Mona," changing her tone from one of extreme joy and thankfulness to another of the deepest censure, "'twas the world an' all of bad behavior to be galavantin' out at this hour."

"The night was so lovely,—so mild," says Mona, faintly, concealment in any form being new to her, and very foreign to her truthful nature; "and I knew Mickey would tell you it was all right."

"An' what brought him home, the murdherin' scamp," says Miss Bridget, with more vehemence than politeness, "instid of stayin' wid ye to see ye came to no harm?"

"He had to see the mare made up, and the pigs fed," says Mona.

"Is that what he towld ye? Oh, the blaggard!" says Bridget. "An' nary sign did he do since his return, but sit be the fire an' smoke his dhudheen. Oh, be the powers of Moll Kelly, but I'll pay him out for his lies? He's soakin' it now, anyhow, as I sint him up to the top of the hill agin, to see what had become of ye."

"Bridget," says Mona, "will you go in and get me a cup of tea before I go to bed? I am tired."

"I will, darlin', shurely," says Bridget, who adores the ground she walks on; and then, turning, she leaves her. Mona lays her hand on Geoffrey's arm.

"Promise me you will not go back to Coolnagurtheen to-night?" she says, earnestly. "At the inn, down in the village, they will give you a bed."

"But, my dearest, why? There is not the slightest danger now, and my horse is a good one, and I sha'n't be any time getting——"

"I won't hear of it!" says Mona, interrupting him vehemently. "You would have to go up *that road* again," with a strong shudder. "I shall not go indoors until you give me your honor you will stay in the village to-night."

Seeing the poor child's terrible fear and anxiety, and that she is completely overwrought, he gives way, and lets her have the desired promise.

"Now, that is good of you," she says, gratefully, and then, as he stoops to kiss her, she throws her arms around his neck and bursts into tears.

"You are worn out, my love, my sweetheart," says Geoffrey, very tenderly, speaking to her as though she is in years the child that, in her soul, she truly is. "Come, Mona, you will not cry on this night of all others that has made me yours and you mine! If this thought made you as happy as it makes me, you *could* not cry. Now lift your head, and let me look at you. There! you have given yourself to me, darling, and there is a good life, I trust, before us; so let us dwell on that, and forget all minor evils. Together we can defy trouble!"

"Yes, that is a thought to dry all tears," she says, very sweetly, checking her sobs and raising her face, on which is dawning an adorable smile. Then, sighing heavily,—a sigh of utter exhaustion,—"You have done me good," she says. "I shall sleep now; and you my dearest, will be safe. Good-night until to-morrow!"

"How many hours there are in the night that we never count!" says Geoffrey, impatiently. "Good-night, Mona! To-morrow's dawn I shall call my dearest friend."

CHAPTER VIII.

HOW GEOFFREY AND MONA PLAN A TRANSFORMATION SCENE.

Time, with lovers, "flies with swallows' wings;" they neither feel nor heed it as it passes, so all too full of haste the moments seem. They are to them replete with love and happiness and sweet content. To-day is an accomplished joy, and to-morrow will dawn for no other purpose but to bring them together. So they think and so they believe.

Rodney has interviewed the old man, her uncle; has told him of his great and lasting love for this pearl among women; has described in a very few words, and without bombast, his admiration for Mona; and Brian Scully (though with sufficient national pride to suppress all undue delight at the young man's proposal) has given a hearty consent to their union, and is in reality flattered and pleased beyond measure at this match for "his girl." For, no matter how the Irish may rebel against landlordism and aristocracy in general, deep down in their hearts lies rooted an undying fealty to old blood.

To his mother, however, he has sent no word of Mona, knowing only too well how the news of his approaching marriage with this "outer barbarian" (as she will certainly deem his darling) will be received. It is not cowardice that holds his pen, as, were all the world to kneel at his feet and implore him or bribe him to renounce his love, all such pleading and bribing would be in vain. It is that, knowing argument to be useless, he puts off the evil hour that may bring pain to his mother to the last moment.

When she knows Mona she will love her,—who could help it? so he argues; and for this reason he keeps silence until such time as, his marriage being a *fait accompli*, hopeless expostulation will be of no avail, and will, therefore, be suppressed.

Meanwhile, the hours go by "laden with golden grain." Every day makes Mona dearer and more dear, her sweet and guileless nature being one calculated to create, with growing knowledge, an increasing admiration and tenderness. Indeed, each happy afternoon spent with her serves but to forge another link in the chain that binds him to her.

To-day is "so cool, so calm, so bright," that Geoffrey's heart grows glad within him as he walks along the road that leads to the farm, his gun upon his shoulder, his trusty dog at his heels.

All through the air the smell of heather, sweet and fragrant, reigns. Far down, miles away, the waves rush inland, glinting and glistening in the sunlight.

"Blue roll the waters, blue the skySpreads like an ocean hung on high."

The birds, as though once more led by the balmy mildness of the day into the belief that summer has not yet forsaken them, are singing in the topmost branches of the trees, from which, with every passing breeze, the leaves fall lightly.

From the cabins pale wreaths of smoke rise slowly, scarce stirred by the passing wind. Going by one of these small tenements, before which the inevitable pig is wallowing in an unsavory pool, a voice comes to him, fresh and joyous, and plainly full of pleasure, that thrills through his whole being. It is to him what no other voice ever has been, or ever can be again. It is Mona's voice!

Again she calls to him from within.

"Is it you?" she says. "Come in here, Geoffrey. I want you."

How sweet it is to be wanted by those we love! Geoffrey, lowering his gun, stoops and enters the lowly cabin (which, to say the truth, is rather uninviting than otherwise) with more alacrity than he would show if asked to enter the queen's palace. Yet what is a palace but the abode of a sovereign? and for the time being, at least, Rodney's sovereign is in possession of this humble dwelling. So it becomes sacred, and almost desirable, in his eyes.

She is sitting before a spinning-wheel, and is deftly drawing the wool through her fingers; brown little fingers they are, but none the less dear in his sight.

"I'm here," she cries, in the glad happy tones that have been ringing their changes in his heart all day.

An old crone is sitting over a turf fire that glows and burns dimly in its subdued fashion. Hanging over it is a three-legged pot, in which boil the "praties" for the "boys'" dinners, who will be coming home presently from their work.

"What luck to find you here," says Geoffrey, stooping over the industrious spinner, and (after the slightest hesitation) kissing her fondly in spite of the presence of the old woman, who is regarding them with silent curiosity, largely mingled with admiration. The ancient dame sees plainly nothing strange in this embrace of Geoffrey's but rather something sweet and to be approved. She smiles amiably, and nods her old head, and mumbles some quaint Irish phrase about love and courtship and happy youth, as though the very sight of these handsome lovers fills her withered breast with glad recollections of bygone days, when she, too, had her "man" and her golden hopes. For deep down in the hearts of all the sons and daughters of Ireland, whether they be young or old, is a spice of romance living and inextinguishable.

Rising, the old dame takes a chair, dusts it, and presents it to the stranger, with a courtesy and a wish that he will make himself welcome. Then she goes back again to the chimney-corner, and taking up the bellows, blows the fire beneath the potatoes, turning her back in this manner upon the young people with a natural delicacy worthy of better birth and better education.

Mona, who has blushed rosy red at his kiss, is now beaming on her lover, and has drawn back her skirts to admit of his coming a little closer to her. He is not slow to avail himself of this invitation, and is now sitting with his arm thrown across the back of the wooden chair that holds Mona, and with eyes full of heartfelt gladness fixed upon her.

"You look like Marguerite. A very lovely Marguerite," says Geoffrey, idly, gazing at her rather dreamily.

"Except that my hair is rolled up, and is too dark, isn't it? I have read about her, and I once saw a picture of Marguerite in the Gallery in Dublin, and it was very beautiful. I remember it brought tears to my eyes, and Aunt Anastasia said I was too fanciful to be happy. Her story is a very sad one, isn't it?"

"Very. And you are not a bit like her, after all," says Geoffrey, with sudden compunction, "because you are going to be as happy as the days are long, if I can make you so."

"One must not hope for perfect happiness on this earth," says Mona, gravely; "but at least I know," with a soft and trusting glance at him, "I shall be happier than most people."

"What a darling you are!" says Rodney, in a low tone; and then something else follows, that, had she seen it, would have caused the weatherbeaten old person at the fire another thrill of tender recollection.

"What are you doing?" asks Geoffrey, presently, when they have returned to everyday life.

"I am spinning flax for Betty, because she has rheumatism in her poor shoulder, and can do nothing, and this much flax must be finished by a certain time. I have nearly got through my portion now," says Mona; "and then we can go home."

"When I bring you to my home," says Geoffrey, "I shall have you painted just in that gown, and with a spinning-wheel before you; and it shall be hung in the gallery among the other—very inferior—beauties."

"Where?" says Mona, looking up quickly.

"Oh! at home, you know," says Mr. Rodney, quickly, discovering his mistake. For the moment he had forgotten his former declaration of poverty, or, at least, his consenting silence, when she had asked him about it.

"In the National Gallery, do you mean?" asks Mona, with a pretty, puzzled frown on her brow. "Oh, no, Geoffrey; I shouldn't like that at all. To be stared at by everybody,—it wouldn't be nice, would it?"

Rodney laughs, in an inward fashion, biting his lip and looking down.

"Very well; you sha'n't be put there," he says. "But nevertheless you must be prepared for the fact that you will undoubtedly be stared at by the common herd, whether you are in the National Gallery or out of it."

"But why?" says Mona, trying to read his face. "Am I so different from other people?"

"Very different," says Rodney.

"That is what I am afraid of always," says Mona, a little wistfully.

"Don't be afraid. It is quite the correct thing to be eccentric nowadays. One is nowhere if not bizarre," says Rodney, laughing; "so I dare say you will find yourself the very height of fashion."

"Now I think you are making fun of me," says Mona, smiling sweetly; and, lifting her hand, she pinches his ear lightly, and very softly, lest she should hurt him.

Here the old woman at the fire, who has been getting up and down from her three-legged stool during the past few minutes, and sniffing at the pot in an anxious manner, gives way to a loud sigh of relief. Lifting the pot from its crook, she lays it on the earthen floor.

Then she strains the water from it, and looks with admiration upon its steaming contents. "The murphies" (as, I fear, she calls the potatoes) are done to a turn.

"Maybe," says Betty Corcoran, turning in a genial fashion to Mona and Geoffrey, "ye'd ate a pratie, would ye, now? They're raal nice an' floury. Ye must be hungry, Miss Mona, afther all the work ye've gone through; an' if you an' your gintleman would condescind to the like of my dinner, 'tis ready for ye, an' welcome ye are to it. Do, now!" heartily. "The praties is gran' this year,—praises be for all mercies. Amen."

"They *do* look nice," says Mona, "and I *am* hungry. If we won't be a great trouble to you, Betty," with graceful Hesitation, "I think we should like some."

"Arrah! throuble is it?" says Betty, scornfully. "Tisn't throuble I'm thinkin' of anyway, when you're by."

"Will you have something to eat Geoffrey?" says Mona.

"Thank you," says Geoffrey, "but——"

"Yes, do, alannah!" says the old lady, standing with one hand upon her hips and the other holding tightly a prodigious "Champion." "'Twill set ye up afther yer walk."

"Then, thank you, Mrs. Corcoran, I *will* have a potato," says Rodney, gratefully, honest hunger and the knowledge that it will please Mona to be friendly with "her people," as she calls them, urging him on. "I'm as hungry as I can be," he says.

"So ye are, bless ye both!" says old Betty, much delighted, and forthwith, going to her dresser, takes down two plates, and two knives and forks, of pattern unknown and of the purest pot-metal, after which she once more returns to the revered potatoes.

Geoffrey, who would be at any moment as polite to a dairymaid as to a duchess, follows her, and, much to her discomfort,—though she is too civil to say so,—helps her to lay the table. He even insists on filling a dish with the potatoes, and having severely burned his fingers, and having nobly suppressed all appearance of pain,—beyond the dropping of two or three of the esculent roots upon the ground,—brings them in triumph to the spot where Mona is sitting.

"It might be that ye'd take a dhrop of new milk, too," says Betty, "on hospitable thoughts intent," placing before her visitors a little jug of milk she has all day been keeping apart, poor soul! for her own delectation.

Not knowing this, Mona and Geoffrey (whose flask is empty) accept the proffered milk, and make merry over their impromptu feast, while in the background, the old woman smiles upon them and utters little kindly sentences.

Ten minutes later, having bidden their hostess a hearty farewell, they step out into the open air and walk towards the farm.

"You have never told me how many people are in your house?" says Mona, presently. "Tell me now. I know about your mother, and," shyly, "about Nicholas; but is there any one else?"

"Well, Jack is home by this time, I suppose,—that's my second brother; at least he was expected yesterday; and Violet Mansergh is very often there; and as a rule, you know, there is always somebody; and that's all."

The description is graphic, certainly.

"Is—is Violet Mansergh a pretty girl?" asks Mona, grasping instinctively at the fact that any one called Violet Mansergh may be a possible rival.

"Pretty? No. But she dresses very swagger, and always looks nice, and is generally correct all through," replies Mr. Rodney, easily.

"I know," says Mona, sadly.

"She's the girl my mother wanted me to marry, you know," goes on Rodney, unobservant, as men always are, of the small signals of distress hung out by his companion.

"Oh, indeed!" says Mona; and then, with downcast eyes, "but I *don't* know, because you never told me before."

"I thought I did," says Geoffrey, waking slowly to a sense of the situation.

"Well, you didn't," says Mona. "Are you engaged to her?"

"If I was, how could I ask you to marry me?" returns he, in a tone so hurt that she grows abashed.

"I hope she isn't in love with you," she says, slowly.

"You may bet anything you like on that," says Geoffrey, cheerfully. "She cares for me just about as much as I care for her,—which means exactly nothing."

"I am very glad," says Mona, in a low tone.

"Why, Mona?"

"Because I could not bear to think any one was made unhappy by me. It would seem as though some evil eye was resting on our love," says Mona, raising her thoughtful, earnest eyes to his. "It must be a sad thing when our happiness causes the misery of others."

"Yet even were it so you would love me, Mona?"

"I shall always love you," says the girl, with sweet seriousness, "better than my life. But in that case I should always, too have a regret."

"There is no need for regret, darling," says he. "I am heart-whole, and I know no woman that loves me, or for whose affection I should ask, except yourself."

"I am indeed dear to you, I think," says Mona, softly and thankfully, growing a little pale through the intensity of her emotion.

"'Perdition catch my soul, but I do love thee,'" replies he, quite as softly.

Then she is pleased, and slips her hand into his, and goes along the quiet road, beside him with a heart in which high jubilee holds sway.

"Now tell me something else," she says, after a little bit. "Do all the women you know dress a great deal?"

"Some of them; not all. I know a considerable few who dress so little that they might as well leave it alone."

"Eh?" says Mona, innocently, and stares at him with an expression so full of bewilderment, being puzzled by his tone more than his words, that presently Mr. Rodney becomes conscious of a feeling akin to shame. Some remembrance of a line that speaks of "a soul as white as heaven" comes to him, and he makes haste to hide the real meaning of his words.

"I mean, some of them dress uncommon badly," he says, with much mendacity and more bad grammar.

"Now, do they?" says Mona. "I thought they always wore lovely clothes. In books they always do; but I was too young when with Aunt Anastasia in Dublin to go out. Somehow, what one imagines is sure to be wrong. I remember," laughing, "when I firmly believed the queen never was seen without her crown on her head."

"Well, it always *is* on her head," says Mr. Rodney, at which ridiculous joke they both laugh as gayly as though it were a *bon-mot* of the first water. That "life is thorny, and youth is vain" has not as yet occurred to either of these two. Nay, more, were you even to name this thought to them, they would rank it as flat blasphemy, and you a false prophet—love and laughter being, up to this, the burden of their song.

Yet after a moment or two the smile fades from Mona's mobile lip that ever looks as if, in the words of the old song, "some bee had stung it newly," and a pensive expression takes its place.

"I think I'd like to see myself in a regular evening gown," she say, wistfully.

"So should I," says Rodney, eagerly, but incorrectly; "at least, not myself, but you,—in something handsome, you know, open at the neck, and with your pretty arms bare, as they were the first day I saw you."

"How you remember that, now!" says Mona, with a heavenly smile, and a faint pressure of the fingers that still rest in his. "Yes, I should like to be sure before I marry you that—that—fashionable clothes would become me. But of course," regretfully, "you will understand I haven't a gown of that sort. I once sat in Lady Crighton's room while her maid dressed her for dinner: so I know all about it."

She sighs, then looks at the sky, and—sighs again.

"And do you know," she says, with charming *naivete*, not looking at him, but biting a blade of grass in a distractingly pretty and somewhat pensive fashion, "do you know her neck and arms are not a patch on mine?"

"You needn't tell me that. I'm positive they couldn't be named in the same day," says Geoffrey, enthusiastically, who never in his life saw Lady Crighton, or her neck or arms.

"No, they are not. Geoffrey, people look much better when they are beautifully dressed, don't they?"

"Well, on the principle that fine feathers make fine birds, I suppose they do," acknowledges Geoffrey, reluctantly.

At this she glances with scorn upon the quakerish and somewhat quaint gray gown in which she is clothed, and in which she is looking far sweeter than she knows, for in her face lie "love enshrined and sweet attractive grace."

"Yet, in spite of all the fine feathers, no one ever crept into my heart but my own Mona," says the young man, putting his hand beneath her chin, which is soft and rounded as a baby's, and turning her face to his. He hates to see the faint chagrin that lingers on it for a moment; for his is one of those tender natures that cannot bear to see the thing it loves endure the smallest torment.

"Some women in the great world overdo it," he goes on, "and choose things and colors utterly unsuited to their style. They are slaves to fashion. But

"'*My* love in her attire doth show her wit;It doth so well become her.'"

"Ah, how you flatter!" says Mona. Nevertheless, being a woman, and the flattery being directed to herself, she takes it kindly.

"No, you must not think that. To wear anything that becomes you must be the perfection of dressing. Why wear a Tam O'Shanter hat when one looks hideous in it? And then too much study spoils effect: you know what Herrick says:—

"'A careless shoe-string in whose tieI see a wild civility,Does more bewitch me than when artIs too precise in every part.'"

"How pretty that is! Yet I should like you to see me, if only for once, as you have seen others," says Mona.

"I should like it too. And it could be managed, couldn't it? I suppose I could get you a dress."

He says this quickly, yet fearfully. If she should take his proposal badly, what shall he do? He stares with flattering persistency upon a distant donkey that adorns a neighboring field, and calmly awaits fate. It is for once kind to him. Mona, it is quite evident, fails to see any impropriety in his speech.

"Could you?" she says hopefully. "How?"

Mr. Rodney, basely forsaking the donkey, returns to his mutton. "There must be a dressmaker in Dublin," he says, "and we could write to her. Don't you know one?"

"*I* don't, but I know Lady Mary and Miss Blake always get their things from a woman called Manning."

"Then Manning it shall be," says Geoffrey, gayly. "I'll run up to Dublin, and if you give me your measure I'll bring a gown back to you."

"Oh, no, don't," says Mona, earnestly. Then she stops short, and blushes a faint sweet crimson.

"But why?" demands he, dense as men will be at times. Then, as she refuses to enlighten his ignorance, slowly the truth dawns upon him.

"Do you mean that you would really miss me if I left you for only one day?" he asks, delightedly. "Mona, tell me the truth."

"Well, then, sure you know I would," confesses she, shyly but honestly. Whereupon rapture ensues that lasts for a full minute.

"Very well, then; I shan't leave you; but you shall have that dress all the same," he says. "How shall we arrange about it?"

"I can give you the size of my waist and my shoulders, and my length," says Mona, thoughtfully, yet with a touch of inspiration.

"And what color becomes you? Blue? that would suit your eyes, and it was blue you used to wear last month."

"Yes, blue looks very nice on me. Geoffrey, if Uncle Brian hears of this, will he be angry?"

"We needn't risk it. And it is no harm, darling, because you will soon be my wife, and then I shall give you everything. When the dress comes I'll send it up to you by my man, and you must manage the rest."

"I'll see about it. And, oh, Geoffrey, I do hope you will like me in it, and think me pretty," she says, anxiously, half fearful of this gown that is meant to transform a "beggar maid" into a queen fit for "King Cophetua." At least such is her reading of the part before her.

And so it is arranged. And that evening Geoffrey indites a letter to Mrs. Manning, Grafton Street, Dublin, that brings a smile to the lips of that cunning modiste.

CHAPTER IX.

HOW GEOFFREY AND MONA DILIGENTLY WORK UP THE TRANSFORMATION SCENE; AND HOW SUCCESS CROWNS THEIR EFFORTS.

In due course the wonderful gown arrives, and is made welcome at the farm, where Geoffrey too puts in an appearance about two hours later.

Mona is down at the gate waiting for him, evidently brimful of information.

"Well have you got it?" asks he, in a whisper. Mystery seems to encircle them and to make heavy the very air they breathe. In truth, I think it is the veil of secrecy that envelops their small intrigue that makes it so sweet to them. They might be children, so delighted are they with the success of their scheme.

"Yes, I have got it," also in a subdued whisper. "And, oh, Geoffrey, it is just too lovely! It's downright delicious; and satin, too! It must"—reproachfully—"have cost a great deal, and after all you told me about being *poor*! But," with a sudden change of tone, forgetting reproach and extravagance and everything, "it is exactly the color I love best, and what I have been dreaming of for years."

"Put it on you," says Geoffrey.

"What! *now?*" with some hesitation, yet plainly filled with an overwhelming desire to show herself to him without loss of time in the adorable gown. "If I should be seen! Well, never mind; I'll risk it. Go down to the little green glade in the wood, and I'll be with you before you can say Jack Robinson."

She disappears, and Geoffrey, obedient to orders, lounges off to the green glade, that now no longer owns rich coloring, but is strewn with leaves from the gaunt trees that stand in solemn order like grave sentries round it.

He might have invoked Jack Robinson a score of times had he so wished, he might even have gone for a very respectable walk, before his eyes are again gladdened by a sight of Mona. Minutes had given place to minutes many times, when, at length, a figure wrapped in a long cloak and with a light woollen shawl covering her head comes quickly towards him across the rustic bridge, and under the leafless trees to where he is standing.

Glancing round fearfully for a moment, as though desirous of making sure that no strange eyes are watching her movements, she lets the loose cloak fall to the ground, and, taking with careful haste the covering from her head, slips like Cinderella from her ordinary garments into all the glories of a *fete* gown. She steps a little to one side, and, throwing up her head with a faint touch of coquetry that sits very sweetly on her, glances triumphantly at Geoffrey, as though fully conscious that she is looking exquisite as a dream.

The dress is composed of satin of that peculiarly pale blue that in some side-lights appears as white. It is opened at the throat, and has no sleeves to speak of. As though some kindly fairy had indeed been at her beck and call, and had watched with careful eyes the cutting of the robe, it fits to a charm. Upon her head a little mob-cap, a very marvel of blue satin and old lace, rests lovingly, making still softer the soft tender face beneath it.

There is a sparkle in Mona's eyes, a slight severing of her lips, that bespeak satisfaction and betray her full of very innocent appreciation of her own beauty. She stands well back, with her head held proudly up, and with her hands lightly clasped before her. Her attitude is full of unstudied grace.

Her eyes, as I tell you, are shining like twin stars. Her whole soul is possessed of this hope, that he for whom almost she lives must think her good to look at. And good indeed she is, and very perfect; for in her earnest face lies such inward godliness and sweet trust as make one feel the better for only a bare glance at her.

Geoffrey is quite dumb, and stands gazing at her surprised at the amazing change a stuff, a color, can make in so short a time. Beautiful she always is in his sight, but he wonders that until now it never occurred to him what a sensation she is likely to create in the London world. When at last he does give way to speech, driven to break his curious silence by something in her face, he says nothing of the gown, but only this.

"Oh, Mona, will you always love me as you do now?"

His tone is full of sadness and longing, and something akin to fear. He has been much in the world, and has seen many of its evil ways, and this is the result of his knowledge. As he gazes on and wonders at her marvellous beauty, for an instant (a most unworthy instant) he distrusts her. Yet surely never was more groundless doubt sustained, as one might know to look upon her eyes and mouth, for in the one lies honest love, and in the other firmness.

Her face changes. He has made no mention of the treasured gown, has said no little word of praise.

"I have disappointed you," she says, tremulously, tears rising quickly. "I am a failure! I am not like the others."

"You are the most beautiful woman I ever saw in all my life," returns Rodney, with some passion.

"Then you are really pleased? I am just what you want me to be? Oh! how you frightened me!" says the girl, laying her hand upon her heart with a pretty gesture of relief.

"Don't ask me to flatter you. You will get plenty to do that by and by," says Geoffrey, rather jealously, rather bitterly.

"'By and by' I shall be your wife," says Mona, archly, "and then my days for receiving flattery will be at an end. Sure you needn't grudge me a few pretty words now."

What a world is to be opened up to her! How severe the test to which she will be exposed! Does she really think the whole earth is peopled with beings pure and perfect as herself?

"Yes, that is true," he says, in a curious tone, in answer to her words, his eyes fixed moodily upon the ground. Then suddenly he lifts his head, and as his gaze meets hers some of the truth and sweetness that belong to her springs from her to him and restores him once again to his proper self.

He smiles, and, turning, kneels before her in mock humility that savors of very real homage. Taking her hand, he presses it to his lips.

"Will your majesty deign to confer some slight sign of favor upon a very devoted servant?"

His looks betray his wish. And Mona, stooping, very willingly bestows upon him one of the sweetest little kisses imaginable.

"I doubt your queen lacks dignity," she says, with a quick blush, when she has achieved her tender crime.

"My queen lacks nothing," says Geoffrey. Then, as he feels the rising wind that is soughing through the barren trees, he says, hurriedly, "My darling, you will catch cold. Put on your wraps again."

"Just in one moment," says the wilful beauty. "But I must first look at myself altogether. I have only seen myself in little bits up to this, my glass is so small."

Running over to the river that flows swiftly but serenely a few yards from her, she leans over the bank and gazes down lingeringly and with love into the dark depths beneath that cast up to her her own fair image.

The place she has chosen as her mirror is a still pool fringed with drooping grasses and trailing ferns that make yet more dark the sanded floor of the stream.

"Yes, I *am* pretty," she says, after a minute's pause, with a long-drawn sigh of deepest satisfaction. Then she glances at Geoffrey. "And for your sake I am glad of it Now, come here and stand beside me," she goes on, presently, holding out her hand backwards as though loath to lose sight of her own reflection. "Let me see how *you* look in the water."

So he takes her hand, and together they lean over the brink and survey themselves in Nature's glass. Lightly their faces sway to and fro as the running water rushes across the pool,—sway, but do not part; they are always together, as though in anticipation of that happy time when their lives shall be one. It seems like a good omen; and Mona, in whose breast rests a little of the superstition that lies innate in every Irish heart, turns to her lover and looks at him.

He, too, looks at her. The same thought fills them both. As they are together there in the water, so (pray they) "may we be together in life." This hope is sweet almost to solemnity.

The short daylight fades; the wind grows higher; the whole scene is curious, and very nearly fantastical. The pretty girl in her clinging satin gown, and her gleaming neck and arms, bare and soft and white, and the tiny lace-fringed cap that crowns her fairness. The gaunt trees branching overhead that are showering down upon her all their fading wealth of orange and crimson and russet-colored leaves, that serve to throw out the glories of her dress. The brown-green sward is beneath her, the river runs with noiseless mirth beside her, rushing with faint music over sand and pebble to the ocean far below. Standing before her is her lover, gazing at her with adoring eyes.

Yet all things in this passing world know an end. In one short moment the perfect picture is spoiled. A huge black dog, bursting through the underwood, flings himself lovingly upon Mona, threatening every moment to destroy her toilet.

"It is Mr. Moore's retriever!" cries Mona, hurriedly, in a startled tone. "I must run. Down, Fan! down! Oh, if he catches me here, in this dress, what will he think? Quick, Geoffrey, give me my shawl!"

She tucks up her dignified train in a most undignified haste, while Geoffrey covers up all the finery with the crimson shawl. The white cloud is once more thrown over the dainty cap; all the pretty coloring vanishes out of sight; and Mona, after one last lingering glance at Geoffrey, follows its example. She, too, flies across the rural bridge into the covert of her own small domain.

It is over; the curtain is down; the charming transformation-scene has reached its end, and the fairy-queen doffing her radiant robes, descends once more to the level of a paltry mortal.

CHAPTER X.

HOW MONA, GROWING INQUISITIVE, ASKS QUESTIONS; AND HOW GEOFFREY, BEING BROUGHT TO BAY, MAKES CONFESSIONS THAT BODE BUT EVIL TO HIS FUTURE PEACE, AND BREED IMMEDIATE WAR.

"Oh! catch him! *do* catch him!" cries Mona, "Look, there he is again! Don't you see?" with growing excitement. "Over there, under that bush. Why on earth can't you see him? Ha! there he is again! Little wretch! Turn him back, Geoffrey; it is our last chance."

She has crossed the rustic bridge that leads into the Moore plantations, in hot pursuit of a young turkey that is evidently filled with a base determination to spend his Sunday out.

Geoffrey is rushing hither and thither, without his hat, and without his temper, in a vain endeavor to secure the rebel and reduce him to order. He is growing warm, and his breath is coming more quickly than is exactly desirable; but, being possessed with the desire to conquer or die, he still holds on. He races madly over the ground, crying "Shoo!" every now and then (whatever that may mean) in a desperate tone, as though impressed with the belief that this simple and apparently harmless expletive must cow the foe.

"Look at him, under that fern there!" exclaims Mona, in her clear treble, that has always something sweet and plaintive in it. "On your right—no! *not* on your left. Sure you know your right, don't you?" with a full, but unconscious, touch of scorn. "Hurry! hurry! or he will be gone again. Was there ever such a hateful bird! With his good food in the yard, and his warm house, and his mother crying for him! Ah! there you have him! No!—yes! no! He is gone again!"

"He isn't!" says Geoffrey, panting "I have him at last!" Whereupon he emerges from a wilderness of ferns, drawing after him and holding up triumphantly to the light the wandering bird, that looks more dead than alive, with all its feathers drooping, and its breath coming in angry cries.

"Oh, you have him!" says Mona, with a beaming smile, that is not reciprocated by the captured turkey. "Hold him tight: you have no idea how artful he is. Sure I knew you'd get him, if any one could!"

There is admiration blended with relief in her tone, and Geoffrey begins to feel like a hero of Waterloo.

"Now carry him over the bridge and put him down there, and he must go home, whether he likes it or not," goes on Mona to her warrior, whereupon that renowned person, armed with the shrieking turkey, crosses the bridge.

Having gained the other side, he places the angry bird on its mother earth, and with a final and almost tender "Shoo!" sends him scuttling along to the farmyard in the distance, where, no doubt, he is received either with open arms and kisses, or with a sounding "spank," as our American cousins would say, by his terrified mamma.

He finds Mona on his return sitting on a bank, laughing and trying to recover her breath.

"I hardly think this is Sunday work," she says, lightly; "but the poor little thing would have died if left out all night. Wasn't it well you saw him?"

"Most fortunate," says Rodney, with deep gravity. "I consider I have been the means of preventing a public calamity. Why, that bird might have haunted us later on."

"Fancy a turkey ghost," says Mona. "How ugly it would be. It would have all its feathers off, of course."

"Certainly not," says Geoffrey: "I blush for you. I never yet heard of a ghost that was not strictly decent. It would have had a winding sheet, of course. Come, let us go for a walk."

"To the old fort?" asks Mona, starting to her feet.

"Anywhere you like. I'm sure we deserve some compensation for the awful sermon that curate gave us this morning."

So they start, in a lazy, happy-go-lucky fashion, for their walk, conversing as they go, of themselves principally as all true lovers will.

But the fort, on this evening at least, is never reached Mona, coming to a stile, seats himself comfortably on the top of it, and looks with mild content around.

"Are you going no farther?" asks Rodney, hoping sincerely she will say "No." She does say it.

"It is so nice here," she says, with a soft sigh, and a dreamy smile, whereupon he too climbs and seats himself beside her. As they are now situated, there is about half a yard between them of passable wall crowned with green sods, across which they can hold sweet converse with the utmost affability. The evening is fine; the heavens promise to be fair; the earth beneath is calm and full of silence as becomes a Sabbath eve; yet, alas! Mona strikes a chord that presently flings harmony to the winds.

"Tell me about your mother," she says, folding her hands easily in her lap. "I mean,—what is she like? Is she cold, or proud, or stand-off?" There is keen anxiety in her tone.

"Eh?" says Geoffrey, rather taken back. "Cold" and "proud" he cannot deny, even to himself, are words that suit his mother rather more than otherwise.

"I mean," says Mona, flushing a vivid scarlet, "is she stern?"

"Oh, no," says Geoffrey, hastily, recovering himself just in time; "she's all right, you know, my mother; and you'll like her awfully when—when you know her, and when—when she knows you."

"Will that take her long?" asks Mona, somewhat wistfully, feeling, without understanding, some want in his voice.

"I don't see how it could take any one long," says Rodney.

"Ah! that is because you are a man, and because you love me," says this astute reader of humanity. "But women are so different. Suppose—suppose she *never* gets to like me?"

"Well, even that awful misfortune might be survived. We can live in our own home 'at ease,' as the old song says, until she comes to her senses. By and by, do you know you have never asked me about your future home,—my own place, Leighton Hall? and yet it is rather well worth asking about, because, though small, it is one of the oldest and prettiest places in the county."

"Leighton Hall," repeats she, slowly, fixing upon him her dark eyes that are always so full of truth and honesty. "But you told me you were poor. That a third son——"

"Wasn't much!" interrupts Geoffrey, with an attempt at carelessness that rather falls through beneath the gaze of those searching eyes. "Well, no more he is, you know, as a rule, unless some kind relative comes to his assistance."

"But you told me no maiden aunt had ever come to your assistance," goes on Mona, remorselessly.

"In that I spoke the truth," says Mr. Rodney, with a shameless laugh, "because it was an uncle who left me some money."

"You have not been quite true with me," says Mona, in a curious way, never removing her gaze and never returning his smile. "Are you rich, then, if you are not poor?"

"I'm a long way off being rich," says the young man, who is palpably amused, in spite of a valiant effort to suppress all outward signs of enjoyment. "I'm awfully poor when compared with some fellows. I dare say I must come in for something when my other uncle dies, but at present I have only fifteen hundred pounds a year."

"*Only!*" says Mona. "Do you know, Mr. Moore has no more than that, and we think him very rich indeed! No, you have not been open with me: you should have told me. I haven't ever thought of you to myself as being a rich man. Now I shall have to begin and think of you a lover again in quite another light." She is evidently deeply aggrieved.

"But, my darling child, I can't help the fact that George Rodney left me the Hall," says Geoffrey, deprecatingly, reducing the space between them to a mere nothing, and slipping his arm round her waist. "And if I was a beggar on the face of the earth, I could not love you more than I do, nor could you, I *hope*"—reproachfully—"love me better either."

The reproachful ring in his voice does its intended work. The soft heart throws out resentment, and once more gives shelter to gentle thoughts alone. She even consents to Rodney's laying his cheek against hers, and faintly returns the pressure of his hand.

"Yet I think you should have told me," she whispers, as a last fading censure. "Do you know you have made me very unhappy?"

"Oh, no, I haven't, now," says Rodney, reassuringly "You don't look a bit unhappy; you only look as sweet as an angel."

"You never saw an angel, so you can't say," says Mona, still sadly severe. "And I *am* unhappy. How will your mother, Mrs. Rodney, like your marrying me, when you might marry so many other people,—that Miss Mansergh, for instance?"

"Oh, nonsense!" says Rodney, who is in high good humor and can see no rocks ahead. "When my mother sees you she will fall in love with you on the spot, as will everybody else. But look here, you know, you mustn't call her Mrs. Rodney!"

"Why?" says Mona. "I couldn't well call her any thing else until I know her."

"That isn't her name at all," says Geoffrey. "My father was a baronet, you know: she is Lady Rodney."

"What!" says Mona And then she grows quite pale, and, slipping off the stile, stands a few yards away from him.

"That puts an end to everything," she says, in a dreadful little voice that goes to his heart, "at once. I could never face any one with a title. What will she say when she hears you are going to marry a farmer's niece? It is shameful of you," says Mona, with as much indignation as if the young man opposite to her, who is making strenuous but vain efforts to speak, has just been convicted of some heinous crime. "It is disgraceful! I wonder at you! That is twice you have deceived me."

"If you would only hear me——"

"I have heard too much already. I won't listen to any more. 'Lady Rodney!' I dare say"—with awful meaning in her tone—"*you* have got a title *too*!" Then, sternly, "Have you?"

"No, no indeed. I give you my honor, no," says Geoffrey, very earnestly, feeling that Fate has been more than kind to him in that she has denied him a handle to his name.

"You are sure?"—doubtfully.

"Utterly certain."

"And your brother?"

"Jack is only Mr. Rodney too."

"I don't mean him,"—severely: "I mean the brother you called 'Old Nick'—*Old Nick* indeed!" with suppressed anger.

"Oh, he is only called Sir Nicholas. Nobody thinks much of that. A baronet is really never of the slightest importance," says Geoffrey, anxiously, feeling exactly as if he were making an apology for his brother.

"That is not correct," says Mona. "We have a baronet here, Sir Owen O'Connor, and he is thought a great deal of. I know all about it. Even Lady Mary would have married him if he had asked her, though his hair is the color of an orange. Mr. Rodney,"—laying a dreadful stress upon the prefix to his name,—"go back to England and"—tragically—"forget me?"

"I shall do nothing of the kind," says Mr. Rodney, indignantly. "And if you address me in that way again I shall cut my throat."

"Much better do that"—gloomily—"than marry me Nothing comes of unequal marriages but worry, and despair, and misery, and *death*," says Mona, in a fearful tone, emphasizing each prophetic word with a dismal nod.

"You've been reading novels," says Rodney, contemptuously.

"No, I haven't," says Mona, indignantly.

"Then you are out of your mind," says Rodney.

"No, I am not. Anything but that; and to be rude"—slowly—"answers no purpose. But I have some common sense, I hope."

"I hate women with common sense. In plainer language it means no heart."

"Now you speak sensibly. The sooner you begin to hate me the better."

"A nice time to offer such advice as that," says Rodney, moodily. "But I shan't take it. Mona,"—seizing her hands and speaking more in passionate excitement than even in love,—"say at once you will keep your word and marry me."

"Nothing on earth shall bring me to say that," says Mona, solemnly. "Nothing!"

"Then don't," says Rodney, furiously, and flinging her hands from him, he turns and strides savagely down the hill, and is lost to sight round the corner.

But, though "lost to sight," to memory he is most unpleasantly "dear." Standing alone in the middle of the deserted field, Mona pulls to pieces, in a jerky, fretful fashion, a blade of grass she has been idly holding during the late warm discussion. She is honestly very much frightened at what she has done, but obstinately declines to acknowledge it even to her own heart. In a foolish but natural manner she tries to deceive herself into the belief that what has happened has been much to her own advantage, and it will be a strict wisdom to rejoice over it.

"Dear me," she says, throwing up her dainty head, and flinging, with a petulant gesture, the unoffending grass far from her, "what an escape I have had! How his mother would have hated me! Surely I should count it lucky that I discovered all about her in time. Because really it doesn't so very much matter; I dare say I shall manage to be quite perfectly happy here again, after a little bit, just as I have been all my life—before he came. And when he is gone"—she pauses, chokes back with stern determination a very heavy sigh, and then goes on hastily and with suspicious bitterness, "What a temper he has! Horrid! The way he flung away my hand, as if he detested me, and flounced down that hill, as if he hoped never to set eyes on me again! With no 'good-by,' or 'by your leave,' or 'with your leave,' or a word of farewell, or a backward glance, or *anything!* I do hope he has taken me at my word, and that he will go straight back, without seeing me again, to his own odious country."

She tells herself this lie without a blush, perhaps because she is so pale at the bare thought that her eyes may never again be gladdened by his presence, that the blood refuses to rise.

A bell tinkles softly in the distance. The early dusk is creeping up from behind the distant hills, that are purple with the soft and glowing heather. The roar of the rushing waves comes from the bay that lies behind those encircling hills, and falls like sound of saddest music on her ear. Now comes

Still evening on, and twilight grayHas in her sober livery all things clad.

And Mona, rousing herself from her unsatisfactory reverie, draws her breath quickly and then moves homeward.

But first she turns and casts a last lingering glance upon the sloping hill down which her sweetheart, filled with angry thoughts, had gone. And as she so stands, with her hand to her forehead, after a little while a slow smile of conscious power comes to her lips and tarries round them, as though fond of its resting-place.

Her lips part. An expression that is half gladness, half amusement, brightens her eyes.

"I wonder," she says to herself, softly, "whether he will be with me at the usual hour to-morrow, or,—a little earlier!"

Then she gathers up her gown and runs swiftly back to the farm.

CHAPTER XI.

HOW GEOFFREY RETURNS TO HIS ALLEGIANCE—HOW HE DISCOVERS HIS DIVINITY DEEP IN THE PERFORMANCE OF SOME MYSTIC RITES WITHIN THE COOL PRECINCTS OF HER TEMPLE—AND HOW HE SEEKS TO REDUCE HER TO REASON FROM THE TOP OF AN INVERTED CHURN.

To-day—that "liberal worldling," that "gay philosopher"—is here; and last night belongs to us only in so far as it deserves a place in our memory or has forced itself there in spite of our hatred and repugnance.

To Rodney, last night is one ever to be remembered as being a period almost without end, and as a perfect specimen of how seven hours can be made to feel like twenty-one.

Thus at odd moments time can treble itself; but with the blessed daylight come comfort and renewed hope, and Geoffrey, greeting with rapture the happy morn, that,

"Waked by the circling hours, with rosy handUnbars the gates of light,"

tells himself that all may yet be right betwixt him and his love.

His love at this moment—which is closing upon noon—is standing in her cool dairy upon business thoughts intent yet with a certain look of expectation and anxiety upon he face,—a *listening* look may best express it.

To-morrow will be market-day in Bantry, to which the week's butter must go; and now the churning is over, and the result of it lies cold and rich and fresh beneath Mona's eyes. She herself is busily engaged printing little pats off a large roll of butter that rests on the slab before her; her sleeves are carefully tucked up, as on that first day when Geoffrey saw her; and in defiance of her own heart—which knows itself to be sad—she is lilting some little foolish lay, bright and shallow as the October sunshine that floods the room, lying in small silken patches on the walls and floor.

In the distance a woman is bending over a keeler making up a huge mass of butter into rolls, nicely squared and smoothed, to make them look their best and handsomest to-morrow.

"An' a nate color too," says this woman, who is bare-footed, beneath her breath, regarding with admiration the yellow tint of the object on which she is engaged. Two pullets, feathered like a partridge, are creeping stealthily into the dairy, their heads turned knowingly on one side, their steps slow and cautious; not even the faintest chirrup escapes them, lest it be the cause of their instant dismissal. There is no sound anywhere but the soft music that falls from Mona's lips.

Suddenly a bell rings in the distance. This is the signal for the men to cease from work and go to their dinners. It must be two o'clock.

Two o'clock! The song dies away, and Mona's brow contracts. So late!—the day is slipping from her, and as yet no word, no sign.

The bell stops, and a loud knock at the hall-door takes its place. Was ever sweeter sound heard anywhere? Mona draws her breath quickly, and then as though ashamed of herself goes on stoically with her task. Yet for all her stoicism her color comes and goes, and now she is pale, and now "celestial, rosy red, love's proper hue," and now a little smile comes up and irradiates her face.

So he has come back to her. There is triumph in this thought and some natural vanity, but above and beyond all else a great relief that lifts from her the deadly fear that all night has been consuming her and has robbed her of her rest. Now anxiety is at an end, and joy reigns, born of the knowledge that by his speedy surrender he has proved himself her own indeed, and she herself indispensable to his content.

"'Tis the English gintleman, miss,—Misther Rodney. He wants to see ye," says the fair Bridget, putting her head in at the doorway, and speaking in a hushed and subdued tone.

"Very well: show him in here," says Mona, very distinctly, going on with the printing of her butter with a courage that deserves credit. There is acrimony in her tone, but laughter in her eyes. While acknowledging a faint soreness at her heart she is still amused at his prompt, and therefore flattering, subjection.

Rodney, standing on the threshold at the end of the small hall, can hear distinctly all that passes.

"Here, miss,—in the dairy? Law, Miss Mona! don't"

"Why?" demands her mistress, somewhat haughtily. "I suppose even the English gentleman, as you call him, can see butter with dying! Show him in at once."

"But in that apron, miss, and wid yer arms bare-like, an' widout yer purty blue bow; law, Miss Mona, have sinse, an' don't ye now."

"Show Mr. Rodney in here, Bridget," says Mona unflinchingly, not looking at the distressed maid, or indeed at anything but the unobservant butter. And Bridget, with a sigh that strongly resembles the snort of a war-horse, ushers Mr. Rodney into the dairy.

"You?" says Mona, with extreme *hauteur* and an unpleasant amount of well-feigned astonishment. She does not deign to go to meet him, or even turn her head altogether in his direction, but just throws a swift and studiously unfriendly glance at him from under her long lashes.

"Yes" replies he, slowly as though regretful that he cannot deny his own identity.

"And what has brought you?" demands she, not rudely or quickly, but as though desirous of obtaining information on a subject that puzzles her.

"An overwhelming desire to see you again," returns this wise young man, in a tone that is absolutely abject.

To this it is difficult to make a telling reply. Mona says nothing she only turns her head completely away from him, as if to conceal something. Is it a smile?—he cannot tell. And indeed presently, as though to dispel all such idea, she sighs softly but audibly.

At this Mr. Rodney moves a shade closer to her.

"What a very charming dairy!" he says, mildly.

"Very uncomfortable for you, I fear, after your long ride," says Mona, coldly but courteously. "Why don't you go into the parlor? I am sure you will find it pleasanter there."

"I am sure I should not," says Rodney.

"More comfortable, at least."

"I am quite comfortable, thank you."

"But you have nothing to sit on."

"Neither have you."

"Oh, I have my work to do; and besides, I often prefer standing."

"So do I, often,—*very* often," says Mr. Rodney, sadly still, but genially.

"Are you sure?"—with cold severity. "It is only two days ago since you told me you loved nothing better than an easy-chair."

"Loved nothing better than a—oh, how you must have misunderstood me!" says Rodney, with mournful earnestness, liberally sprinkled with reproach.

"I have indeed misunderstood you in *many* ways." This is unkind, and the emphasis makes it even more so. "Norah, if the butter is finished, you can go and feed the calves." There is a business-like air about her whole manner eminently disheartening to a lover out of court.

"Very good, miss; I'm going," says the woman, and with a last touch to the butter she covers it over with a clean wet cloth and moves to the yard door. The two chickens on the threshold, who have retreated and advanced a thousand times, now retire finally with an angry "cluck-cluck," and once more silence reigns.

"We were talking of love, I think," says Rodney, innocently, as though the tender passion as subsisting between the opposite sexes had been the subject of the conversation.

"Of love generally?—no," with a disdainful glance,—"merely of your love of comfort."

"Yes, quite so: that is exactly what I meant," returns he, agreeably. It was *not* what he meant; but that doesn't count. "How awfully clever you are," he says, presently, alluding to her management of the little pats, which, to say truth, are faring but ill at her hands.

"Not clever," says Mona. "If I were clever I should not take for granted—as I always do—that what people say they must mean. I myself could not wear a double face."

"That is just like me," says Mr. Rodney, unblushingly—"the very image of me."

"Is it?"—witheringly. Then, with some impatience, "You will be far happier in an arm-chair: do go into the parlor. There is really no reason why you should remain here."

"There is,—a reason not to be surpassed. And as to the parlor,"—in a melancholy tone,—"I could not be happy there, or anywhere, just at present. Unless, indeed,"—this in a very low but carefully distinct tone,—"it be here!"

A pause. Mona mechanically but absently goes on with her work, avoiding all interchange of glances with her deceitful lover. The deceitful lover is plainly meditating a fresh attack. Presently he overturns an empty churn and seats himself on the top of it in a dejected fashion.

"I never saw the easy-chair I could compare with this," he says, as though to himself, his voice full of truth.

This is just a little too much. Mona gives way. Standing well back from her butter, she lets her pretty rounded bare arms fall lightly before her to their full length, and as her fingers clasp each other she turns to Rodney and breaks into a peal of laughter sweet as music.

At this he would have drawn her into his arms, hoping her gayety may mean forgiveness and free absolution for all things said and done the day before; but she recoils from him.

"No, no," she says; "all is different now, you know, and you should never have come here again at all; but"—with charming inconsequence—"*why* did you go away last evening without bidding me good-night?"

"My heart was broken, and by you: that was why. How could you say the cruel things you did? To tell me it would be better for me to cut my throat than marry you! That was abominable of you, Mona, wasn't it now? And to make me believe you meant it all, too!" says this astute young man.

"I did mean it. Of course I cannot marry you," says Mona, but rather weakly. The night has left her in a somewhat wavering frame of mind.

"If you can say that again now, in cold blood, after so many hours of thought, you must be indeed heartless," says Rodney; "and"—standing up—"I may as well go."

He moves towards the door with "pride in his port, defiance in his eye," as Goldsmith would say.

"Well, well, wait for one moment," says Mona, showing the white feather at last, and holding out to him one slim little hand. He seizes it with avidity, and then, placing his arm round her waist with audacious boldness, gives her an honest kiss, which she returns with equal honesty.

"Now let us talk no more nonsense," says Rodney, tenderly. "We belong to each other, and always shall, and that is the solution of the whole matter."

"Is it?" says she, a little wistfully. "You think so now; but if afterwards you should know regret, or——"

"Oh, if—if—if!" interrupts he. "Is it that you are afraid for yourself? Remember there is 'beggary in the love that can be reckoned.'"

"That is true," says Mona; "but it does not apply to me; and it is for you only I fear. Let me say just this: I have thought it all over; there were many hours in which to think, because I could not sleep——"

"Neither could I," puts in Geoffrey. "But it was hard on you, my darling."

"And this is what I would say: in one year from this I will marry you, if"—with a faint tremble in her tone—"you then still care to marry me. But not before."

"A year! An eternity!"

"No; only twelve months,"—hastily; "say no more now: my mind is quite made up."

"Last week, Mona, you gave me your promise to marry me before Christmas; can you break it now? Do you know what an old writer says? 'Thou oughtest to be nice even to superstition in keeping thy promises; and therefore thou shouldst be equally cautious in making them.' Now, you have made yours in all good faith, how can you break it again?"

"Ah! then I did not know all," says Mona. "That was your fault. No; if I consent to do you this injury you shall at least have time to think it over."

"Do you distrust me?" says Rodney,—this time really hurt, because his love for her is in reality deep and strong and thorough.

"No,"—slowly,—"I do not. If I did, I should not love you as—as I do."

"It is all very absurd," says Rodney, impatiently. "If a year, or two, or twenty, were to go by, it would be all the same; I should love you then as I love you to-day, and no other woman. Be reasonable, darling; give up this absurd idea."

"Impossible," says Mona.

"Impossible is a word only to be found in the dictionary of fools. *You* are not a fool. This is a mere fad of yours and I think you hardly know why you are insisting on it."

"I do know," says Mona. "First, because I would have you weigh everything carefully, and——"

"Yes, and——"

"You know your mother will object to me," says Mona, with an effort, speaking hurriedly, whilst a little fleck of scarlet flames into her cheeks.

"Stuff!" says Mr. Rodney; "that is only piling Ossa upon Pelion: it will bring you no nearer the clouds. Say you will go back to the old arrangement and marry me next month, or at least the month after."

"No."

She stands away from him, and looks at him with a face so pale, yet so earnest and intense, that he feels it will be unwise to argue further with her just now. So instead he takes both her hands and draws her to his side again.

"Oh, Mona, if you could only know how wretched I was all last night," he says; "I never put in such a bad time in my life."

"Yes; I can understand you," said Mona, softly, "for I too was miserable."

"Do you recollect all you said, or one-half of it? You said it would be well if I hated you."

"That was very nasty of me," confesses Mona. "Yet," with a sigh, "perhaps I was right."

"Now, that is nastier," says Geoffrey; "unsay it."

"I will," says the girl, impulsively, with quick tears in her eyes. "Don't hate me, my dearest, unless you wish to kill me; for that would be the end of it."

"I have a great mind to say something uncivil to you, if only to punish you for your coldness," says Geoffrey, lightly, cheered by her evident sincerity. "But I shall refrain, lest a second quarrel be the result, and I have endured so much during these past few hours that

'As I am a Christian faithful manI would not spend another such a nightThough 'twere to buy a world of happy days.'

From the hour I parted from you till I saw you again I felt downright suicidal."

"But you didn't cut your throat, after all," says Mona, with a wicked little grimace.

"Well, no; but I dare say I shall before I am done with you. Besides, it occurred to me I might as well have a last look at you before consigning my body to the grave."

"And an unhallowed grave, too. And so you really felt miserable when angry with me? How do you feel now?" She is looking up at him, with love and content and an adorable touch of coquetry in her pretty face.

"'I feel that I am happier than I know,'" quotes he, softly, folding her closely to his heart.

So peace is restored, and presently, forsaking the pats of butter and the dairy, they wander forth into the open air, to catch the last mild breezes that belong to the dying day.

CHAPTER XII.

HOW GEOFFREY TELLS HOME SECRETS, AND HOW MONA COMMENTS THEREON—HOW DEATH STALKS RAMPANT IN THEIR PATH—AND HOW, THOUGH GEOFFREY DECLINES TO "RUN AWAY," HE STILL "LIVES TO FIGHT ANOTHER DAY."

"And you really mustn't think us such very big people," says Geoffrey, in a deprecating tone, "because we are any thing but that, and, in fact,"—with a sharp contraction of his brow that betokens inward grief,—"there is rather a cloud over us just now."

"A cloud?" says Mona. And I think in her inmost heart she is rather glad than otherwise that her lover's people are not on the top rung of the ladder.

"Yes,—in a regular hole, you know," says Mr. Rodney. "It is rather a complicated story, but the truth is, my grandfather hated his eldest son—my uncle who went to Australia—like poison, and when dying left all the property—none of which was entailed—to his second son, my father."

"That was a little unfair, wasn't it?" says Mona. "Why didn't he divide it?"

"Well, that's just it," returns he. "But, you see, he didn't. He willed the whole thing to my father. He had a long conversation with my mother the very night before his death, in which he mentioned this will, and where it was locked up, and all about it; yet the curious part of the whole matter is this, that on the morning after his death, when they made search for this will, it was nowhere to be found! Nor have we heard tale or tidings of it ever since Though of the fact that it was duly signed, sealed, and delivered there is no doubt."

"How strange!" says Mona. "But how then did you manage?"

"Well, just then it made little difference to us, as, shortly after my grandfather went off the hooks, we received what we believed to be authenticated tidings of my uncle's death."

"Yes?" says Mona, who looks and is, intensely interested.

"Well, belief, however strong, goes a short way sometimes. An uncommon short way with us."

"But your uncle's death made it all right, didn't it?"

"No, it didn't: it made it all wrong. But for that lie we should not be in the predicament in which we now find ourselves. You will understand me better when I tell you that the other day a young man turned up who declares himself to be my uncle George's son, and heir to his land and title. That *was* a blow. And, as this wretched will is not forthcoming, I fear he will inherit everything. We are disputing it, of course, and are looking high and low for the missing will that should have been sought for at the first. But it's very shaky the whole affair."

"It is terrible," says Mona, with such exceeding earnestness that he could have hugged her on the spot.

"It is very hard on Nick," he says disconsolately.

"And he is your cousin, this strange young man?"

"Yes, I suppose so," replies Mr. Rodney, reluctantly. "But he don't look like it. Hang it, you know," exclaims he, vehemently, "one can stand a good deal, but to have a fellow who wears carbuncle rings, and speaks of his mother as the 'old girl,' call himself your cousin, is more than flesh and blood can put up with: it's—it's worse than the lawsuit."

"It is very hard on Sir Nicholas," says Mona, who would not call him "Nick" now for the world.

"Harder even than you know. He is engaged to one of the dearest little girls possible, but of course if this affair terminates in favor of—" he hesitates palpably, then says with an effort—"my cousin, the engagement comes to an end."

"But why?" says Mona.

"Well, he won't be exactly a catch after that, you know," says Rodney, sadly. "Poor old Nick! it will be a come-down for him after all these years."

"But do you mean to tell me the girl he loves will give him up just because fortune is frowning on him?" asks Mona, slowly. "Sure she couldn't be so mean as that."

"It won't be her fault; but of course her people will object, which amounts to the same thing. She can't go against her people, you know."

"I *don't* know," says Mona unconvinced. "I would go against all the people in the world rather than be bad to you. And to forsake him, too, at the very time when he will most want sympathy, at the very hour of his great trouble. Oh! that is shameful! I shall not like her, I think."

"I am sure you will, notwithstanding. She is the gayest, brightest creature imaginable, just such another as yourself. If it be true that 'birds of a feather flock together,' you and she must amalgamate. You may not get on well with Violet Mansergh, who is somewhat reserved, but I know you will be quite friends with Doatie."

"What is her name?"

"She is Lord Steyne's second daughter. The family name is Darling. Her name is Dorothy."

"A pretty name, too."

"Yes, old-fashioned. She is always called Doatie Darling by her familiars, which sounds funny. She is quite charming, and loved by every one."

"Yet she would renounce her love, would betray him for the sake of filthy lucre," says Mona, gravely. "I cannot understand that."

"It is the way of her world. There is more in training than one quite knows. Now, you are altogether different. I know that; it is perhaps the reason why you have made my heart your own. Do not think it flattery when I tell you there are very few like you, Mona, in the world; but I would have you be generous. Do not let your excellence make you harsh to others. That is a common fault; and all people, darling, are not charactered alike."

"Am I harsh?" says Mona, wistfully.

"No, you are not," says Geoffrey, grieved to the heart that he could have used such a word towards her. "You are nothing that is not sweet and adorable. And, besides all this, you are, I know, sincerity itself. I feel (and am thankful for the knowledge) that were fate to 'steep me in poverty to the very lips,' you would still be faithful to me."

"I should be all the more faithful: it is then you would feel your need of me," says Mona, simply. Then, as though puzzled, she goes on with a little sigh, "In time perhaps, I shall understand it all, and how other people feel, and— if it will please you, Geoffrey—I shall try to like the girl you call Doatie."

"I wish Nick didn't like her so much," says Geoffrey, sadly. "It will cut him up more than all the rest, if he has to give her up."

"Geoffrey," says Mona, in a low tone, slipping her hand into his in a half-shamed fashion, "I have five hundred pounds of my own, would it—would it be of any use to Sir Nicholas?"

Rodney is deeply touched.

"No, darling, no; I am afraid not," he says, very gently. But for the poor child's tender earnestness and good faith, he could almost have felt some faint amusement; but this offering of hers is to him a sacred thing, and to treat her words as a jest is a thought far from him. Indeed, to give wilful offence to any one, by either word or action, would be very foreign to his nature. For if "he is gentil that doth gentil dedis" be true, Rodney to his finger-tips is gentleman indeed.

It is growing dusk; "the shades of night are falling fast," the cold pale sun, that all day long has cast its chill October beams upon a leafless world, has now sunk behind the distant hill, and the sad silence of the coming night hath set her finger with deep touch upon creation's brow.

"Do you know," says Mona, with a slight shiver, and a little nervous laugh, pressing closer to her side, "I have lost half my courage of late? I seem to be always anticipating evil."

Down from the mountain's top the shadows are creeping stealthily: all around is growing dim, and vague, and mysterious, in the uncertain light.

"Perhaps I feel nervous because of all the unhappy things one hears daily," goes on Mona, in a subdued voice. "That murder at Oola, for instance: that was horrible.'

"Well but a murder at Oola isn't a murder here, you know," says Mr. Rodney, airily. "Let us wait to be melancholy until it comes home to ourselves,— which indeed, may be at any moment, your countrymen are of such a very playful disposition. Do you remember what a lively time we had of it the night we ran to Maxwell's assistance, and what an escape he had?"

"Ay! so he had, an escape *you* will never know," says a hoarse voice at this moment, that makes Mona's heart almost cease to beat. An instant later, and two men jump up from the dark ditch in which they have been evidently hiding, and confront Rodney with a look of savage satisfaction upon their faces.

At this first glance he recognizes them as being the two men with whom Mona had attempted argument and remonstrance on the night elected for Maxwell's murder. They are armed with guns, but wear no disguise, not even the usual band of black crape across the upper half of the face.

Rodney casts a quick glance up the road, but no human creature is in sight; nor, indeed, were they here, would they have been of any use. For who in these lawless days would dare defy or call in question the all-powerful Land League?

"You, Ryan?" says Mona, with an attempt at unconcern, but her tone is absolutely frozen with fear.

"You see me," says the man, sullenly; "an' ye may guess my errand." He fingers the trigger of his gun in a terribly significant manner as he speaks.

"I do guess it," she answers, slowly. "Well, kill us both, if it must be so." She lays her arms round Rodney's neck as she speaks, even before he can imagine her meaning, and hides her face on his breast.

"Stand back," says Ryan, savagely. "Stand back, I tell ye, unless ye want a hole in yer own skin, for his last moment is come."

"Let me go, Mona," says Geoffrey, forcing her arms from round him and almost flinging her to one side. It is the first and last time he ever treats a woman with roughness.

"Ha! That's right," says Ryan. "You hold her, Carthy, while I give this English gentleman a lesson that will carry him to the other world. I'll teach him how to balk me of my prey a second time. D'ye think I didn't know about Maxwell, eh? an' that my life is in yer keepin'! But yours is in mine now," with a villanous leer "an' I wouldn't give a thraneen for it."

Carthy, having caught Mona's arms from behind just a little above the elbow, holds her as in a vice. There is no escape, no hope! Finding herself powerless, she makes no further effort for freedom, but with dilated eyes and parted, bloodless lips, though which her breath comes in quick agonized gasps, waits to see her lover murdered almost at her feet. "Now say a short prayer," says Ryan, levelling his gun; "for yer last hour has come."

"Has it?" says Rodney, fiercely. "Then I'll make the most of it," and before the other can find time to fire he flings himself upon him, and grasps his throat with murderous force.

In an instant they are locked in each other's arms. Ryan wrestles violently, but is scarcely a match for Rodney, whose youth and training tell, and who is actually fighting for dear life. In the confusion the gun goes off, and the bullet, passing by Rodney's arm, tears away a piece of the coat with it, and also part of the flesh. But this he hardly knows till later on.

To and fro they sway, and then both men fall heavily to the ground. Presently they are on their feet again, but this time Rodney is master of the unloaded gun.

"Leave the girl alone, and come here," shouts Ryan furiously to Carthy, who is still holding Mona captive. The blood is streaming from a large cut on his forehead received in his fall.

"Coward!" hisses Rodney between his teeth. His face is pale as death; his teeth are clenched; his gray eyes are flaming fire. His hat has fallen off in the struggle, and his coat, which is a good deal torn, betrays a shirt beneath deeply stained with blood. He is standing back a little from his opponent, with his head thrown up, and his fair hair lying well back from his brow.

"Come on," he says, with a low furious laugh, that has no mirth in it, but is full of reckless defiance. "But first," to Ryan, "I'll square accounts with you."

Advancing with the empty gun in his hands, he raises it, and, holding it by the barrel, brings it down with all his might upon his enemy's skull. Ryan reels, staggers, and once more licks the dust. But the wretched weapon—sold probably at the back of some miserable shebeen in Bantry for any price ranging from five-and-six to one guinea—snaps in two at this moment from the force of the blow, so leaving Rodney, spent and weak with loss of blood, at the mercy of his second opponent.

Carthy, having by this time freed himself from Mona's detaining grasp,—who, seeing the turn affairs have taken, has clung to him with all her strength, and so hampered his efforts to go to his companion's assistance,—comes to the front.

But a hand-to-hand encounter is not Mr. Carthy's forte. He prefers being propped up by friends and acquaintances, and thinks a duel *a la mort* a poor speculation. Now, seeing his whilom accomplice stretched apparently lifeless upon the ground, his courage (what he has of it), like Bob Acres', oozes out through his palms, and a curious shaking, that surely can't be fear, takes possession of his knees.

Moreover, he has never before had a gun in his own keeping; and the sensation, though novel, is not so enchanting as he had fondly hoped it might have been. He is plainly shy about the managing of it, and in his heart is not quite sure which end of it goes off. However, he lifts it with trembling fingers, and deliberately covers Rodney.

Tyro as he is, standing at so short a distance from his antagonist, he could have hardly failed to blow him into bits, and probably would have done so, but for one little accident.

Mona, whose Irish blood by this time is at its hottest, on finding herself powerless to restrain the movements of Carthy any longer, had rushed to the wall near, and, made strong by love and excitement, had torn from its top a heavy stone.

Now, turning back, she aims carefully for Carthy's head, and flings the missile from her. A woman's eye in such cases is seldom sure, and now the stone meant for his head falls short, and, hitting his arm, knocks the gun from his nerveless fingers.

This brings the skirmish to an end. Carthy, seeing all is lost, caves in, and, regardless of the prostrate figure of his companion, jumps hurriedly over the low wall, and disappears in the night-mist that is rolling up from the bay.

Rodney, lifting the gun, takes as sure aim as he can at the form of the departing hero; but evidently the bullet misses its mark, as no sound of fear or pain comes to disturb the utter silence of the evening.

Then he turns to Mona.

"You have saved my life," he says, in a tone that trembles for the first time this evening, "my love! my brave girl! But what an ordeal for you!"

"I felt nothing, nothing, but the one thing that I was powerless to help you," says Mona, passionately; "that was bitter."

"What spirit, what courage, you displayed! At first I feared you would faint——"

"While you still lived? While I might be of some use to you? No!" says Mona, her eyes gleaming. "To myself I said, there will be time enough for that later on." Then, with a little dry sob, "There will be time to *die* later on."

Here her eyes fall upon Ryan's motionless figure, and a shudder passes over her.

"Is he dead?" she asks, in a whisper, pointing without looking at their late foe. Rodney, stooping, lays his hand on the ruffian's heart.
"No, he breathes," he says. "He will live, no doubt. Vermin are hard to kill. And if he does die," bitterly, "what matter? Dog! Let him die there! The road is too good a place for him."
"Come home," says Mona, faintly. Now the actual danger is past, terror creeps over her, rendering her a prey to imaginary sights and sounds. "There may be others. Do not delay."
In ignorance of the fact that Geoffrey has been hurt in the fray, she lays her hand upon the injured arm. Instinctively he shrinks from the touch.
"What is it?" she says, fearfully, and then, "Your coat is wet—I feel it. Oh Geoffrey, look at your shirt. It is blood!" Her tone is full of horror. "What have they done to you?" she says, pitifully. "You are hurt, wounded!"
"It can't be much," says Geoffrey, who, to confess the truth, is by this time feeling a little sick and faint. "I never knew I was touched till now. Come, let us get back to the farm."

"I wonder you do not hate me," says Mona, with a brokenhearted sob, "when you remember I am of the same blood as these wretches."

"Hate you!" replies he, with a smile of ineffable fondness, "my preserver and my love!"

She is comforted in a small degree by his words, but fear and depression still hold her captive. She insists upon his leaning on her, and he, seeing she is bent on being of some service to him, lays his hand lightly on her shoulder, and so they go slowly homeward.

CHAPTER XIII.

HOW MONA PROVES HERSELF EQUAL—IF NOT SUPERIOR—TO DR. MARY WALKER; AND HOW GEOFFREY, BY A BASE THREAT, CARRIES HIS POINT.

Old Brian Scully is in his parlor, and comes to meet them as they enter the hall,—his pipe behind his back.

"Come in, come in," he begins, cheerily, and then, catching sight of Mona's pale face, stops short. "Why, what has come to ye?" cries he, aghast, glancing from his niece to Rodney's discolored shirt and torn coat; "what has happened?"

"It was Tim Ryan," returns Mona, wearily, feeling unequal to a long story just at present.

"Eh, but this is bad news!" says old Scully, evidently terrified and disheartened by his niece's words. "Where will it all end? Come in, Misther Rodney: let me look at ye, boy. No, not a word out of ye now till ye taste something. 'Tis in bits ye are; an' good coat it was this mornin'. There's the whiskey, Mona, agra, an' there's the wather. Oh! the black villain! Let me examine ye, me son. Why, there's blood on ye! Oh! the murthering thief!"

So runs on the kindly farmer, smitten to the heart that such things should be,—and done upon Rodney of all men. He walks round the young man, muttering his indignation in a low tone, while helping him with gentle care to remove his coat,—or at least what remains of that once goodly garment that had for parent Mr. Poole.

"Where's the docther at all, at all?" says he, forcing Geoffrey into a chair, and turning to Biddy, who is standing open-mouthed in the doorway, and who, though grieved, is plainly finding some pleasure in the situation. Being investigated, she informs them the "docther" is to-night on the top of Carrigfoddha Mountain, and, literally, "won't be home until morning."

"Now, what's to be done?" says old Brian, in despair. "I know, as well as if ye tould me, it is Norry Flannigan! Just like those wimmen to be always troublesome! Are ye sure Biddy?"

"Troth I am, sir. I see him goin' wid me own two eyes not an hour ago, in the gig an' the white horse, wid the wan eye an' the loose tail,—that looks for all the world as if it was screwed on to him. An' 'tisn't Norry is callin' for him nayther (though I don't say but she'll be on the way), but Larry Moloney the sweep. 'Tis a stitch he got this morning, an' he's gone intirely this time, the people say. An' more's the pity too, for a dacent sowl he was, an' more nor a mortial sweep."

This eulogy on the departing Larry she delivers with much unction, and a good deal of check apron in the corner of one eye.

"Never mind Larry," says the farmer, impatiently. "This is the seventh time he has died this year. But think of Misther Rodney here. Can't ye do something for him?"

"Sure Miss Mona can," says Biddy, turning to her young mistress, and standing in the doorway in her favorite position,—that is, with her bare arms akimbo, and her head to one side like a magpie. "She's raal clever at dhressin' an' doctherin' an' that."

"Oh, no, I'm not clever," says Mona; "but"—nervously and with downcast eyes, addressing Geoffrey—"I might perhaps be able to make you a little more comfortable."

A strange feeling of shyness is weighing upon her. Her stalwart English lover is standing close beside her, having risen from his chair with his eyes on hers, and in his shirt-sleeves looking more than usually handsome because of his pallor, and because of the dark circles that, lying beneath his eyes, throw out their color, making them darker, deeper, than is their nature. How shall she bare the arm of this young Adonis?—how help to heal his wound? Oh, Larry Moloney, what hast thou not got to answer for!

She shrinks a little from the task, and would fain have evaded it altogether; though there is happiness, too, in the thought that here is an occasion on which she may be of real use to him. Will not the very act itself bring her nearer to him? Is it not sweet to feel that it is in her power to ease his pain? And is she not only doing what a tender wife would gladly do for her husband?

Still she hesitates, though betraying no vulgar awkwardness or silly *mauvaise honte*. Indeed, the only sign of emotion she does show is a soft slow blush, that, mounting quickly, tips even her little ears with pink.

"Let her thry," says old Brian, in his soft, Irish brogue, that comes kindly from his tongue. "She's mighty clever about most things."

"I hardly like to ask her to do it," says the young man, divided between an overpowering desire to be made "comfortable," as she has expressed it, and a chivalrous fear that the sight of the nasty though harmless flesh-wound will cause her some distress. "Perhaps it will make you unhappy,—may shock you," he says to her, with some anxiety.

"No, it will not shock me," returns Mona, quietly; whereupon he sits down, and Biddy puts a basin on the table, and Mona, with trembling fingers, takes a scissors, and cuts away the shirt-sleeve from his wounded arm. Then she bathes it.

After a moment she turns deadly pale, and says, in a faint tone, "I know I am hurting you: I *feel* it." And in truth I believe the tender heart does feel it, much more than he does. There is an expression that amounts to agony in her beautiful eyes.

"*You* hurt me!" replies he, in a peculiar tone, that is not so peculiar but it fully satisfies her. And then he smiles, and, seeing old Brian has once more returned to the fire and his pipe, and Biddy has gone for fresh water, he stoops over the reddened basin, and, in spite of all the unromantic surroundings, kisses her as fondly as if roses and moonbeams and dripping fountains and perfumed exotics were on every side. And this, because true romance—that needs no outward fire to keep it warm—is in his heart.

And now Mona knows no more nervousness, but with a steady and practised hand binds up his arm, and when all is finished pushes him gently (*very* gently) from her, and "with heart on her lips, and soul within her eyes," surveys with pride her handiwork.

"Now I hope you will feel less pain," she says, with modest triumph.

"I feel no pain," returns he, gallantly.

"Well said!" cries the old man from the chimney-corner, slapping his knee with delight; "well said, indeed! It reminds me of the ould days when we'd swear to any lie to please the lass we loved. Ay, very good, very good."

At this Mona and Geoffrey break into silent laughter, being overcome by the insinuation about lying.

"Come here an' sit down, lad," says old Scully, unknowing of their secret mirth, "an' tell me all about it, from start to finish,—that Ryan's a thundering rogue,—while Mona sees about a bed for ye."

"Oh, no," says Rodney, hastily. "I have given quite too much trouble already. I assure you I am quite well enough now to ride back again to Bantry."

"To Bantry," says Mona, growing white again,—"to-night! Oh, do you want to kill me and yourself?"

"She has reason," says the old man, earnestly and approvingly, rounding his sentence after the French fashion, as the Irish so often will: "she has said it," he goes on, "she always does say it; she has brains, has my colleen. Ye don't stir out of this house to-night, Mr. Rodney; so make up yer mind to it. With Tim Ryan abroad, an' probably picked up and carried home by this time, the counthry will be all abroad, an' no safe thravellin' for man or baste. Here's a cosey sate for ye by the fire: sit down, lad, an' take life aisy."

"If I was quite sure I shouldn't be dreadfully in the way," says Geoffrey, turning to Mona, she being mistress of the ceremonies.

"Be quite sure," returns she, smiling.

"And to-morrow ye can go into Banthry an' prosecute that scoundrel Ryan," says Scully, "an' have yer arm properly seen afther."

"So I can," says Geoffrey. Then, not for any special reason, but because, through very love of her, he is always looking at her, he turns his eyes on Mona. She is standing by the table, with her head bent down.

"Yes, to-morrow you can have your arm re-dressed," she says, in a low tone, that savors of sadness; and then he knows she does not want him to prosecute Ryan.

"I think I'll let Ryan alone," he says, instantly, turning to her uncle and addressing him solely, as though to prove himself ignorant of Mona's secret wish. "I have given him enough to last him for some time." Yet the girl reads him him through and through, and is deeply grateful to him for this quick concession to her unspoken desire.

"Well, well, you're a good lad at heart," says Scully, glad perhaps in his inmost soul, as his countrymen always are and will be when a compatriot cheats the law and escapes a just judgment. "Mona, look after him for awhile, until I go an' see that lazy spalpeen of mine an' get him to put a good bed undher Mr. Rodney's horse."

When the old man has gone, Mona goes quietly up to her lover, and, laying her hand upon his arm,—a hand that seems by some miraculous means to have grown whiter of late,—says, gratefully,—

"I know why you said that about Ryan, and I thank you for it. I should not like to think it was your word had transported him."

"Yet, I am letting him go free that he may be the perpetrator of even greater crimes."

"You err, nevertheless, on the side of mercy, if you err at all; and—perhaps there may be no other crimes. He may have had his lesson this evening,—a lasting one. To-morrow I shall go to his cabin, and——"

"Now, once for all, Mona," interrupts he, with determination, "I strictly forbid you ever to go to Ryan's cottage again."

It is the first time he has ever used the tone of authority towards her, and involuntarily she shrinks from him, and glances up at him from under her long lashes in a half frightened, half-reproachful fashion, as might an offended child.

Following her, he takes both her hands, and, holding them closely, draws her back to her former position beside him.

"Forgive me: it was an ugly word," he says, "I take it back. I shall never forbid you to do anything, Mona, if my doing so must bring that look into your eyes. Yet surely there are moments in every woman's life when the man who loves her, and whom she loves, may claim from her obedience, when it is for her own good. However, let that pass. I now entreat you not to go again to Ryan's cabin."

Releasing her hands from his firm grasp, the girl lays them lightly crossed upon his breast, and looks up at him with perfect trust,—

"Nay," she says, very sweetly and gravely, "you mistake me. I am glad to obey you. I shall not go to Ryan's house again."

There is both dignity and tenderness in her tone. She gazes at him earnestly for a moment, and then suddenly slips one arm round his neck.

"Geoffrey," she says with a visible effort.

"Yes, darling."

"I want you to do something for my sake."

"I will do anything, my own."

"It is for my sake; but it will break my heart."

"Mona! what are you going to say to me?"

"I want you to leave Ireland—not next month, or next week, but at once. To-morrow, if possible."

"My darling, why?"

"Because you are not safe here: your life is in danger. Once Ryan is recovered, he will not be content to see you living, knowing his life is in your hands; every hour you will be in danger. Whatever it may cost me, you must go."

"That's awful nonsense, you know," says Rodney, lightly. "When he sees I haven't taken any steps about arresting him, he will forget all about it, and bear no further ill will."

"You don't understand this people as I do. I tell you he will never forgive his downfall the other night, or the thought that he is in your power."

"Well, at all events I shan't go one moment before I said I should," says Rodney.

"It is now my turn to demand obedience," says Mona, with a little wan attempt at a smile. "Will you make every hour of my life unhappy? Can I live in the thought that each minute may bring me evil news of you,—may bring me tidings of your death?" Here she gives way to a passionate burst of grief, and clings closer to him, as though with her soft arms to shield him from all danger. Her tears touch him.

"Well, I will go," he says, "on one condition,—that you come with me."

"Impossible!" drawing back from him. "How could I be ready? and, besides, I have said I will not marry you until a year goes by. How can I break my word?"

"That word should never have been said. It is better broken."

"Oh, no."

"Very well. I shall not ask you to break it. But I shall stay on here. And if," says this artful young man, in a purposely doleful tone, "anything *should* happen, it will——"

"Don't say it! don't!" cries Mona, in an agony, stopping his mouth with her hand. "Do not! Yes, I give in. I will go with you. I will marry you any time you like, the sooner the better,"—feverishly; "anything to save your life!"

This is hardly complimentary, but Geoffrey passes it over.

"This day week, then," he says, having heard, and taken to heart the wisdom of, the old maxim about striking while the iron is hot.

"Very well," says Mona, who is pale and thoughtful.

And then old Brian comes in, and Geoffrey opens out to him this newly-devized plan; and after a while the old farmer, with tears in his eyes, and a strange quiver in his voice that cuts through Mona's heart, gives his consent to it, and murmurs a blessing on this hasty marriage that is to deprive him of all he best loves on earth.

And so they are married, and last words are spoken, and adieux said, and sad tears fall, and for many days her own land knows Mona no more.

And that night, when she is indeed gone, a storm comes up from the sea, and dashes the great waves inward upon the rocky coast. And triumphantly upon their white bosoms the sea-mews ride, screaming loudly their wild sweet song that mingles harmoniously with the weird music of the winds and waves.

And all the land is rich with angry beauty beneath the rays of the cold moon, that

"O'er the dark her silver mantle throws;"

and the sobbing waves break themselves with impotent fury upon the giant walls of granite that line the coast, and the clouds descend upon the hills, and the sea-birds shriek aloud, and all nature seems to cry for Mona.

But to the hill of Carrickdhuve, to sit alone and gaze in loving silence on the heaven-born grandeur of earth and sky and sea, comes Mona Scully no more forever.

CHAPTER XIV.

HOW GEOFFREY WRITES A LETTER THAT POSSESSES ALL THE PROPERTIES OF DYNAMITE—AND HOW CONFUSION REIGNS AT THE TOWERS.

In the house of Rodney there is mourning and woe. Horror has fallen upon it, and something that touches on disgrace. Lady Rodney, leaning back in her chair with her scented handkerchief pressed close to her eyes, sobs aloud and refuses to be comforted.

The urn is hissing angrily, and breathing forth defiance with all his might. It is evidently possessed with the belief that the teapot has done it some mortal injury, and is waging on it war to the knife.

The teapot, meanwhile, is calmly ignoring its rage, and is positively turning up its nose at it. It is a very proud old teapot, and is looking straight before it, in a very dignified fashion, at a martial row of cups and saucers that are drawn up in battle-array and are only waiting for the word of command to march upon the enemy.

But this word comes not. In vain does the angry urn hiss. The teapot holds aloft its haughty nose for naught. The cups and saucers range themselves in military order all for nothing. Lady Rodney is dissolved in tears.

"Oh! Nicholas, it can't be true! it really *can't*!" she says, alluding to the news contained in a letter Sir Nicholas is reading with a puzzled brow.

He is a tall young man, about thirty-two, yet looking younger, with a somewhat sallow complexion, large dreamy brown eyes, and very fine sleek black hair. He wears neither moustache nor whiskers, principally for the very good reason that Nature has forgotten to supply them. For which perhaps he should be grateful, as it would have been a cruel thing to hide the excessive beauty of his mouth and chin and perfectly-turned jaw. These are his chief charms, being mild and thoughtful, yet a trifle firm, and in perfect accordance with the upper part of his face. He is hardly handsome, but is certainly attractive.

In manner he is somewhat indolent, silent, perhaps lazy. But there is about him a subtle charm that endears him to all who know him. Perhaps it is his innate horror of offending the feelings of any one, be he great or small, and perhaps it is his inborn knowledge of humanity, and the power he possesses (with most other sensitive people) of being able to read the thoughts of those with whom he comes in contact, that enables him to avoid all such offence. Perhaps it is his honesty, and straightforwardness, and general, if inactive, kindliness of disposition.

He takes little trouble about anything, certainly none to make himself popular, yet in all the countryside no man is so well beloved as he is. It is true that a kindly word here, or a smile in the right place, does more to make a man a social idol than substantial deeds of charity doled out by an unsympathetic hand. This may be unjust; it is certainly beyond dispute the fact.

Just now his forehead is drawn up into a deep frown, as he reads the fatal letter that has reduced his mother to a Niobe. Another young man, his brother, Captain Rodney, who is two or three years younger than he, is looking over his shoulder, while a slight, brown-haired, very aristocratic looking girl is endeavoring, in a soft, modulated voice, to convey comfort to Lady Rodney.

Breakfast is forgotten; the rolls and the toast and the kidneys are growing cold. Even her own special little square of home-made bread is losing its crispness and falling into a dejected state, which shows almost more than anything else could that Lady Rodney is very far gone indeed.

Violet is growing as nearly frightened as good breeding will permit at the protracted sobbing, when Sir Nicholas speaks.

"It is inconceivable!" he says to nobody in particular. "What on earth does he mean?" He turns the letter round and round between his fingers as though it were a bombshell; though, indeed, he need not at this stage of the proceedings have been at all afraid of it, as it has gone off long ago and reduced Lady Rodney to atoms. "I shouldn't have thought Geoffrey was that sort of fellow."

"But what is it?" asks Miss Mansergh from behind Lady Rodney's chair, just a little impatiently.

"Why, Geoffrey's been and gone and got married," says Jack Rodney, pulling his long fair moustache, and speaking rather awkwardly. It has been several times hinted to him, since his return from India, that, Violet Mansergh being reserved for his brother Geoffrey, any of his attentions in that quarter will be eyed by the family with disfavor. And now to tell her of her quondam lover's defection is not pleasant. Nevertheless he watches her calmly as he speaks.

"Is that all?" says Violet, in a tone of surprise certainly, but as certainly in one of relief.

"No, it is *not* all," breaks in Sir Nicholas. "It appears from this," touching the bombshell, "that he has married a—a—young woman of very inferior birth."

"Oh! that is really shocking," says Violet, with a curl of her very short upper lip.

"I do hope she isn't the under-housemaid," said Jack, moodily. "It has grown so awfully common. Three fellows this year married under-housemaids, and people are tired of it now; one can't keep up the excitement always. Anything new might create a diversion in his favor, but he's done for if he has married another under-housemaid."

"It is worse," says Lady Rodney, in a stifled tone, coming out for a brief instant from behind the deluged handkerchief. "He has married a common farmer's niece!"

"Well, you know that's better than a farmer's common niece," says Jack, consolingly.

"What does he say about it?" asks Violet, who shows no sign whatever of meaning to wear the willow for this misguided Benedict, but rather exhibits all a woman's natural curiosity to know exactly what he has said about the interesting event that has taken place.

Sir Nicholas again applies himself to the deciphering of the detested letter. "'He would have written before, but saw no good in making a fuss beforehand,'" he reads slowly.

"Well, there's good deal of sense in that," says Jack.

"'Quite the loveliest girl in the world,' with a heavy stroke under the 'quite.' That's always so, you know: nothing new or striking about that." Sir Nicholas all through is speaking in a tone uniformly moody and disgusted.

"It is a point in her favor nevertheless," says Jack, who is again looking over his shoulder at the letter.

"'She is charming at all points,'" goes on Sir Nicholas deliberately screwing his glass into his eye, "'with a mind as sweet as her face.' Oh, it is absurd!" says Sir Nicholas, impatiently. "He is evidently in the last stage of imbecility. Hopelessly bewitched."

"And a very good thing, too," puts in Jack, tolerantly: "it won't last, you know, so he may as well have it strong while he is about it."

"What do you know about it?" says Sir Nicholas, turning the tables in the most unexpected fashion upon his brother, and looking decidedly ruffled, for no reason that one can see, considering it is he himself is condemning the whole matter so heartily. "As he is married to her, I sincerely trust his affection for her may be deep and lasting, and not misplaced. She may be a very charming girl."

"She may," says Jack. "Well go on. What more does he say?"

"'He will write again. And he is sure we shall all love her when we see her.' That is another sentence that goes without telling. They are always sure of that beforehand. They absolutely arrange our feelings for us! I hope he will be as certain of it this time six months, for all our sakes."

"Poor girl! I feel honestly sorry for her," says Jack, with a mild sigh. "What an awful ass he has made of himself!"

"And 'he is happier now than he has ever been in all his life before.' Pshaw!" exclaims Sir Nicholas, shutting up the letter impatiently. "He is mad!"

"Where does he write from?" asks Violet.

"From the Louvre. They are in Paris."

"He has been married a whole fortnight and never deigned to tell his own mother of it until now," says Lady Rodney, hysterically.

"A whole fortnight! And he is as much in love with her as ever! Oh! she can't be half bad," says Captain Rodney, hopefully.

"Misfortunes seem to crowd upon us," says Lady Rodney, bitterly.

"I suppose she is a Roman Catholic," says Sir Nicholas musingly.

At this Lady Rodney sits quite upright, and turns appealingly to Violet. "Oh, Violet, I do hope not," she says.

"Nearly all the Irish farmers are," returns Miss Mansergh, reluctantly. "When I stay with Uncle Wilfrid in Westmeath, I see them all going to mass every Sunday morning. Of course"—kindly—"there are a few Protestants, but they are very few."

"This is too dreadful!" moans Lady Rodney, sinking back again in her chair, utterly overcome by this last crowning blow. She clasps her hands with a deplorable gesture, and indeed looks the very personification of disgusted woe.

"Dear Lady Rodney, I shouldn't take that so much to heart," says Violet, gently leaning over her. "Quite good people are Catholics now, you know. It is, indeed, the fashionable religion, and rather a nice one when you come to think of it."

"I don't want to think of it," says her friend, desperately.

"But do," goes on Violet, in her soft, even monotone, that is so exactly suited to her face. "It is rather pleasant thinking. Confession, you know, is so soothing; and then there are always the dear saints, with their delightful tales of roses and lilies, and tears that turn into drops of healing balm, and their bones that lie in little glass cases in the churches abroad. It is all so picturesque and pretty, like an Italian landscape. And it is so comfortable, too, to know that, no matter how naughty we may be here, we can still get to heaven at last by doing some great and charitable deed."

"There is something in that, certainly," says Captain Rodney, with feeling. "I wonder, now, what great and charitable deed I could do."

"And then isn't it sweet to think," continues Violet, warming to her subject, "that when one's friends are dead one can still be of some service to them, in praying for their souls? It seems to keep them always with one. They don't seem so lost to us as they would otherwise."

"Violet, please do not talk like that; I forbid it," says Lady Rodney, in a horrified tone. "Nothing could make me think well of anything connected with this—this odious girl; and when you speak like that you quite upset me. You will be having your name put in that horrid list of perverts in the 'Whitehall Review' if you don't take care."

"You really will, you know," says Captain Rodney, warningly; then, as though ambitious of piling up the agony, he says, *sotto voce*, yet loud enough to be heard, "I wonder if Geoff will go to mass with her?"

"It is exactly what I expect to hear next," says Geoff's mother, with the calmness of despair.

Then there is silence for a full minute, during which Miss Mansergh casts a reproachful glance at the irrepressible Jack.

"Well, I hope he has married a good girl, at all events," says Sir Nicholas, presently, with a sigh. But at this reasonable hope Lady Rodney once more gives way to bitter sobs.

"Oh, to think Geoffrey should marry 'a good girl'!" she says, weeping sadly. "One would think you were speaking of a servant! Oh! it is *too* cruel!" Here she rises and makes for the door, but on the threshold pauses to confront Sir Nicholas with angry eyes. "To hope the wretched boy had married 'a good girl'!" she says, indignantly: "I never heard such an inhuman wish from one brother to another!"

She withers Sir Nicholas with a parting glance, and then quits the room, Violet in her train, leaving her eldest son entirely puzzled.

"What does she mean?" asks he of his brother, who is distinctly amused. "Does she wish poor old Geoff had married a bad one? I confess myself at fault."

And so does Captain Rodney.

Meantime, Violet is having rather a bad time in the boudoir. Lady Rodney refuses to see light anywhere, and talks on in a disjointed fashion about this disgrace that has befallen the family.

"Of course I shall never receive her; that is out of the question, Violet: I could not support it."

"But she will be living only six miles from you, and the county will surely call, and that will not be nice for you," says Violet.

"I don't care about the county. It must think what it likes; and when it knows her it will sympathize with me. Oh! what a name! Scully! Was there ever so dreadful a name?"

"It is not a bad name in Ireland. There are very good people of that name: the Vincent Scullys,—everybody has heard of them," says Violet, gently. But her friend will not consent to believe anything that may soften the thought of Mona. The girl has entrapped her son, has basely captured him and made him her own beyond redemption; and what words can be bad enough to convey her hatred of the woman who has done this deed?

"I meant him for you," she says, in an ill-advised moment, addressing the girl who is bending over her couch assiduously and tenderly applying eau-de-cologne to her temples. It is just a little too much. Miss Mansergh fails to see the compliment in this remark. She draws her breath a little quickly, and as the color comes her temper goes.

"Dear Lady Rodney, you are really too kind," she says, in a tone soft and measured as usual, but without the sweetness. In her heart there is something that amounts as nearly to indignant anger as so thoroughly well-bred and well regulated a girl can feel. "You are better, I think," she says, calmly, without any settled foundation for the thought; and then she lays down the perfume-bottle, takes up her handkerchief, and, with a last unimportant word or two, walks out of the room.

CHAPTER XV.

HOW LADY RODNEY SPEAKS HER MIND—HOW GEOFFREY DOES THE SAME—AND HOW MONA DECLARES HERSELF STRONG TO CONQUER.

It is the 14th of December, and "bitter chill." Upon all the lawns and walks at the Towers, "Nature, the vicar of the almightie Lord," has laid its white winding-sheet. In the long avenue the gaunt and barren branches of the stately elms are bowed down with the weight of the snow, that fell softly but heavily all last night, creeping upon the sleeping world with such swift and noiseless wings that it recked not of its visit till the chill beams of a wintry sun betrayed it.

Each dark-green leaf in the long shrubberies bears its own sparkling burden. The birds hide shivering in the lourestine—that in spite of frost and cold is breaking into blossom,—and all around looks frozen.

"Full knee-deep lies the winter snow,And the winter winds are wearily sighing;"

yet there is grandeur, too, in the scene around, and a beauty scarcely to be rivalled by June's sweetest efforts.

Geoffrey, springing down from the dog-cart that has been sent to the station to meet him, brushes the frost from his hair, and stamps his feet upon the stone steps.

Sir Nicholas, who has come out to meet him, gives him a hearty hand-shake, and a smile that would have been charming if it had not been funereal. Altogether, his expression in such as might suit the death-bed of a beloved friend, His countenance is of an unseemly length, and he plainly looks on Geoffrey as one who has fallen upon evil days.

Nothing daunted, however, by this reception, Geoffrey returns his grasp with interest, and, looking fresh and young and happy, runs past him, up the stairs, to his mother's room, to beard—as he unfilially expresses it—the lioness in her den. It is a very cosey den, and, though claws maybe discovered in it, nobody at the first glance would ever suspect it of such dangerous toys. Experience, however, teaches most things, and Geoffrey has donned armor for the coming encounter.

He had left Mona in the morning at the Grosvenor, and had run down to have it out with his mother and get her permission to bring Mona to the Towers to be introduced to her and his brothers. This he preferred to any formal calling on their parts.

"You see, our own house is rather out of repair from being untenanted for so long, and will hardly be ready for us for a month or two," he said to Mona: "I think I will run down to the Towers and tell my mother we will go to her for a little while."

Of course this was on the day after their return to England, before his own people knew of their arrival.

"I shall like that very much," Mona had returned, innocently, not dreaming of the ordeal that awaited her,—because in such cases even the very best men will be deceitful, and Geoffrey had rather led her to believe that his mother would be charmed with her, and that she was most pleased than otherwise at their marriage.

When she made him this little trustful speech, however, he had felt some embarrassment, and had turned his attention upon a little muddy boy who was playing pitch-and-toss, irrespective of consequences, on the other side of the way.

And Mona had marked his embarrassment, and had quickly, with all the vivacity that belongs to her race, drawn her own conclusions therefrom, which were for the most part correct.

But to Geoffrey—lest the telling should cause him unhappiness—she had said nothing of her discovery; only when the morning came that saw him depart upon his mission (now so well understood by her), she had kissed him, and told him to "hurry, hurry, *hurry* back to her," with a little sob between each word. And when he was gone she had breathed an earnest prayer, poor child, that all might yet be well, and then told herself that, no matter what came, she would at least be a faithful, loving wife to him.

To her it is always as though he is devoid of name. It is always "he" and "his" and "him," all through, as though no other man existed upon earth.

"Well, mother?" says Geoffrey, when he has gained her room and received her kiss, which is not exactly all it ought to be after a five months' separation. He is her son, and of course she loves him, but—as she tells herself—there are some things hard to forgive.

"Of course it was a surprise to you," he says.

"It was more than a 'surprise.' That is a mild word," says Lady Rodney. She is looking at him, is telling herself what a goodly son he is, so tall and strong and bright and handsome. He might have married almost any one! And now—now——? No, she cannot forgive. "It was, and must always be, a lasting grief," she goes on, in a low tone.

This is a bad beginning. Mr. Rodney, before replying, judiciously gains time, and makes a diversion by poking the fire.

"I should have written to you about it sooner," he says at last, apologetically, hoping half his mother's resentment arises from a sense of his own negligence, "but I felt you would object, and so put it off from day to day."

"I heard of it soon enough," returns his mother, gloomily, without lifting her eyes from the tiny feathered fire-screen she is holding. "Too soon! That sort of thing seldom tarries. 'For evil news rides post, while good news baits.'"

"Wait till you see her," says Geoffrey, after a little pause, with full faith in his own recipe.

"I don't want to see her," is the unflinching and most ungracious reply.

"My dear mother, don't say that," entreats the young man, earnestly, going over to her and placing his arm round her neck. He is her favorite son, of which he is quite aware, and so hopes on. "What is it you object to?"

"To everything! How could you think of bringing a daughter-in-law of—of—her description to your mother?"

"How can you describe her, when you have not seen her?"

"She is not a lady," says Lady Rodney, as though that should terminate the argument.

"It entirely depends on what you consider a lady," says Geoffrey, calmly, keeping his temper wonderfully, more indeed for Mona's sake than his own. "You think a few grandfathers and an old name make one: I dare say it does. It ought, you know; though I could tell you of several striking exceptions to that rule. But I also believe in a nobility that belongs alone to nature. And Mona is as surely a gentlewoman in thought and deed as though all the blood of all the Howards was in her veins."

"I did not expect you would say anything else," returns she, coldly. "Is she quite without blood?"

"Her mother was of good family, I believe."

"You believe!" with ineffable disgust. "And have you not even taken the trouble to make sure? How late in life you have developed a trusting disposition!"

"One might do worse than put faith in Mona," says, Geoffrey, quickly. "She is worthy of all trust. And she is quite charming,—quite. And the very prettiest girl I ever saw. You know you adore beauty, mother,"—insinuatingly,—"and she is sure to create a *furor* when presented."

"Presented!" repeats Lady Rodney, in a dreadful tone. "And would you present a low Irish girl to your sovereign? And just now, too, when the whole horrid nation is in such disrepute."

"You mustn't call her names, you know; she is my wife," says Rodney, gently, but with dignity,—"the woman I love and honor most on earth. When you see her you will understand how the word 'low' could never apply to her. She looks quite correct, and is perfectly lovely."

"You are in love," returns his mother, contemptuously. "At present you can see no fault in her; but later on when you come to compare her with the other women in your own set, when you see them together, I only hope you will see no difference between them, and feel no regret."

She says this, however, as though it is her one desire he may know regret, and feel a difference that be overwhelming.

"Thank you," says Geoffrey, a little dryly, accepting her words as they are said, not as he feels they are meant.

Then there is another pause, rather longer than the last, Lady Rodney trifles with the fan in a somewhat excited fashion, and Geoffrey gazes, man-like, at his boots. At last his mother breaks the silence.

"Is she—is she noisy?" she asks, in a faltering tone.

"Well, she can laugh, if you mean that," says Geoffrey somewhat superciliously. And then, as though overcome with some recollection in which the poor little criminal who is before the bar bore a humorous part, he lays his head down upon the mantelpiece and gives way to hearty laughter himself.

"I understand," says Lady Rodney, faintly, feeling her burden is "greater than she can bear." "She is, without telling, a young woman who laughs uproariously, at everything,—no matter what,—and takes good care her vulgarity shall be read by all who run."

Now, I can't explain why but I never knew a young man who was not annoyed when the girl he loved was spoken of as a "young woman." Geoffrey takes it as a deliberate insult.

"There is a limit to everything,—even my patience," he says, not looking at his mother. "Mona is myself, and even from you, my mother, whom I love and reverence, I will not take a disparaging word of her."

There is a look upon his face that recalls to her his dead father, and Lady Rodney grows silent. The husband of her youth had been dear to her, in a way, until age had soured him, and this one of all his three children most closely resembled him, both in form and in feature; hence, perhaps, her love for him. She lowers her eyes, and a slow blush—for the blood rises with difficulty in the old—suffuses her face.

And then Geoffrey, marking all this, is vexed within himself, and, going over to her, lays his arm once more around her neck, and presses his cheek to hers.

"Don't let us quarrel," he says, lovingly. And this time she returns his caress very fondly, though she cannot lose sight of the fact that he has committed a social error not to be lightly overlooked.

"Oh, Geoffrey, how could you do it?" she says, reproachfully, alluding to his marriage,—"you whom I have so loved. What would your poor father have thought had he lived to see this unhappy day? You must have been mad."

"Well, perhaps I was," says Geoffrey, easily: "we are all mad on one subject or another, you know; mine may be Mona. She is an excuse for madness, certainly. At all events, I know I am happy, which quite carries out your theory, because, as Dryden says,—

'There is a pleasure sureIn being mad, which none but madmen know.'

I wish you would not take it so absurdly to heart. I haven't married an heiress, I know; but the whole world does not hinge on money."

"There was Violet," says Lady Rodney.

"I wouldn't have suited her at all," says Geoffrey. "I should have bored her to extinction, even if she had condescended to look at me, which I am sure she never would."

He is not sure of anything of the kind, but he says it nevertheless, feeling he owes so much to Violet, as the conversation has drifted towards her, and he feels she is placed—though unknown to herself—in a false position.

"I wish you had never gone to Ireland!" says Lady Rodney, deeply depressed. "My heart misgave me when you went, though I never anticipated such a climax to my fears. What possessed you to fall in love with her?"

"'She is pretty to walk with,And witty to talk with,And pleasant, too, to think on.'"

quotes Geoffrey, lightly, "Are not these three reasons sufficient? If not, I could tell you a score of others. I may bring her down to see you?"

"It will be very bitter to me," says Lady Rodney.

"It will not: I promise you that; only do not be too prejudiced in her disfavor. I want you to know her,—it is my greatest desire,—or I should not say another word after your last speech, which is not what I hoped to hear from you. Leighton, as you know, is out of repair, but if you will not receive us we can spend the rest of the winter at Rome or anywhere else that may occur to us."

"Of course you must come here," says Lady Rodney, who is afraid of the county and what it will say if it discovers she is at loggerheads with her son and his bride. But there is no welcome in her tone. And Geoffrey, greatly discouraged, yet determined to part friends with her for Mona's sake,—and trusting to the latter's sweetness to make all things straight in the future,— after a few more desultory remarks takes his departure, with the understanding on both sides that he and his wife are to come to the Towers on the Friday following to take up their quarters there until Leighton Hall is ready to receive them.

With mingled feelings he quits his home, and all the way up to London in the afternoon train weighs with himself the momentous question whether he shall or shall not accept the unwilling invitation to the Towers, wrung from his mother.

To travel here and there, from city to city and village to village, with Mona, would be a far happier arrangement. But underlying all else is a longing that the wife whom he adores and the mother whom he loves should be good friends.

Finally, he throws up the mental argument, and decides on letting things take their course, telling himself it will be a simple matter to leave the Towers at any moment, should their visit there prove unsatisfactory. At the farthest, Leighton must be ready for them in a month or so.

Getting back to the Grosvenor, he runs lightly up the stairs to the sitting-room, and, opening the door very gently,—bent in a boyish fashion on giving her a "rise,"—enters softly, and looks around for his darling.

At the farthest end of the room, near a window, lying back in an arm-chair, lies Mona, sound asleep.

One hand is beneath her cheek,—that is soft and moist as a child's might be in innocent slumber,—the other is thrown above her head. She is exquisite in her *abandon*, but very pale, and her breath comes unevenly.

Geoffrey, stooping over to wake her with a kiss, marks all this, and also that her eyelids are tinged with pink, as though from excessive weeping.

Half alarmed, he lays his hand gently on her shoulder, and, as she struggles quickly into life again, he draws her into his arms.

"Ah, it is you!" cries she, her face growing glad again.

"Yes; but you have been crying, darling! What has happened?"

"Oh, nothing," says Mona, flushing. "I suppose I was lonely. Don't mind me. Tell me all about yourself and your visit."

"Not until you tell me what made you cry."

"Sure you know I'd tell you if there was anything to tell," replies she, evasively.

"Then do so," returns he, quite gravely, not to be deceived by her very open attempts at dissimulation. "What made you unhappy in my absence?"

"If you must know, it is this," says Mona, laying her hand in his and speaking very earnestly. "I am afraid I have done you an injury in marrying you!"

"Now, that is the first unkind thing you have ever said to me," retorts he.

"I would rather die than be unkind to you," says Mona, running her fingers with a glad sense of appropriation through his hair. "But this is what I mean; your mother will never forgive your marriage; she will not love me, and I shall be the cause of creating dissension between her and you." Again tears fill her eyes.

"But there you are wrong. There need be no dissensions; my mother and I are very good friends, and she expects us both to go to the Towers on Friday next."

Then he tells her all the truth about his interview with his mother, only suppressing such words as would be detrimental to the cause he has in hand, and might give her pain.

"And when she sees you all will be well," he says, still clinging bravely to his faith in this panacea for all evils. "Everything rests with you.'

"I will do my best," says Mona, earnestly; "but if I fail,—if after all my efforts your mother still refuses to love me, how will it be then?"

"As it is now; it need make no difference to us; and indeed I will not make the trial at all if you shrink from it, or if it makes you in the faintest degree unhappy."

"I do not shrink from it," replies she, bravely: "I would brave anything to be friends with your mother."

"Very well, then: we will make the attempt," says he, gayly. "'Nothing venture, nothing have.'"

"And 'A dumb priest loses his benefice,'" quotes Mona, in her turn, almost gayly too.

"Yet remember, darling, whatever comes of it," says Rodney, earnestly, "that you are more to me than all the world,—my mother included. So do not let defeat—if we should be defeated—cast you down. Never forget how I love you." In his heart he dreads for her the trial that awaits her.

"I do not," she says, sweetly. "I could not: it is my dearest remembrance; and somehow it has made me strong to conquer, Geoffrey,"—flushing, and raising herself to her full height, as though already arming for action,—"I feel, I *know*, I shall in the end succeed with your mother."

She lifts her luminous eyes to his, and regards him fixedly as she speaks, full of hopeful excitement. Her eyes have always a peculiar fascination of their own, apart from the rest of her face. Once looking at her, as though for the first time impressed with this idea, Geoffrey had said to her, "I never look at your eyes that I don't feel a wild desire to close them with a kiss." To which she had made answer in her little, lovable way, and with a bewitching glance from the lovely orbs in question, "If that is how you mean to do it, you may close them just as often as ever you like."

Now he takes advantage of this general permission, and closes them with a soft caress.

"She must be harder-hearted than I think her, if she can resist *you*," he says, fondly.

CHAPTER XVI.

HOW GEOFFREY AND MONA ENTER THE TOWERS—AND HOW THEY ARE RECEIVED BY THE INHABITANTS THEREOF.

The momentous Friday comes at last, and about noon Mona and Geoffrey start for the Towers. They are not, perhaps, in the exuberant spirits that should be theirs, considering they are going to spend their Christmas in the bosom of their family,—at all events, of Geoffrey's family which naturally for the future she must acknowledge as hers. They are indeed not only silent, but desponding, and as they get out of the train at Greatham and enter the carriage sent by Sir Nicholas to meet them their hearts sink nearly into their boots, and for several minutes no words pass between them.

To Geoffrey perhaps the coming ordeal bears a deeper shade; as Mona hardly understands all that awaits her. That Lady Rodney is a little displeased at her son's marriage she can readily believe, but that she has made up her mind beforehand to dislike her, and intends waging with her war to the knife, is more than has ever entered into her gentle mind.

"Is it a long drive, Geoff?" she asks, presently, in a trembling tone, slipping her hand into his in the old fashion. "About six miles. I say, darling, keep up your spirits; if we don't like it, we can leave, you know. But"—alluding to her subdued voice—"don't be imagining evil."

"I don't think I am," says Mona; "but the thought of meeting people for the first time makes me feel nervous. Is your mother tall, Geoffrey?"

"Very."

"And severe-looking? You said she was like you."

"Well, so she is; and yet I suppose our expressions are dissimilar. Look here," says Geoffrey, suddenly, as though compelled at the last moment to give her a hint of what is coming. "I want to tell you about her,—my mother I mean: she is all right, you know, in every way, and very charming in general, but just at first one might imagine her a little difficult!"

"What's that?" asked Mona. "Don't speak of your mother as if she were a chromatic scale."

"I mean she seems a trifle cold, unfriendly, and—er—that," says Geoffrey. "Perhaps it would be a wise thing for you to make up your mind what you will say to her on first meeting her. She will come up to you, you know, and give you her hand like this," taking hers, "and——"

"Yes, I know," said Mona, eagerly interrupting him. "And then she will put her arms round me, and kiss me just like this," suiting the action to the word.

"Like *that?* Not a bit of it," says Geoffrey, who had given her two kisses for her one: "you mustn't expect it. She isn't in the least like that. She will meet you probably as though she saw you yesterday, and say, 'How d'ye do? I'm afraid you have had a very long and cold drive.' And then you will say——"

A pause.

"Yes, I shall say——" anxiously.

"You—will—say——" Here he breaks down ignominiously, and confesses by his inability to proceed that he doesn't in the least know what it is she can say.

"I know," says Mona, brightening, and putting on an air so different from her own usual unaffected one as to strike her listener with awe. "I shall say, 'Oh! thanks, quite too awfully much, don't you know? but Geoffrey and I didn't find it a bit long, and we were as warm as wool all the time.'"

At this appalling speech Geoffrey's calculations fall through, and he gives himself up to undisguised mirth.

"If you say all that," he says, "there will be wigs on the green: that's Irish, isn't it? or something like it, and very well applied too. The first part of your speech sounded like Toole or Brough, I'm not sure which."

"Well, it *was* in a theatre I heard it," confesses Mona, meekly: "it was a great lord who said it on the stage, so I thought it would be all right."

"Great lords are not necessarily faultlessly correct, either on or off the stage," says Geoffrey. "But, just for choice, I prefer them off it. No, that will not do at all. When my mother addresses you, you are to answer her back again in tones even colder than her own, and say——"

"But, Geoffrey, why should I be cold to your mother? Sure you wouldn't have me be uncivil to her, of all people?"

"Not uncivil, but cool. You will say to her, 'It was rather better than I anticipated, thank you.' And then, if you can manage to look bored, it will be quite correct, so far, and you may tell yourself you have scored one."

"I may say that horrid speech, but I certainly can't pretend I was bored during our drive, because I am not," says Mona.

"I know that. If I was not utterly sure of it I should instantly commit suicide by precipitating myself under the carriage-wheels," says Geoffrey. "Still—'let us dissemble.' Now say what I told you."

So Mrs. Rodney says, "It was rather better than I anticipated, thank you," in a tone so icy that his is warm beside it.

"But suppose she doesn't say a word about the drive?" says Mona, thoughtfully. "How will it be then?"

"She is safe to say something about it, and that will do for anything," says Rodney, out of the foolishness of his heart.

And now the horses draw up before a brilliantly-lighted hall, the doors of which are thrown wide as though in hospitable expectation of their coming.

Geoffrey, leading his wife into the hall, pauses beneath a central swinging lamp, to examine her critically. The footman who is in attendance on them has gone on before to announce their coming: they are therefore for the moment alone.

Mona is looking lovely, a little pale perhaps from some natural agitation, but her pallor only adds to the lustre of her great blue eyes and lends an additional sweetness to the ripeness of her lips. Her hair is a little loose, but eminently becoming, and altogether she looks as like an exquisite painting as one can conceive.

"Take off your hat," says Geoffrey, in a tone that gladdens her heart, so full it is of love and admiration; and, having removed her hat, she follows him though halls and one or two anterooms until they reach the library, into which the man ushers them.

It is a very pretty room, filled with a subdued light, and with a blazing fire at one end. All bespeaks warmth, and home, and comfort, but to Mona in her present state it is desolation itself. The three occupants of the room rise as she enters, and Mona's heart dies within her as a very tall statuesque woman, drawing herself up languidly from a lounging-chair, comes leisurely up to her. There is no welcoming haste in her movements, no gracious smile, for which her guest is thirsting, upon her thin lips.

She is dressed in black velvet, and has a cap of richest old lace upon her head. To the quick sensibilities of the Irish girl it becomes known without a word that she is not to look for love from this stately woman, with her keen scrutinizing glance and cold unsmiling lips.

A choking sensation, rising from her heart, almost stops Mona's breath; her mouth feels parched and dry; her eyes widen. A sudden fear oppresses her. How is it going to be in all the future? Is Geoffrey's—her own husband's—mother to be her enemy?

Lady Rodney holds out her hand, and Mona lays hers within it.

"So glad you have come," says Lady Rodney, in a tone that belies her words, and in a sweet silvery voice that chills the heart of her listener. "We hardly thought we should see you so soon, the trains here are so unpunctual. I hope the carriage was in time?"

She waits apparently for an answer, at which Mona grows desperate. For in reality she has heard not one word of the labored speech made to her, and is too frightened to think of anything to say except the unfortunate lesson learned in the carriage and repeated secretly so often since. She looks round helplessly for Geoffrey; but he is laughing with his brother, Captain Rodney, whom he has not seen since his return from India, and so Mona, cast upon her own resources, says,—

"It was rather better than I anticipated, thank you," not in the haughty tone adopted by her half an hour ago, but, in an unnerved and frightened whisper.

At this remarkable answer to a very ordinary and polite question, Lady Rodney stares at Mona for a moment, and then turns abruptly away to greet Geoffrey. Whereupon Captain Rodney, coming forward, tells Mona he is glad to see her, kindly but carelessly; and then a young man, who has been standing up to this silently upon the hearthrug, advances, and takes Mona's hand in a warm clasp, and looks down upon her with very friendly eyes.

At his touch, at his glance, the first sense of comfort Mona has felt since her entry into the room falls upon her. This man, at least, is surely of the same kith and kin as Geoffrey, and to him her heart opens gladly, gratefully.

He has heard the remarkable speech made to his mother, and has drawn his own conclusions therefrom. "Geoffrey has been coaching the poor little soul, and putting absurd words into her mouth, with—as is usual in all such cases—a very brilliant result." So he tells himself, and is, as we know, close to the truth.

He tells Mona she is very welcome, and, still holding her hand, draws her over to the fire, and moves a big arm-chair in front of it, in which he ensconces her, bidding her warm herself, and make herself (as he says with a kindly smile that has still kinder meaning in it) "quite at home."

Then he stoops and unfastens her sealskin jacket, and takes it off her, and in fact pays her all the little attentions that lie in his power.

"You are Sir Nicholas?" questions she at last, gaining courage to speak, and raising her eyes to his full of entreaty, and just a touch of that pathos that seems of right to belong to the eyes of all Irishwomen.

"Yes," returns he with a smile. "I am Nicholas." He ignores the formal title. "Geoffrey, I expect, spoke to you of me as 'old Nick;' he has never called me anything else since we were boys."

"He has often called you that; but,"—shyly,—"now that I have seen you, I don't think the name suits you a bit."

Sir Nicholas is quite pleased. There is a sort of unconscious flattery in the gravity of her tone and expression that amuses almost as much as it pleases him. What a funny child she is! and how unspeakably lovely! Will Doatie like her?

But there is yet another introduction to be gone through. From the doorway Violet Mansergh comes up to Geoffrey clad in some soft pale shimmering stuff, and holds out to him her hand.

"What a time you have been away!" she says, with a pretty, slow smile, that has not a particle of embarrassment or consciousness in it, though she is quite aware that Jack Rodney is watching her closely. Perhaps, indeed, she is secretly amused at his severe scrutiny.

"You will introduce me to your wife?" she asks, after a few minutes, in her even, *trainante* voice, and is then taken up to the big arm-chair before the fire, and is made known to Mona.

"Dinner will be ready in a few minutes: of course we shall excuse your dressing to-night," says Lady Rodney, addressing her son far more than Mona, though the words presumably are meant for her. Whereupon Mona, rising from her chair with a sigh of relief, follows Geoffrey out of the room and upstairs.

"Well?" says Sir Nicholas, as a deadly silence continues for some time after their departure, "what do you think of her?"

"She is painfully deficient; positively without brains," says Lady Rodney, with conviction. "What was the answer she made me when I asked about the carriage? Something utterly outside the mark."

"She is not brainless; she was only frightened. It certainly was an ordeal coming to a house for the first time to be, in effect, stared at. And she is very young."

"And perhaps unused to society," puts in Violet, mildly. As she speaks she picks up a tiny feather that has clung to her gown, and lightly blows it away from her into the air.

"She looked awfully cut up, poor little thing," says Jack, kindly. "You were the only one she opened her mind to, Nick What did she say? Did she betray the ravings of a lunatic or the inanities of a fool?"

"Neither."

"Then, no doubt, she heaped upon you priceless gems of Irish wit in her mother-tongue?"

"She said very little; but she looks good and true. After all, Geoffrey might have done worse."

"Worse!" repeats his mother, in a withering tone. In this mood she is not nice, and a very little of her suffices.

"She is decidedly good to look at, at all events," says Nicholas, shifting ground. "Don't you think so, Violet?"

"I think she is the loveliest woman I ever saw," returns Miss Mansergh, quietly, without enthusiasm, but with decision. If cold, she is just, and above the pettiness of disliking a woman because she may be counted more worthy of admiration than herself.

"I am glad you are all pleased," says Lady Rodney, in a peculiar tone; and then the gong sounds, and they all rise, as Geoffrey and Mona once more make their appearance. Sir Nicholas gives his arm to Mona, and so begins her first evening at the Towers.

CHAPTER XVII.

HOW MONA RISES BETIMES—AND HOW SHE ENCOUNTERS A STRANGER AMIDST THE MORNING DEWS.

All through the night Mona scarcely shuts her eyes, so full is her mind of troubled and perplexing thoughts. At last her brain grows so tired that she cannot pursue any subject to its end, so she lies silently awake, watching for the coming of the tardy dawn.

At last, as she grows weary for wishing for it,—

"Morning fairComes forth with pilgrim steps in amice gray"

and light breaks through shutter and curtain, and objects pale and ghostly at first soon grow large and intimate.

"Brown night retires; young day pours in apace,And opens all a lawny prospect wide."

Naturally an early riser, Mona slips noiselessly from her bed, lest she shall wake Geoffrey,—who is still sleeping the sleep of the just,—and, going into his dressing-room, jumps into his bath, leaving hers for him.

The general bath-room is to Geoffrey an abomination; nothing would induce him to enter it. His own bath, and nothing but his own bath, can content him. To have to make uncomfortable haste to be first, or else to await shivering the good pleasure of your next-door neighbor, is according to Mr. Rodney, a hardship too great for human endurance.

Having accomplished her toilet without the assistance of a maid (who would bore her to death), and without disturbing her lord and master, she leaves her room, and, softly descending the stairs, bids the maid in the hall below a "fair good-morning," and bears no malice in that the said maid is so appalled by her unexpected appearance that she forgets to give her back her greeting. She bestows her usual bonnie smile upon this stricken girl, and then, passing by her, opens the hall door, and sallies forth into the gray and early morning.

"The first low fluttering breath of waking dayStirs the wide air. Thin clouds of pearly hazeFloat slowly o'er the sky, to meet the raysOf the unrisen sun."

But which way to go? To Mona all round is an undiscovered country, and for that reason possesses an indiscribable charm. Finally, she goes up the avenue, beneath the gaunt and leafless elms, and midway, seeing a path that leads she knows not whither, she turns aside and follows it until she loses herself in the lonely wood.

The air is full of death and desolation. It is cold and raw, and no vestige of vegetation is anywhere. In the distance, indeed, she can see some fir-trees that alone show green amidst a wilderness of brown, and are hailed with rapture by the eye, tired of the gray and sullen monotony. But except for these all is dull and unfruitful.

Still, Mona is happy: the walk has done her good, and warmed her blood, and brought a color soft and rich as carmine, to her cheeks. She has followed the winding path for about an hour, briskly, and with a sense of *bien-etre* that only the young and godly can know, when suddenly she becomes aware that some one was following her.

She turns slowly, and finds her fellow-pedestrian is a young man clad in a suit of very impossible tweed: she blushes hotly, not because he is a young man, but because she has no hat on her head, having covered her somewhat riotous hair with a crimson silk handkerchief she had found in Geoffrey's room, just before starting. It covers her head completely, and is tied under the chin Connemara fashion, letting only a few little love-locks be seen, that roam across her forehead, in spite of all injunctions to the contrary.

Perhaps, could she only know how charmingly becoming this style of headdress is to her flower-like face, she would not have blushed at all.

The stranger is advancing slowly: he is swarthy, and certainly not prepossessing. His hair is of that shade and texture that suggests unpleasantly the negro. His lips are a trifle thick, his eyes like sloes. There is, too, an expression of low cunning in these latter features that breeds disgust in the beholder.

He does not see Mona until he is within a yard of her, a thick bush standing between him and her. Being always a creature of impulse, she has stood still on seeing him, and is lost in wonder as to who he can be. One hand is lifting up her gown, the other is holding together the large soft white fleecy shawl that covers her shoulders, and is therefore necessarily laid upon her breast. Her attitude is as picturesque as it is adorable.

The stranger, having come quite near, raises his head, and, seeing her, starts naturally, and also comes to a standstill. For a full half-minute he stares unpardonably, and then lifts his hat. Mona—who, as we have seen, is not great in emergencies—fails to notice the rudeness, in her own embarrassment, and therefore bows politely in return to his salutation.

She is still wondering vaguely who he can be, when he breaks the silence.

"It is an early hour to be astir," he says, awkwardly; then, finding she makes no response, he goes on, still more awkwardly. "Can you tell me if this path will lead me to the road for Plumston?"

Plumston is a village near. The first remark may sound Too free and easy, but his manner is decorous in the extreme. In spite of the fact that her pretty head is covered with a silk handkerchief in lieu of a hat, he acknowledges her "within the line," and knows instinctively that her clothes, though simplicity itself, are perfect both in tint and in texture.

He groans within him that he cannot think of any speech bordering on the Grandisonian, that may be politely addressed to this sylvan nymph; but all such speeches fail him. Who can she be? Were ever eyes so liquid before, or lips so full of feeling?

"I am sorry I can tell you nothing," says Mona, shaking her head. "I was never in this wood before; I know nothing of it."

"*I* should know all about it," says the stranger, with a curious contraction of the muscles of his face, which it may be he means for a smile. "In time I shall no doubt, but at present it is a sealed book to me. But the future will break all seals as far at least as Rodney Towers is concerned."

Then she knows she is speaking to "the Australian," (as she has heard him called), and, lifting her head, examines his face with renewed interest. Not a pleasant face by any means, yet not altogether bad, as she tells herself in the generosity of her heart.

"I am a stranger; I know nothing," she says again, hardly knowing what to say, and moving a little as though she would depart.

"I suppose I am speaking to Mrs. Rodney," he says, guessing wildly, yet correctly as it turns out, having heard, as all the country has besides, that the bride is expected at the Towers during the week. He has never all this time removed his black eyes from the perfect face before him with its crimson headgear. He is as one fascinated, who cannot yet explain where the fascination lies.

"Yes, I am Mrs. Rodney," says Mona, feeling some pride in her wedded name, in spite of the fact that two whole months have gone by since first she heard it. At this question, though, as coming from a stranger, she recoils a little within herself, and gathers up her gown more closely with a gesture impossible to misunderstand.

"You haven't asked me who I am," says the stranger, as though eager to detain her at any cost, still without a smile, and always with his eyes fixed upon her face. It seems as though he positively cannot remove them, so riveted are they.

"No;" she might in all truth have added, "because I did not care to know," but what she does say (for incivility even to an enemy would be impossible to Mona) is, "I thought perhaps you might not like it."

Even this is a small, if unconscious, cut, considering what objectionable curiosity he evinced about her name. But the Australian is above small cuts, for the good reason that he seldom sees them.

"I am Paul Rodney," he now volunteers,—"your husband's cousin, you know. I suppose," with a darkening of his whole face, "now I have told you who I am, it will not sweeten your liking for me."

"I have heard of you," says Mona, quietly. Then, pointing towards that part of the wood whither he would go, she says, coldly, "I regret I cannot tell you where this path leads to. Good-morning."

With this she inclines her head, and without another word goes back by the way she has come.

Paul Rodney, standing where she has left him, watches her retreating figure until it is quite out of sight, and the last gleam of the crimson silk handkerchief is lost in the distance, with a curious expression upon his face. It is an odd mixture of envy, hatred, and admiration. If there is a man on earth he hates with cordial hatred, it is Geoffrey Rodney who at no time has taken the trouble to be even outwardly civil to him. And to think this peerless creature is his wife! For thus he designates Mona,—the Australian being a man who would be almost sure to call the woman he admired a "peerless creature."

When she is quite gone, he pulls himself together with a jerk, and draws a heavy sigh, and thrusting his hands deep into his pockets, continues his walk.

At breakfast Mona betrays the fact that she has met Paul Rodney during her morning ramble, and tells all that passed between him and her,—on being closely questioned,—which news has the effect of bringing a cloud to the brow of Sir Nicholas and a frown to that of his mother.

"Such presumption, walking in our wood without permission," she says, haughtily.

"My dear mother, you forget the path leading from the southern gate to Plumston Road has been open to the public for generations. He was at perfect liberty to walk there."

"Nevertheless, it is in very bad taste his taking advantage of that absurd permission, considering how he is circumstanced with regard to us," says Lady Rodney. "You wouldn't do it yourself, Nicholas, though you find excuses for him."

A very faint smile crosses Sir Nicholas's lips.

"Oh, no, I shouldn't," he says, gently; and then the subject drops.

And here perhaps it will be as well to explain the trouble that at this time weighs heavily upon the Rodney family.

CHAPTER XVIII.

HOW OLD SIR GEORGE HATED HIS FIRSTBORN—AND HOW HE MADE HIS WILL—AND HOW THE EARTH SWALLOWED IT.

Now, old Sir George Rodney, grandfather of the present baronet, had two sons, Geoffrey and George. Now, Geoffrey he loved, but George he hated. And so great by years did this hatred grow that after a bit he sought how he should leave the property away from his eldest-born, who was George, and leave it to Geoffrey, the younger,—which was hardly fair; for "what," says Aristotle, "is justice?—to give every man his own." And surely George, being the elder, had first claim. The entail having been broken during the last generation, he found this easy to accomplish; and so after many days he made a will, by which the younger son inherited all, to the exclusion of the elder.

But before this, when things had gone too far between father and son, and harsh words never to be forgotten on either side had been uttered, George, unable to bear longer the ignominy of his position (being of a wild and passionate yet withal generous disposition), left his home, to seek another and happier one in foreign lands.

Some said he had gone to India, others to Van Diemen's Land, but in truth none knew, or cared to know, save Elspeth, the old nurse, who had tended him and his father before him, and who in her heart nourished for him an undying affection.

There were those who said she clung to him because of his wonderful likeness to the picture of his grandfather in the south gallery, Sir Launcelot by name, who in choicest ruffles and most elaborate *queue*, smiled gayly down upon the passers-by.

For this master of the Towers (so the story ran) Elspeth, in her younger days, had borne a love too deep for words, when she herself was soft and rosy-cheeked, with a heart as tender and romantic as her eyes were blue, and when her lips, were for all the world like "cherries ripe."

But this, it may be, was all village slander, and was never borne out by anything. And Elspeth had married the gardener's son, and Sir Launcelot had married an earl's daughter; and when the first baby was born at the "big house," Elspeth came to the Towers and nursed him as she would have nursed her own little bairn, but that Death, "dear, beauteous Death, the jewel of the just, shining nowhere but in the dark," sought and claimed her own little one two days after its birth.

After that she had never again left the family, serving it faithfully while strength stayed with her, knowing all its secrets and all its old legends, and many things, it may be, that the child she nursed at her bosom never knew.

For him—strange as it may seem—she had ever but little love. But when he married, and George, the eldest boy, was given into her arms, and as he grew and developed and showed himself day by day to be the very prototype of his grandsire, she "took to him," as the servants said, and clung to him—and afterwards to his memory—until her dying day.

When the dark, wayward, handsome young man went away, her heart went with him, and she alone perhaps knew anything of him after his departure. To his father his absence was a relief; he did not disguise it; and to his brother (who had married, and had then three children, and had of late years grown estranged from him) the loss was not great. Nor did the young madam,—as she was called,—the mother of our present friends, lose any opportunity of fostering and keeping alive the ill will and rancor that existed for him in his father's heart.

So the grudge, being well watered, grew and flourished, and at last, as I said, the old man made a will one night, in the presence of the gardener and his nephew, who witnessed it, leaving all he possessed—save the title and some outside property, which he did not possess—to his younger son. And, having made this will, he went to his bed, and in the cold night, all alone, he died there, and was found in the morning stiff and stark, with the gay spring sunshine pouring in upon him, while the birds sang without as though to mock death's power, and the flowers broke slowly into life.

But when they came to look for the will, lo! it was nowhere to be found. Each drawer and desk and cabinet was searched to no avail. Never did the lost document come to light.

Day after day they sought in vain; but there came a morning when news of the lost George's demise came to them from Australia, and then the search grew languid and the will was forgotten. And they hardly took pains even to corroborate the tidings sent them from that far-off land but, accepting the rightful heir's death as a happy fact, ascended the throne, and reigned peacefully for many years.

And when Sir George died, Sir Nicholas, as we know, governed in his stead, and "all went merry as a marriage-bell," until a small cloud came out of the south, and grew and grew and waxed each day stronger, until it covered all the land.

For again news came from Australia that the former tidings of George Rodney's death had been false; that he had only died a twelvemonth since;

that he had married almost on first going out, and that his son was coming home to dispute Sir Nicholas's right to house and home and title.

And now where was the missing will? Almost all the old servants were dead or scattered. The gardener and his nephew wore no more; even old Elspeth was lying at rest in the cold churchyard, having ceased long since to be even food for worms. Only her second nephew—who had lived with her for years in the little cottage provided for her by the Rodneys, when she was too old and infirm to do aught but sit and dream of days gone by—was alive, and he, too, had gone to Australia on her death and had not been heard of since.

It was all terrible,—this young man coming and the thought that, no matter how they might try to disbelieve in his story, still it might be true.

And then the young man came, and they saw that he was very dark, and very morose, and very objectionable. But he seemed to have more money than he quite know what to do with; and when he decided on taking a shooting-box that then was vacant quite close to the Towers, their indignation knew no bounds. And certainly it was execrable taste, considering he came there with the avowed determination to supplant, as lord and master, the present owner of the Towers, the turrets of which he could see from his dining room windows.

But, as he had money, some of the county, after the first spasm, rather acknowledged him, as at least a cousin, if not *the* cousin. And because he was somewhat unusual, and therefore amusing, and decidedly liberal, and because there was no disgrace attaching to him, and no actual reason why he should not be received, many houses opened their doors to him. All which was bitter as wormwood to Lady Rodney.

Indeed, Sir Nicholas himself had been the very first to set the example. In his curious, silent, methodical fashion, he had declared to his mother (who literally detested the very mention of the Australian's name, as she called him, looking upon him as a clean-born Indian might look upon a Pariah) his intention of being civil to him all round, as he was his father's brother's child; and as he had committed no sin, beyond trying to gain his own rights, he would have him recognized, and treated by every one, if not with cordiality, at least with common politeness.

But yet there were those who did not acknowledge the new-comer, in spite of his wealth and the romantic story attaching to him, and the possibility that he might yet be proved to be the rightful baronet and the possessor of all the goodly lands that spread for miles around. Of these the Duchess of Lauderdale was one; but then she was always slow to acknowledge new blood, or people unhappy enough to have a history. And Lady Lilias Eaton was another; but she was a young and earnest disciple of æstheticism, and gave little thought to anything save Gothic windows, lilies, and unleavened bread. There were also many of the older families who looked askance upon Paul Rodney, or looked through him, when brought into contact with him, in defiance of Sir Nicholas's support, which perhaps was given to this undesirable cousin more in pride than generosity.

And so matters stood when Mona came to the Towers.

CHAPTER XIX.

HOW FATE DEALS HARSHLY WITH MONA, AND HOW SHE DROOPS—AS MIGHT A FLOWER—BENEATH ITS UNKINDLY TOUCH.

To gain Lady Rodney's friendship is a more difficult thing than Mona in her ignorance had imagined, and she is determined to be ice itself to her poor little guest. As for her love, when first Mona's eyes lit upon her she abandoned all hope of ever gaining that.

With Captain Rodney and Sir Nicholas she makes way at once, though she is a little nervous and depressed, and not altogether like her usual gay *insouciant* self. She is thrown back upon herself, and, like a timid snail, recoils sadly into her shell.

Yet Nature, sooner or later, must assert itself; and after a day or two a ringing laugh breaks from her, or a merry jest, that does Geoffrey's heart good, and brings an answering laugh and jest to the lips of her new brothers.

Of Violet Mansergh—who is still at the Towers, her father being abroad and Lady Rodney very desirous of having her with her—she knows little. Violet is cold, but quite civil, as Englishwomen will be until they know you. She is, besides, somewhat prejudiced against Mona, because—being honest herself—she has believed all the false tales told her of the Irish girl. These silly tales, in spite of her belief in her own independence of thought, weigh upon her; and so she draws back from Mona, and speaks little to her, and then of only ordinary topics, while the poor child is pining for some woman to whom she can open her mind and whom she may count as an honest friend "For talking with a friend," says Addison, "is nothing else but thinking aloud."

Of Lady Rodney's studied dislike Mona's sensitive nature could not long remain in ignorance; yet, having a clear conscience, and not knowing in what she has offended,—save in cleaving to the man she loves, even to the extent of marrying him,—she keeps a calm countenance, and bravely waits what time may bring.

To quarrel with Geoffrey's people will be to cause Geoffrey silent but acute regret, and so for his sake, to save him pain, she quietly bears many things, and waits for better days. What is a month or two of misery, she tells herself, but a sigh amidst the pleasures of one's life? Yet I think it is the indomitable pluck and endurance of her race that carries her successfully through all her troubles.

Still, she grows a little pale and dispirited after a while, for

"Dare, when it once is entered in the breast,Will have the whole possession ere it rest."

One day, speaking of Sir Nicholas to Lady Rodney, she had—as was most natural—called him "Nicholas." But she had been cast back upon herself and humiliated to the earth by his mother's look of cold disapproval and the emphasis she had laid upon the "Sir" Nicholas when next speaking of him.

This had widened the breach more than all the rest, though Nicholas himself, being quite fascinated by her, tries earnestly to make her happy and at home with him.

About a week after her arrival—she having expressed her admiration of ferns the night before—he draws her hand through his arm and takes her to his own special sanctum,—off which a fernery has been thrown, he being an enthusiastic grower of that lovely weed.

Mona is enchanted with the many varieties she sees that are unknown to her, and, being very much not of the world, is not ashamed to express her delight. Looking carefully through all, she yet notices that a tiny one, dear to her, because common to her sweet Killarney, is not among his collection.

She tells him of it, and he is deeply interested; and when she proposes to write and get him one from her native soil, he is glad as a schoolboy promised a new bat, and her conquest of Sir Nicholas is complete.

And indeed the thought of this distant fern is as dear to Mona as to him. For to her comes a rush of tender joy, as she tells herself she may soon be growing in this alien earth a green plant torn from her fatherland.

"But I hope you will not be disappointed when you see it," she says, gently. "You have the real Killarney fern, Sir Nicholas, I can see; the other, I speak of, though to me almost as lovely, is not a bit like it."

She is very careful to give him his title ever since that encounter with his mother.

"I shall not be disappointed. I have read all about it," returns he, enthusiastically. Then, as though the thought has just struck him, he says,—

"Why don't you call me Nicholas, as Geoffrey does?"

Mona hesitates, then says, shyly, with downcast eyes,—

"Perhaps Lady Rodney would not like it."

Her face betrays more than she knows.

"It doesn't matter in the least what any one thinks on this subject," says Nicholas, with a slight frown, "I shall esteem it a very great honor if you will call me by my Christian name. And besides, Mona, I want you to try to care for me,—to love me, as I am your brother."

The ready tears spring into Mona's eyes. She is more deeply, passionately grateful to him for this small speech than he will ever know.

"Now, that is very kind of you," she says, lifting her eyes, humid with tears, to his. "And I think it will take only a very little time to make me love you!"

After this, she and Sir Nicholas are even better friends than they have been before,—a silent bond of sympathy seeming to exist between them. With Captain Rodney, though he is always kind to her, she makes less way, he being devoted to the society of Violet, and being besides of such a careless disposition as prevents his noticing the wants of those around,—which is perhaps another name for selfishness.

Yet selfish is hardly the word to apply to Jack Rodney, because at heart he is kindly and affectionate, and, if a little heedless and indifferent, is still good *au fond*. He is light hearted and agreeable, and singularly hopeful:—

"A man he seems of cheerful yesterdaysAnd confident to morrow."

During the past month he has grown singularly domestic, and fond of home and its associations. Perhaps Violet has something to do with this, with her little calm thoroughbred face, and gentle manners, and voice low and *trainante*. Yet it would be hard to be sure of this, Captain Rodney being one of those who have "sighed to many," without even the saving clause of having "loved but one." Yet with regard to Mona there is no mistake about Jack Rodney's sentiments. He likes her well (could she but know it) in all sincerity.

Of course everybody that is anybody has called on the new Mrs. Rodney. The Duchess of Lauderdale who is an old friend of Lady Rodney's, and who is spending the winter at her country house to please her son the young duke, who is entertaining a houseful of friends, is almost the first to come. And Lady Lillias Eaton, the serious and earnest-minded young æsthetic,—than whom nothing can be more coldly and artistically correct according to her own school,—is perhaps the second: but to both, unfortunately, Mona is "not at home."

And very honestly, too, because at the time of their visits, when Lady Rodney was entertaining them in the big drawing-room and uttering platitudes and pretty lies by the score, she was deep in the recesses of the bare brown wood, roaming hither and thither in search of such few flowers as braved the wintry blasts.

For all this Lady Rodney is devoutly thankful. She is glad of the girl's absence. She has no desire to exhibit her, prejudice making Mona's few defects to look monstrous in her eyes. Yet these same defects might perhaps be counted on the fingers of one hand.

There is, for example, her unavoidable touch of brogue, her little gesture of intense excitement, and irrepressible exclamation when anything is said that affects or interests her, and her laugh, which, if too loud for ordinary drawing-room use, is yet so sweet and catching that involuntarily it brings an answering laugh to the lips of those who hear it.

All these faults, and others of even less weight, are an abomination in the eyes of Lady Rodney, who has fallen into a prim mould, out of which it would now be difficult to extricate her.

"There is a set of people whom I cannot bear," says Chalmers, "the pinks of fashionable propriety, whose every word is precise, and whose every movement is unexceptionable, but who, though versed in all the categories of polite behavior, have not a particle of soul or cordiality about them."

Such folk Chalmers hated; and I agree with Chalmers. And of this class is Lady Rodney, without charity or leniency for the shortcomings of those around her. Like many religious people,—who are no doubt good in their own way,—she fails to see any grace in those who differ from her in thought and opinion.

And by degrees, beneath her influence, Mona grows pale and *distrait* and in many respects unlike her old joyous self. Each cold, reproving glance and sneering word,—however carefully concealed—falls like a touch of ice upon her heart, chilling and withering her glad youth. Up to this she has led a bird's life, gay, *insouciant*, free and careless. Now her song seems checked, her sweetest notes are dying fast away through lack of sympathy. She is "cribbed, cabined, and confined," through no fault of her own, and grows listless and dispirited in her captivity.

And Geoffrey, who is blind to nothing that concerns her notices all this, and secretly determines on taking her away from all this foolish persecution, to London or elsewhere, until such time as their own home shall be ready to receive them.

But at this break in my history, almost as he forms this resolution, an event occurs that brings friends to Mona, and changes *in toto* the aspect of affairs.

CHAPTER XX.

HOW MONA DANCES A COUNTRY DANCE BEFORE A HYPERCRITICAL AUDIENCE—AND HOW MORE EYES THAN SHE WOTS OF MARK HER PERFORMANCE.

"I hope you have had a nice walk?" says Violet, politely, drawing her skirts aside to make room for Mona, who had just come in.

It is quite half-past six; and though there is no light in the room, save the glorious flames given forth by the pine logs that lie on the top of the coals, still one can see that the occupants of the apartment are dressed for dinner.

Miss Darling—Sir Nicholas's *fiancée*—and her brother are expected to night; and so the household generally has dressed itself earlier than usual to be in full readiness to receive them.

Lady Rodney and Violet are sitting over the fire, and now Mona joins them, gowned in the blue satin dress in which she had come to meet Geoffrey, not so many months ago, in the old wood behind the farm.

"Very nice," she says, in answer to Violet's question, sinking into the chair that Miss Mansergh, by a small gesture, half languid, half kindly, has pushed towards her, and which is close to Violet's own. "I went up the avenue, and then out on the road for about half a mile."

"It is a very late hour for any one to be on the public road," says Lady Rodney, unpleasantly, quite forgetting that people, as a rule, do not go abroad in pale-blue satin gowns, and that therefore some time must have elapsed between Mona's return from her walk and the donning of her present attire. And so she overreaches herself, as clever people will do, at times.

"It was two hours ago," says Mona, gently. "And then it was quite daylight, or at least"—truthfully—"only the beginning of dusk."

"I think the days are lengthening," says Violet, quietly, defending Mona unconsciously, and almost without knowing why. Yet in her heart—against her will as it were—she is making room for this Irish girl, who, with her great appealing eyes and tender ways, is not to be resisted.

"I had a small adventure," says Mona, presently, with suppressed gayety. All her gayety of late has been suppressed. "Just as I came back to the gate here, some one came riding by, and I turned to see who it was, at which his horse—as though frightened by my sudden movement—shied viciously, and then reared so near me as almost to strike me with his fore-paws. I was frightened rather, because it was all so sudden, and sprang to one side. Then the gentleman got down, and, coming to me, begged my pardon. I said it didn't matter, because I was really uninjured, and it was all my fault. But he seemed very sorry, and (it was dusk as I told you, and I believe he is short sighted) stared at me a great deal."

"Well?" says Violet, who is smiling, and seems to see a joke where Mona fails to see anything amusing.

"When he was tired of staring, he said, 'I suppose I am speaking to——' and then he stopped. 'Mrs. Rodney,' replied I; and then he raised his hat, and bowed, and gave me his card. After that he mounted again, and rode away."

"But who was this gentleman?" says Lady Rodney, superciliously. "No doubt some draper from the town."

"No; he was not a draper," says Mona, gently, and without haste.

"Whoever he was, he hardly excelled in breeding," says Lady Rodney; "to ask your name without an introduction! I never heard of such a thing. Very execrable form, indeed. In your place I should not have given it. And to manage his horse so badly that he nearly ran you down. He could hardly be any one we know. Some petty squire, no doubt."

"No; not a petty squire," says Mona; "and I think you do know him. And why should I be ashamed to tell my name to any one?"

"The question was strictly in bad taste," says Lady Rodney again. "No well-bred man would ask it. I can hardly believe I know him. He must have been some impossible person."

"He was the Duke of Lauderdale," says Mona, simply. "Here is his card."

A pause.

Lady Rodney is plainly disconcerted, but says nothing. Violet follows suit, but more because she is thoroughly amused and on the point of laughter, than from a desire to make matters worse.

"I hope you had your hat on," says Lady Rodney, presently, in a severe tone, meant to cover the defeat. She had once seen Mona with the crimson silk handkerchief on her head,—Irish fashion,—and had expressed her disapproval of all such uncivilized headdresses.

"Yes; I wore my big Rubens hat, the one with——"

"I don't care to hear about the contents of your wardrobe," interrupts Lady Rodney, with a slight but unkind shrug. "I am glad, at least, you were not seen in that objectionable headdress you so often affect."

"Was it the Rubens hat with the long brown feather?" asks Violet, sweetly, turning to Mona, as though compelled by some unknown force to say anything that shall restore the girl to evenness of mind once more.

"Yes; the one with the brown feather," returns Mona, quickly, and with a smile radiant and grateful, that sinks into Violet's heart and rests there.

"You told the duke who you were?" breaks in Lady Rodney at this moment, who is in one of her worst moods.

"Yes; I said I was Mrs. Rodney."

"Mrs. Geoffrey Rodney, would have been more correct. You forget your husband is the youngest son. When Captain Rodney marries, *his* wife will be Mrs. Rodney."

"But surely until then Mona may lay claim to the title," says Violet, quickly.

"I do not wish to lay claim to anything," says Mona, throwing up her head with a little proud gesture,—"least of all to what does not by right belong to me. To be Mrs. Geoffrey is all I ask."

She leans back in her chair, and brings her fingers together, clasping them so closely that her very nails grow white. Her thin nostrils dilate a little, and her breath comes quickly, but no angry word escapes her. How can her lips give utterance to a speech that may wound the mother of the man she loves!

Violet, watching her, notes the tumult in her mind, and, seeing how her will gains mastery over her desire, honors her for her self-control.

Then Jack comes in, and Sir Nicholas, and later on Geoffrey.

"No one can say we are not in time," says Jack, gayly. "It is exactly"—examining closely the ormolu-clock upon the mantelpiece—"one hour before we can reasonably expect dinner."

"And three-quarters. Don't deceive yourself, my dear fellow: they can't be here one moment before a quarter to eight."

"Then, in the meantime, Violet, I shall eat you," says Captain Rodney, amiably, "just to take the edge off my appetite. You would be hardly sufficient for a good meal!" He laughs and glances significantly at her slight but charming figure, which is *petite* but perfect, and then sinks into a low chair near her.

"I hear this dance at the Chetwoodes' is to be rather a large affair," says Geoffrey, indifferently. "I met Gore to-day, and he says the duchess is going, and half the county."

"Does he mean going himself?" says Nicholas, idly. "He is here to-day, I know, but one never knows where he may be to-morrow, he is so erratic."

"He is a little difficult; but, on the whole, I think I like Sir Mark better than most men," says Violet, slowly.

Whereupon Jack Rodney instantly conceives a sudden and uncalled for dislike towards the man in question.

"Lilian is such a dear girl," says Lady Rodney; "she is a very general favorite. I have no doubt her dance will be a great success."

"You are speaking of Lady Chetwoode? Was it her that called last week?" asks Mona, timidly, forgetting grammar in her nervousness.

"Yes; it was her that called last week," returns her amiable mother-in-law, laying an unmistakable stress upon the pronoun.

No one is listening, fortunately, to this gratuitous correction, or hot words might have been the result. Sir Nicholas and Geoffrey are laughing over some old story that has been brought to their recollection by this idle chattering about the Chetwoodes' ball; Jack and Violet are deep in some topic of their own.

"Well, she danced like a fairy, at all events, in spite of her size," says Sir Nicholas, alluding to the person the funny story had been about.

"You dance, of course," says Lady Rodney, turning to Mona, a little ashamed, perhaps, of her late rudeness.

"Oh, yes," says Mona, brightening even under this small touch of friendliness. "I'm very fond of it, too. I can get through all the steps without a mistake."

At this extraordinary speech, Lady Rodney stares in bewilderment.

"Ah! Walzes and polkas, you mean?" she says, in a puzzled tone.

"Eh?" says Mrs. Geoffrey.

"You can waltz?"

"Oh, no!" shaking her lovely head emphatically, with a smile. "It's country dances I mean. Up the middle and down again, and all that," moving her hand in a soft undulating way as though keeping it in accord with some music that is ringing in her brain. Then, sweetly, "Did *you* ever dance a country dance?"

"Never!" says Lady Rodney, in a stony fashion. "I don't even know what you mean."

"No?" arching her brows, and looking really sorry for her. "What a pity! They all come quite naturally to me. I don't remember ever being taught them. The music seemed to inspire me, and I really dance them very well. Don't I Geoff?"

"I never saw your equal," says Geoffrey, who, with Sir Nicholas, has been listening to the last half of the conversation, and who is plainly suppressing a strong desire to laugh.

"Do you remember the evening you taught me the country dance that I said was like an old-fashioned minuet? And what an apt pupil I proved! I really think I could dance it now. By the by, my mother never saw one danced. She"—apologetically—"has not been out much. Let us go through one now for her benefit."

"Yes, let us," says Mona, gayly.

"Pray do not give yourselves so much trouble on my account," says Lady Rodney, with intense but subdued indignation.

"It won't trouble us, not a *bit*," says Mrs. Geoffrey, rising with alacrity. "I shall love it, the floor is so nice and slippery. Can any one whistle?"

At this Sir Nicholas gives way and laughs out loud, whereon Mona laughs too, though she reddens slightly, and says, "Well, of course the piano will do, though the fiddle is best of all."

"Violet, play us something," says Geoffrey, who has quite entered into the spirit of the thing, and who doesn't mind his mothers "horrors" in the least, but remembers how sweet Mona used to look when going slowly and with that quaint solemn dignity of hers "through her steps."

"I shall be charmed," says Violet; "but what is a country dance? Will 'Sir Roger' do?"

"No. Play anything monotonous, that is slow and dignified besides, and it will answer; in fact, anything at all," says Geoffrey, largely, at which Violet smiles and seats herself at the piano.

"Well, just wait till I tuck up the tail of my gown," says Mrs. Geoffrey, airily flinging her pale-blue skirt over her white bare arm.

"You may as well call it a train; people like it better," says Geoffrey. "I'm sure I don't know why, but perhaps it sounds better."

"There can be scarcely any question about that," says Lady Rodney, unwilling to let any occasion pass that may permit a slap at Mona.

"Yet the Princess D—— always calls her train a 'tail,'" says Violet, turning on her piano-stool to make this remark, which is balm to Mona's soul: after which she once more concentrates her thoughts on the instrument before her, and plays some odd old-fashioned air that suits well the dance of which they have been speaking.

Then Geoffrey offers Mona his hand, and leads her to the centre of the polished floor. There they salute each other in a rather Grandisonian fashion, and then separate.

The light from the great pine fire streams over all the room, throwing a rich glow upon the scene, upon the girl's flushed and earnest face, and large happy eyes, and graceful rounded figure, betraying also the grace and poetry of her every movement.

She stands well back from Geoffrey, and then, without any of the foolish, unlovely bashfulness that degenerates so often into awkwardness in the young, begins her dance.

It is a very curious and obsolete, if singularly charming, performance, full of strange bows, and unexpected turnings, and curtseys dignified and deep.

As she advances and retreats, with her *svelte* figure drawn to its fullest height, and her face eager and intent upon the business in hand, and with her whole heart thrown apparently into the successful accomplishment of her task, she is looking far lovelier than she herself is at all aware.

Even Lady Rodney for the moment has fallen a prey to her unpremeditated charms, and is leaning forward anxiously watching her. Jack and Sir Nicholas are enchanted.

The shadows close them in on every side. Only the firelight illumines the room, casting its most brilliant and ruddy rays upon its central figures, until they look like beings conjured up from the olden times, as they flit to and fro in the slow mysterious mazes of the dance.

Mona's waxen arms gleam like snow in the uncertain light. Each movement of hers is full of grace and *verve*. Her entire action is perfect.

"Her feet beneath her petticoatLike little mice, stole in and out,As if they feared the light.And, oh! she dances such a way,No sun upon an Easter dayIs half so fine a sight."

The music, soft and almost mournful, echoes through the room; the feet keep time upon the oaken floor; weird-like the two forms move through the settled gloom.

The door at the farthest end of the room has been opened, and two people who are as yet invisible stand upon the threshold, too surprised to advance, too enthralled, indeed, by the sight before them to do so.

Only as Mrs. Geoffrey makes her final curtesy, and Geoffrey, with a laugh, stoops forward to kiss her lips instead of her hand, as acknowledgment of her earnest and very sweet performance, thereby declaring the same to have come to a timely end, do the new-comers dare to show themselves.

"Oh, how pretty!" cries one of them from the shadow as though grieved the dance has come so quickly to an end "How lovely!"

At this voice every one starts! Mona, slipping her hand into Geoffrey's, draws him to one side; Lady Rodney rises from her sofa, and Sir Nicholas goes eagerly towards the door.

"You have come!" cries he, in a tone Mona has never heard before, and then—there is no mistake about the fact that he and the shadow have embraced each other heartily.

"Yes, we have indeed," says the same sweet voice again, which is the merriest and softest voice imaginable, "and in very good time too, as it seems. Nolly and I have been here for fully five minutes, and have been so delighted with what we have seen that we positively could not stir. Dear Lady Rodney, how d'ye do?"

She is a very little girl, quite half a head shorter than Mona, and, now that one can see her more plainly as she stands on the hearthrug, something more than commonly pretty.

Her eyes are large and blue, with a shade of green in them; her lips are soft and mobile; her whole expression is *debonnaire*, yet full of tenderness. She is brightness itself; each inward thought, be it of grief or gladness, makes itself outwardly known in the constant changes of her face. Her hair is cut above her forehead, and is quite golden, yet perhaps it is a degree darker than the ordinary hair we hear described as yellow. To me, to think of Dorothy Darling's head is always to remind myself of that line in Milton's "Comus," where he speaks of

"The loose train of thy amber-drooping hair."

She is very sweet to look at, and attractive and lovable.

"Her angel's faceAs the great eye of heaven shined bright,And made a sunshine in the shady place."

Such is Nicholas's betrothed, to whom, as she gazes on her, all at once, in the first little moment, Mona's whole soul goes out.

She has shaken hands with everybody, and has kissed Lady Rodney, and is now being introduced to Mona.

"Your wife, Geoffrey?" she says, holding Mona's hand all the time, and gazing at her intently. Then, as though something in Mrs. Geoffrey's beautiful face attracts her strangely, she lifts her face and presses her soft lips to Mona's cheek.

A rush of hope and gladness thrills Mona's bosom at this gentle touch. It is the very first caress she has ever received from one of Geoffrey's friends or relations.

"I think somebody might introduce me," says a plaintive voice from the background, and Dorothy's brother, putting Dorothy a little to one side, holds out his hand to Mona. "How d'ye do, Mrs. Rodney?" he says, pleasantly. "There's a dearth of etiquette about your husband that no doubt you have discovered before this. He has evidently forgotten that we are comparative strangers; but we sha'n't be long so, I hope?"

"I hope not, indeed," says Mona giving him her hand with a very flattering haste.

"You have come quite half an hour earlier than we expected you," says Sir Nicholas, looking with fond satisfaction into Miss Darling's eyes. "These trains are very uncertain."

"It wasn't the train so much," says Doatie, with a merry laugh, "as Nolly: we weren't any time coming, because he got out and took the reins from Hewson, and after that I rather think he took it out of your bays, Nicholas."

"Well, I never met such a blab! I believe you'd peach on your grandmother," says her brother, with supreme contempt. "I didn't do 'em a bit of harm, Rodney I give you my word."

"I'll take it," says Nicholas; "but, even if you did, I should still owe you a debt of gratitude for bringing Doatie here thirty minutes before we hoped for her."

"Now make him your best curtsey, Dolly," says Mr. Darling, seriously; "it isn't everyday you will get such a pretty speech as that."

"And see what we gained by our haste," says Dorothy, smiling at Mona. "You can't think what a charming sight it was. Like an old legend or a fairy-tale. Was it a minuet you were dancing?"

"Oh, no; only a country dance," says Mona, blushing.

"Well, it was perfect: wasn't it, Violet?"

"I wish I could have seen it better," returns Violet, "but, you see, I was playing."

"I wish I could have seen it forever," says Mr. Darling, gallantly, addressing Mona; "but all good things have an end too soon. Do you remember some lines like these? they come to me just now:

When you do dance, I wish youA wave o' the sea, that you might ever doNothing but that."

"Yes, I recollect; they are from the 'Winter's Tale.' I think," says Mona, shyly; "but you say too much for me."

"Not half enough," says Mr. Darling, enthusiastically.

"Don't you think, sir, you would like to get ready for dinner?" says Geoffrey, with mock severity. "You can continue your attentions to my wife later on,—at your peril."

"I accept the risk," says Nolly, with much stateliness and forthwith retires to make himself presentable.

CHAPTER XXI.

HOW NOLLY HAVING MADE HIMSELF PRESENTABLE, TRIES ALSO TO MAKE HIMSELF AGREEABLE—AND HOW HE SUCCEEDS.

Mr. Darling is a flaxen-haired young gentleman of about four-and-twenty, with an open and ingenuous countenance, and a disposition cheerful to the last degree. He is positively beaming with youth and good spirits, and takes no pains whatever to suppress the latter; indeed, if so sweet-tempered a youth could be said to have a fault, it lies in his inability to hold his tongue. Talk he must, so talk he does,—anywhere and everywhere, and under all circumstances.

He succeeds in taking Mona down to dinner, and shows himself particularly devoted through all the time they spend in the dining-room, and follows her afterwards to the drawing-room, as soon as decency will permit. He has, in fact, fallen a hopeless victim to Mona's charms, and feels no shame in the thought that all the world must notice his subjugation. On the contrary, he seems to glory in it.

"I was in your country, the other day," he says, pushing Mona's skirts a little to one side, and sinking on to the ottoman she has chosen as her own resting-place. "And a very nice country it is."

"Ah! were you really there!" says Mona, growing at once bright and excited at the bare mention of her native land. At such moments she falls again unconsciously into the "thens," and "sures," and "ohs!" and "ahs!" of her Ireland.

"Yes, I was indeed. Down in a small place cabled Castle-Connell, near Limerick. Nice people in Limerick, but a trifle flighty, don't you think? Fond of the merry blunderbuss, and all that, and with a decided tendency towards midnight maraudings."

"I am afraid you went to almost the worst part of Ireland," says Mona, shaking her head. "New Pallas, and all round Limerick, is so dreadfully disloyal."

"Well, that was just my luck, you see," says Darling "We have some property there. And, as I am not of much account at home, 'my awful dad' sent me over to Ireland to see why the steward didn't get in the rents. Perhaps he hoped the natives might pepper me; but, if so, it didn't come off. The natives, on the contrary, quite took to me, and adopted me on the spot. I was nearly as good as an original son of Erin in a week."

"But how did you manage to procure their good graces?"

"I expect they thought me beneath their notice, and, as they wouldn't hate me, they were forced to love me. Of course they treated the idea of paying up as a good joke, and spoke a great deal about a most unpleasant person called Griffith and his valuation, whatever that may be. So I saw it was of no use, and threw it up,—my mission, I mean. I had capital shooting, as far as partridges were concerned, but no one dreamed of wasting a bullet upon me. They positively declined to insert a bit of lead in my body. And, considering I expected some civility of the kind on going over, I felt somewhat disappointed, and decidedly cheap."

"We are not so altogether murderous as you seem to think," says Mona, half apologetically.

"Murderous! They are a delightful people, and the scenery is charming, you know, all round. The Shannon is positively lovely. But they wouldn't pay a farthing. And, 'pon my life, you know," says Mr. Darling, lightly, "I couldn't blame 'em. They were as poor as poor could be, regular out-at-elbows, you know, and I suppose they sadly wanted any money they had. I told the governor so when I came back, but I don't think he seemed to see it; sort of said *he* wanted it too, and then went on to make some ugly and most uncalled-for remarks about my tailor's bill, which of course I treated with the contempt they deserved."

"Well, but it was a little hard on your father, wasn't it?" says Mona, gently.

"Oh, it wasn't much," says the young man, easily; "and he needn't have cut up so rough about it. I was a failure, of course, but I couldn't help it; and, after all, I had a real good time in spite if everything, and enjoyed myself when there down to the ground."

"I am glad of that," says Mona, nicely, as he pauses merely through a desire for breath, not from a desire for silence.

"I had, really. There was one fellow, a perfect giant,—Terry O'Flynn was his name,—and he and I were awful chums. We used to go shooting together every day, and got on capitally. He was a tremendously big fellow, could put me in his pocket, you know, and forget I was there until I reminded him. He was a farmer's son, and a very respectable sort of man. I gave him my watch when I was coming away, and he was quite pleased. They don't have much watches, by the by, the lower classes, do they."

At this Mona breaks into a sweet but ringing laugh, that makes Lady Rodney (who is growing sleepy, and, therefore, irritable) turn, and fix upon her a cold, reproving glance.

Geoffrey, too, raises his head and smiles, in sympathy with his wife's burst of merriment, as does Miss Darling, who stops her conversation with Sir Nicholas to listen to it.

"What are you talking about?" asks Geoffrey, joining Mona and her companion.

"How could I help laughing," says Mona. "Mr. Darling has just expressed surprise at the fact that the Irish peasantry do not as a rule possess watches." Then suddenly her whole face changes from gayety to extreme sorrow. "Alas! poor souls!" she says, mournfully, "they don't, as a rule, have even meat!"

"Well, I noticed that, too. There *did* seem to be a great scarcity of that raw material," answers Darling, lightly. "Yet they are a fine race in spite of it. I'm going over again to see my friend Terry before very long. He is the most amusing fellow, downright brilliant. So is his hair, by the by,—the very richest crimson."

"But I hope you were not left to spend your days with Terry?" says Mona, smiling.

"No. All the county people round when they heard of me—which, according to my own mental calculations on the subject, must have been exactly five minutes after my arrival—quite adopted me. You are a very hospitable nation, Mrs. Rodney; nobody can deny that. Positively, the whole time I was in Limerick I could have dined three times every day had I so chosen."

"Bless me!" says Geoffrey; "what an appalling thought! it makes me feel faint."

"Rather so. In their desire to feed me lay my only danger of death. But I pulled through. And I liked every one I met,—really you know," to Mona, "and no humbug. Yet I think the happiest days I knew over there were those spent with Terry. It was rather a sell, though, having no real adventure, particularly as I had promised one not only to myself but to my friends when starting for Paddy-land. I beg your pardon a thousand times! Ireland, I mean."

"I don't mind," says Mona. "We are Paddies, of course."

"I wish I was one!" says Mr. Darling, with considerable effusion. "I envy the people who can claim nationality with you. I'd be a Paddy myself to-morrow if I could, for that one reason."

"What a funny boy you are!" says Mona, with a little laugh.

"So they all tell me. And of course what every one says is true. We're bound to be friends, aren't we?" rattles on Darling pleasantly. "Our mutual love for Erin should be a bond between us."

"I hope we shall be; I am sure we shall," returns Mona, quickly. It is sweet to her to find a possible friend in this alien land.

"Not a doubt of it," says Nolly, gayly. "Every one likes me, you know. 'To see me is to love me, and love but me forever,' and all that sort of thing; we shall be tremendous friends in no time. The fact is, I'm not worth hating; I'm neither useful nor ornamental, but I'm perfectly harmless, and there is something in that, isn't there? Every one can't say the same. I'm utterly certain *you* can't," with a glance of admiration.

"Don't be unkind to me," says Mona, with just a touch of innocent and bewitching coquetry. She is telling herself she likes this absurd young man better than any one she has met since she came to England, except perhaps Sir Nicholas.

"That is out of my power," says Darling, whom the last speech—and glance that accompanied it—has completely finished. "I only pray you of your grace never to be unkind to me."

"What a strange name yours is!—Nolly," says Mona, presently.

"Well, I wasn't exactly born so," explains Mr. Darling, frankly; "Oliver is my name. I rather fancy my own name, do you know; it is uncommon, at all events. One don't hear it called round every corner, and it reminds one of that 'bold bad man' the Protector. But they shouldn't have left out the Cromwell. That would have been a finishing stroke. To hear one's self announced as Oliver Cromwell Darling in a public room would have been as good as a small fortune."

"Better," says Mona, laughing gayly.

"Yes, really, you know. I'm in earnest," declares Mr. Darling, laughing too. He is quite delighted with Mona. To find his path through life strewn with people who will laugh with him, or even at him, is his idea of perfect bliss. So he chatters on to her until, bed-hour coming, and candles being forced into notice, he is at length obliged to tear himself away from her and follow the men to the smoking-room.

Here he lays hands on Geoffrey.

"By Jove, you know, you've about done it," he says, bestowing upon Geoffrey's shoulder a friendly pat that rather takes the breath out of that young man's body. "Gave you credit for more common sense. Why, such a proceeding as this is downright folly. You are bound to pay for your fun, you know, sooner or later."

"Sir," says Mr. Rodney, taking no notice of this preamble, "I shall trouble you to explain what you mean by reducing an inoffensive shoulder-blade to powder."

"Beg pardon, I'm sure," says Nolly, absently. "But"—with sudden interest—"do you know what you have done? You have married the prettiest woman in England."

"I haven't," says Geoffrey.

"You have," says Nolly.

"I tell you I have not," says Geoffrey. "Nothing of the sort. You are wool-gathering."

"Good gracious! he can't mean that he is tired of her already," exclaims Mr. Darling, in an audible aside. "That would be too much even for our times."

At this Geoffrey gives way to mirth. He and Darling are virtually alone, as Nicholas and Captain Rodney are talking earnestly about the impending lawsuit in a distant corner.

"My dear fellow, you have overworked your brain," he says, ironically: "You don't understand me. I am not tired of her. I shall never cease to bless the day I saw her,"—this with great earnestness,—"but you say I have married the handsomest woman in England, and she is not English at all."

"Oh, well, what's the odds?" says Nolly. "Whether she is French, or English, Irish or German, she has just the loveliest face I ever saw, and the sweetest ways. You've done an awfully dangerous thing. You will be Mrs. Rodney's husband in no time,—nothing else, and you positively won't know yourself in a year after. Individuality lost. Name gone. Nothing left but your four bones. You will be quite thankful for *them*, even, after a bit."

"You terrify me," says Geoffrey, with a grimace. "You think, then, that Mona is pretty?"

"Pretty doesn't express it. She is quite intense; and new style, too, which of course is everything. You will present her next season, I suppose? You must, you know, if only in the cause of friendship, as I wouldn't miss seeing Mrs. Laintrie's and Mrs. Whelon's look of disgust when your wife comes on the scene for worlds!"

"Her eyes certainly are——" says Geoffrey.

"She is all your fancy could possibly paint her; she is lovely and divine. Don't try to analyze her charms, my dear Geoff. She is just the prettiest and sweetest woman I ever met. She is young, in the 'very May morn of delight,' yet there is nothing of that horrid shyness—that *mauvaise honte*—about her that, as a rule, belongs to the 'freshness of morning.' Her laugh is so sweet, so full of enjoyment."

"If you mean me to repeat all this back again, you will find yourself jolly well mistaken; because, understand at once, I sha'n't do it," says Geoffrey. "I'm not going to have a hand in my undoing; and such unqualified praise is calculated to turn any woman's head. Seriously, though," says Geoffrey, laying his hands on Darling's shoulders, "I'm tremendously glad you like her."

"Don't!" says Darling, weakly. "Don't put it in that light. It's too feeble. If you said I was madly in love with your wife you would be nearer the mark, as insanity touches on it. I haven't felt so badly for years. It is right down unlucky for me, this meeting with Mrs. Rodney."

"Poor Mona!" says Geoffrey; "don't tell her about it, as remorse may sadden her."

"Look here," says Mr. Darling, "just try one of these, do. They are South American cigarettes, and nearly as strong as the real thing, and quite better: they are a new brand. Try 'em; they'll quite set you up."

"Give me one, Nolly," says Sir Nicholas, rousing from his reverie.

CHAPTER XXII.

HOW MONA GOES TO HER FIRST BALL—AND HOW SHE FARES THEREAT.

It is the day of Lady Chetwoode's ball, or to be particular, for critics "prove unkind" these times, it is the day to which belongs the night that has been selected for Lady Chetwoode's ball; all which sounds very like the metre of the house that Jack built.

Well, never mind! This ball promises to be a great success. Everybody who is anybody is going, from George Beatoun, who has only five hundred pounds a year in the world, and the oldest blood in the county, to the duchess, who "fancies" Lilian Chetwoode, and has, in fact, adopted her as her last "rave." Nobody has been forgotten, nobody is to be chagrined: to guard against this has cost both Sir Guy and Lilian Chetwoode many an hour of anxious thought.

To Mona, however, the idea of this dance is hardly pure nectar. It is half a terror, half a joy. She is nervous, frightened, and a little strange. It is the first time she has ever been to any large entertainment, and she cannot help looking forward to her own *debut* with a longing mingled largely with dread.

Now, as the hour approaches that is to bring her face to face with half the county, her heart fails her, and almost with a sense of wonder she contrasts her present life with the old one in her emerald isle, where she lived happily, if with a certain dulness, in her uncle's farmhouse.

All day long the rain has been pouring, pouring; not loudly or boisterously, not dashing itself with passionate force against pane and gable, but falling with a silent and sullen persistency.

"No walks abroad to-night," says Mr. Darling, in a dismal tone, staring in an injured fashion upon the drenched lawns and *pleasaunces* outside. "No Chinese lanterns, no friendly shrubberies,—*nothing!*"

Each window presents an aspect in a degree more dreary than the last,—or so it appears. The flower-beds are beaten down, and are melancholy in the extreme. The laurels do nothing but drip drip, in a sad aside, "making mournful music for the mind." Whilst up and down the elm walk the dreary wind goes madly, sporting and playing with the raindrops, as it rushes here and there.

Indoors King Bore stalks rampant. Nobody seems in a very merry mood. Even Nolly, who is generally game for anything, is a prey to despair. He has, for the last hour, lost sight of Mona!

"Let us do something, anything, to get rid of some of these interminable hours," says Doatie, flinging her book far from her. It is not interesting, and only helps to add insult to injury. She yawns as much as breeding will permit, and then crosses her hands behind her dainty head. "Oh! here comes Mona. Mona, I am so bored that I shall die presently, unless you suggest a remedy."

"Your brother is better at suggestions than I am," says Mona, gently, who is always somewhat subdued when in the room with Lady Rodney.

"Nolly, do you hear that? Come over to the fire directly, and cease counting those hateful raindrops. Mona believes in you. Isn't that joyful news? Now get out of your moody fit at once, like a dear boy."

"I sha'n't," says Mr. Darling, in an aggrieved tone. "I feel slighted. Mrs. Rodney has of *malice prepense* secluded herself from public gaze at least for an hour. I can't forget all *that* in one moment."

"Where have you been?" asks Lady Rodney, slowly turning her head to look at Mona. "Out of doors?" Her tone is unpleasant.

"No. In my own room," says Mona.

"Oh, Nolly! do think of some plan to cheat the afternoon of an hour or two," persists Doatie, eagerly.

"I have it," says her brother with all the air of one who has discovered a new continent. "Let's talk of graves, of worms, and epitaphs."

At this Doatie turns her back on him, while Mona breaks into a peal of silver laughter.

"Would you not like to do that?" demands Nolly, sadly "I should. I'm quite in the humor for it."

"I am afraid we are not," says Violet, smiling too. "Think of something else."

"Well, if you all *will* insist upon a change, and desire something more lively, then,—

'For heaven's sake, let us sit upon the ground, And tell sad stories of the death of kings.'

Perhaps after all you are right, and that will be better It will be rather effective, too, if uncomfortable, our all sitting on the polished floor."

"Fancy Nolly quoting Shakspeare," says Geoffrey, who has just entered, and is now leaning over Mona's chair. He stoops and whispers something in her ear that makes her flush and glance appealingly at Doatie. Whereon Miss

Darling, who is quick to sympathize, rises, and soon learns what the whisper has been about.

"Oh! how charming!" she cries, clapping her hands. "The very thing! Why did we not think of it before? To teach Mona the last new step! It will be delicious." Good-natured Doatie, as she says this, springs to her feet and runs her hand into Mona's. "Come," she says. "Before to-night, I promise you, you shall rival Terpsichore herself."

"Yes, she certainly must learn before to-night," says Violet, with sudden and unexpected interest, folding and putting away her work as though bent on other employment. "Let us come into the ballroom."

"Do you know no other dances but those—er—very Irish performances?" asks Lady Rodney, in a supercilious tone, alluding to the country dance Mona and Geoffrey had gone through on the night of Doatie's arrival.

"No. I have never been to a ball in all my life," says Mona distinctly. But she pales a little at the note of contempt in the other's voice. Unconsciously she moves a few steps nearer to Geoffrey, and holds out her hand to him in a childish entreating fashion.

He clasps it and presses it lightly but fondly to his lips. His brow darkens. The little stern expression, so seldom seen upon his kindly face, but which is inherited from his father, creeps up now and alters him preceptibly.

"You mistake my mother," he says to Mona, in a peculiar tone, looking at Lady Rodney, not at her. "My wife is, I am sure, the last person she would choose to be rude to; though, I confess, her manner just now would mislead most people."

With the frown still on his forehead, he draws Mona's hand through his arm, and leads her from the room.

Lady Rodney has turned pale. Otherwise she betrays no sign of chagrin, though in her heart she feels deeply the rebuke administered by this, her favorite son. To have Mona be a witness of her defeat is gall and wormwood to her. And silently, without any outward gesture, she registers a vow to be revenged for the insult (as she deems it) that has just been put upon her.

Dorothy Darling, who has been listening anxiously to all that has passed, and who is very grieved thereat, now speaks boldly.

"I am afraid," she says to Lady Rodney, quite calmly, having a little way of her own of introducing questionable topics without giving offence,—"I am afraid you do not like Mona?"

At this Lady Rodney flings down her guard and her work at the same time, and rises to her feet.

"Like her," she says, with suppressed vehemence. "How should I like a woman who has stolen from me my son, and who can teach him to be rude even to his own mother?"

"Oh, Lady Rodney, I am sure she did not mean to do that."

"I don't care what she meant; she has at all events done it. Like her! A person who speaks of 'Jack Robinson,' and talks of the 'long and short of it.' How could you imagine such a thing! As for you, Dorothy, I can only feel regret that you should so far forget yourself as to rush into a friendship with a young woman so thoroughly out of your own sphere."

Having delivered herself of this speech, she sweeps from the room, leaving Violet and Dorothy slightly nonplussed.

"Well, I never heard anything so absurd!" says Doatie, presently, recovering her breath, and opening her big eyes to their widest. "Such a tirade, and all for nothing. If saying 'Jack Robinson' is a social crime, I must be the biggest sinner living, as I say it just when I like. I think Mona adorable, and so does every one else. Don't you?"

"I am not sure. I don't fall in love with people at first sight. I am slow to read character," says Violet, calmly. "You, perhaps, possess that gift?"

"Not a bit of it, my dear. I only say to myself, such and such a person has kind eyes or a loving mouth, and then I make up my mind to them. I am seldom disappointed; but as to reading or studying character, that isn't in my line at all. It positively isn't in me. But don't you think Lady Rodney is unjust to Mona?"

"Yes, I think she is. But of course there are many excuses to be made for her. An Irish girl of no family whatever, no matter how sweet, is not the sort of person one would select as a wife for one's son. Come to the ballroom. I want to make Mona perfect in dancing."

"You want to make her a success to-night," says Dorothy, quickly. "I know you do. You are a dear thing, Violet, if a little difficult. And I verily believe you have fallen as great a victim to the charms of this Irish siren 'without family' as any of us. Come, confess it."

"There is nothing to confess. I think her very much to be liked, if you mean that," says Violet, slowly.

"She is a perfect pet," says Miss Darling, with emphasis, "and you know it."

Then they adjourn to the ballroom, and Sir Nicholas is pressed into the service, and presently Jack Rodney, discovering where Violet is, drops in too, and after a bit dancing becomes universal. Entering into the spirit of the thing, they take their "preliminary canter" now, as Nolly expresses it, as though to get into proper training for the Chetwoodes' ball later on. And they all dance with Mona, and show a great desire that she shall not be found wanting when called upon by the rank, beauty, and fashion of Lauderdale to trip it on the "light fantastic toe."

Even Jack Rodney comes out of himself, and, conquering his habitual laziness, takes her in hand, and, as being the best dancer present, *par excellence*, teaches and tutors, and encourages her until Doatie cries "enough," and protests with pathos she will have no more of it, as she is not going to be cut out by Mona at all events in the dancing line.

So the day wears to evening; and the rain ceases, and the sullen clouds scud with a violent haste across the tired sky. Then the stars come out, first slowly, one by one, as though timid early guests at the great gathering, then with a brilliant rush, until all the sky,

"Bespangled with those isles of lightSo wildly, spiritually bright."

shows promise of a fairer morrow.

Mona, coming slowly downstairs, enters with lagging steps the library, where tea is awaiting them before they start.

She is gowned in a cream-colored satin that hangs in severe straight lines, and clings to her lissom rounded figure as dew clings to a flower. A few rows of tiny pearls clasp her neck. Upon her bosom some Christmas roses, pure and white as her own soul, lie softly; a few more nestle in her hair, which is drawn simply back and coiled in a loose knot behind her head; she wears no earrings and very few bracelets.

One of the latter, however, is worthy of note. It is a plain gold band on which stands out a figure of Atalanta posed as when she started for her famous race. It had been sent to her on her marriage by Mr. Maxwell, in hearty remembrance, no doubt, of the night when she by her fleetness had saved his life.

She is looking very beautiful to-night. As she enters the room, nearly every one stops talking, and careless of good breeding, stares at her. There is a touch of purity about Mona that is perhaps one of her chiefest charms.

Even Lady Rodney can hardly take her eyes from the girl's face as she advances beneath the full glare of the chandelier, utterly unconscious of the extent of the beauty that is her rich gift.

Sir Nicholas, going up to her, takes her by both hands, and leads her gently beneath the huge bunch of mistletoe that still hangs from the centre-lamp.

Here, stooping, he embraces her warmly. Mona, coloring, shrinks involuntarily a few steps backward.

"Forgive me, my sister," says Nicholas, quickly. "Not the kiss, but the fact that until now I never quite understood how very beautiful you are!"

Mona smiles brightly—as might any true woman—at so warm a compliment. But Doatie, putting on a pathetic little *moue* that just suits her baby face, walks over to her *fiancé* and looks up at him with appealing eyes.

"Don't altogether forget *me*, Nicholas," she says, in her pretty childish way, pretending (little rogue that she is) to be offended.

"You, my own!" responds Nicholas, in a very low tone, that of course means everything, and necessitates a withdrawal into the curtained recess of the window, where whisperings may be unheard.

Then the carriages are announced, and every one finishes his and her tea, and many shawls are caught up and presently all are driving rapidly beneath the changeful moon to Chetwoode.

Now, strange as it may seem, the very moment Mona sets her foot upon the polished ballroom floor, and sees the lights, and hears the music, and the distant splashing of water in some unknown spot, and breathes the breath of dying flowers, all fears, all doubts, vanish; and only a passionate desire to dance, and be in unison with the sweet sounds that move the air, overfills her.

Then some one asks her to dance, and presently—with her face lit up with happy excitement, and her heart throbbing—she is actually mingling with the gay crowd that a moment since she has been envying. In and out among the dancers they glide, Mona so happy that she barely has time for thought, and so gives herself up entirely to the music to the exclusion of her partner. He has but a small place in her enjoyment. Perhaps, indeed, she betrays her satisfaction rather more than is customary or correct in an age when the *nil admirari* system reigns supreme. Yet there are many in the room who unconsciously smile in sympathy with her happy smile, and feel warmed by the glow of natural gladness that animates her breast.

After a little while, pausing beside a doorway, she casts an upward glance at her companion.

"I am glad you have at last deigned to take some small notice of me," says he, with a faint touch of pique in his tone. And then, looking at him again, she sees it is the young man who had nearly ridden over her some time ago, and tells herself she has been just a little rude to his Grace the Duke of Lauderdale.

"And I went to the utmost trouble to get an introduction," goes on Lauderdale, in an aggrieved voice; "because I thought you might not care about that impromptu ceremony at the lodge-gate; and yet what do I receive for my pains but disappointment? Have you quite forgotten me?"

"No. Of course I remember you now," says Mona, taking all this nonsense as quite *bona fide* sense in a maddeningly fascinating fashion. "How unkind I have been! But I was listening to the music, not to our introduction, when Sir Nicholas brought you up to me, and—and that is my only excuse." Then, sweetly, "You love music?"

"Well, I do," says the duke. "But I say that perhaps as a means of defence. If I said otherwise, you might think me fit only 'for treasons, stratagems, and spoils.'"

"Oh, no! you don't look like that," says Mona, with a heavenly smile. "You do not seem like a man that could not be 'trusted.'"

He is delighted with her ready response, her gayety, her sweetness, her freshness; was there ever so fair a face? Every one in the room by this time is asking who is the duke's partner, and Lady Chetwoode is beset with queries. All the women, except a very few, are consumed with jealousy; all the men are devoured with envy of the duke. Beyond all doubt the pretty Irish bride is the rage of the hour.

She chatters on gayly to the duke, losing sight of the fact of his rank, and laughing and making merry with him as though he were one of the ordinary friends of her life. And to Lauderdale, who is susceptible to beauty and tired of adulation, such manner has its charm, and he is perhaps losing his head a little, and is conning a sentence or two of a slightly tender nature, when another partner coming up claims Mona, and carries her away from what might prove dangerous quarters.

"Malcolm, who was that lovely creature you were talking to just now?" asks his mother, as Lauderdale draws near her.

"That? Oh, that was the bride, Mrs. Rodney," replies he. "She is lovely, if you like."

"Oh, indeed!" says the duchess, with some faint surprise. Then she turns to Lady Rodney, who is near her, and who is looking cold and supercilious. "I congratulate you," she says, warmly. "What a face that child has! How charming! How full of feeling! You are fortunate in securing so fair a daughter."

"Thank you," says Lady Rodney, coldly, letting her lids fall over her eyes.

"I am sorry I have missed her so often," says the duchess, who had been told that Mona was out when she called on her the second time, and who had been really not at home when Mona returned her calls. "But you will introduce me to her soon, I hope."

Just at this moment Mona comes up to them, smiling and happy.

"Ah! here she is," says the duchess, looking at the girl's bright face with much interest, and turning graciously towards Mona. And then nothing remains but for Lady Rodney to get through the introduction as calmly as she can, though it is sorely against her will, and the duchess, taking her hand, says something very pretty to her, while the duke looks on with ill-disguised admiration in his face.

They are all standing in a sort of anteroom, curtained off, but only partly concealed from the ballroom. Young Lady Chetwoode, who, as I have said, is a special pet with the duchess, is present, with Sir Guy and one or two others.

"You must give me another dance, Mrs. Rodney, before your card is quite full," says the duke, smiling. "If, indeed, I am yet in time."

"Yes, quite in time," says Mona. Then she pauses, looking at him so earnestly that he is compelled to return her gaze. "You shall have another dance," she says, in her clear voice, that is perfectly distinct to every one; "but you must not call me Mrs. Rodney: I am only Mrs. Geoffrey!"

A dead silence follows. Lady Rodney raises her head, scenting mischief in the air.

"No?" says Lauderdale, laughing. "But why, then? There is no other Mrs. Rodney, is there?"

"No. But there will be when Captain Rodney marries. And Lady Rodney says I have no claim to the name at all. I am only Mrs. Geoffrey."

She says it all quite simply, with a smile, and a quick blush that arises merely from the effort of having to explain, not from the explanation itself. There is not a touch of malice in her soft eyes or on her parted lips.

Lady Chetwoode looks at her fan and then at Sir Guy. The duchess, with a grave expression, looks at Lady Rodney. Can her old friend have proved herself unkind to this pretty stranger? Can she have already shown symptoms of that tyrannical temper which, according to the duchess, is Lady Rodney's chief bane? She says nothing, however, but, moving her fan with a beckoning gesture, draws her skirts aside, and motions to Mona, to seat herself beside her.

Mona obeys, feeling no shrinking from the kindly stout lady who is evidently bent on being "all things" to her. It does occur, perhaps, to her laughter-loving mind that there is a paucity of nose about the duchess, and a rather large amount of "too, too solid flesh;" but she smothers all such iniquitous reflections, and commences to talk with her gayly and naturally.

CHAPTER XXIII.

HOW MONA INTERVIEWS THE DUCHESS—AND HOW SHE SUSTAINS CONVERSATION WITH THE RODNEYS' EVIL GENIUS.

For some time they talk together, and then the duchess, fearing lest she may be keeping Mrs. Geoffrey from the common amusement of a ballroom, says, gently,—

"You are not dancing much?"

"No," says Mona, shaking her head. "Not—not to-night. I shall soon."

"But why not to-night?" asks her Grace, who has noticed with curiosity the girl's refusal to dance with a lanky young man in a hussar uniform, who had evidently made it the business of the evening to get introduced to her. Indeed, for an hour he had been feasting his eyes upon her fresh young beauty, and, having gone to infinite trouble to get presented to her, had been rewarded for his trouble by a little friendly smile, a shake of the head, and a distinct but kindly refusal to join in the mazy dance.

"But why?" asks the duchess.

"Because"—with a quick blush—"I am not accustomed to dancing much. Indeed, I only learned to-day, and I might not be able to dance with every one."

"But you were not afraid to dance with Lauderdale, my son?" says the duchess, looking at her.

"I should never be afraid of him," returns Mona. "He has kind eyes. He is"— slowly and meditatively—"very like you."

The duchess laughs.

"He may be, of course," she says. "But I don't like to see a gay child like you sitting still. You should dance everything for the night."

"Well, as I say, I shall soon," returns Mona, brightening, "because Geoffrey has promised to teach me."

"If I were 'Geoffrey,' I think I shouldn't," says the duchess, meaningly.

"No?" raising an innocent face. "To much trouble, you think, perhaps. But, bless you, Geoffrey wouldn't mind that, so long as he was giving me pleasure." At which answer the duchess is very properly ashamed of both her self and her speech.

"I should think very few people would deem it a trouble to serve you," she says, graciously. "And perhaps, after all, you don't much care about dancing."

"Yes, I do," says Mona, truthfully. "Just now, at least. Perhaps"—sadly—"when I am your age I sha'n't."

This is a *betise* of the first water. And Lady Rodney, who can hear—and is listening to—every word, almost groans aloud.

The duchess, on the contrary, gives way to mirth, and, leaning back in her chair, laughs softly but with evident enjoyment. Mona contemplates her curiously, pensively.

"What have I said?" she asks, half plaintively. "You laugh, yet I did not mean to be funny. Tell me what I said."

"It was only a little touch of nature," explains her Grace. "On that congratulate yourself. Nature is at a discount these days. And I—I love nature. It is so rare, a veritable philosopher's stone. You only told me what my glass tells me daily,—that I am not so young as I once was,—that, in fact, when sitting next pretty children like you, I am quite old."

"*Did* I say all that?" asks Mrs. Geoffrey, with wide eyes. "Indeed, I think you mistake. Old people have wrinkles, and they do not talk as you do. And when one is sweet to look at, one is never old."

To pay a compliment perfectly one must, I think, have at least a few drops of Irish blood in one's veins. As a rule, the happy-go-lucky people of Ireland can bring themselves to believe thoroughly, and without hypocrisy, in almost anything for the time being,—can fling themselves heart and soul into their flatteries, and come out of them again as victors. And what other nation is capable of this? To make sweet phrases is one thing; to look as if you felt or meant them is quite another.

The little suspicion of blarney trips softly and naturally from Mona's tongue. She doesn't smile as she speaks, but looks with eyes full of flattering conviction at the stout but comely duchess. And in truth it may be that in Mona's eyes she is sweet to look at, in that she has been kind and tender towards her in her manner.

And the duchess is charmed, pleased beyond measure That faint touch about the wrinkles was the happiest of the happy. Only that morning her Grace, in spite of her unapproachable maid and unlimited care, had seen an additional line around her mouth that had warned her of youth's decline, and now to meet some one oblivious of this line is sweet to her.

"Then you didn't go out much in Ireland?" she says, thinking it more graceful to change the conversation at this point.

"Out? Oh, ever so much," says Mrs. Geoffrey.

"Ah!" says the duchess, feeling puzzled. "Then perhaps they don't dance in Ireland.

"Yes, they do indeed, a great deal; at least I have heard so."

"Then I suppose when there you were too young to go out?" pursues the poor duchess, striving for information.

"I wasn't," says Mona: "I went out a great deal. All day long I was in the open air. That is what made my hands so brown last autumn."

"Were they brown?"

"As berries," says Mona, genially.

"At least they are a pretty shape," says the duchess glancing at the slim little hands lying gloved in their owner's lap. "But I don't think you quite understood the 'going out' in the light that I did. I mean, did you go much into society?"

"There wasn't much society to go into," says Mona, "and I was only fifteen when staying with Aunt Anastasia. She," confidentially, "made rather a grand match for us, you know." (Lady Rodney grinds her teeth, and tells herself she is on the point of fainting.) "She married the Provost of Trinity College; but I don't think he did her any good. She is the oddest old thing! Even to think of her now makes me laugh. You should have seen her," says Mrs. Geoffrey, leaning back in her chair, and giving way to her usual merry laugh, that rings like a peal of silver bells, "with her wig that had little curls all over it, and her big poke-bonnet like a coal-scuttle!"

"Well, I really wish I had seen her," says the good-humored duchess, smiling in sympathy, and beginning to feel herself more capable of thorough enjoyment than she has been for years. "Was she witty, as all Irish people are said to be?"

"Oh, dear, no," says Mona, with an emphatic shake of her lovely head. "She hadn't the least little bit of wit in her composition. She was as solemn as an Eng——I mean a Spaniard (they are all solemn, are they not?), and never made a joke in her life, but she was irresistibly comic all the same." Then suddenly, "What a very pretty little woman that is over there, and what a lovely dress!"

"Very pretty indeed, and quite good taste and that. She's a Mrs. Lennox, and her husband is our master of the hounds. She is always quite correct in the matter of *clothes*." There is an awful reservation in her Grace's tone, which is quite lost upon Mona. "But she is by no means little in her own opinion, and in fact rather prides herself upon her—er—form generally," concludes the duchess, so far at a loss for a word as to be obliged to fall back upon slang.

"Her form!" says Mrs. Geoffrey, surveying the tiny Mrs. Lennox from head to foot in sheer wonderment. "She need hardly pride herself on that. She hasn't much of it, has she?"

"Yes,—in her own estimation," says the duchess, somewhat severely, whose crowning horror is a frisky matron, to which title little Mrs. Lennox may safely lay claim.

"Well, I confess that puzzles me," says Mona, knitting her straight brows and scanning the small lady before her with earnest eyes, who is surrounded by at least a dozen men, with all of whom she is conversing without any apparent effort. "I really think she is the smallest woman I ever saw. Why, I am only medium height, but surely I could make two of her. At least I have more figure, or form, as you call it, than she has."

The duchess gives it up. "Yes, and a far better one, too," she says, amiably, declining to explain. Indeed, she is delighted to meet a young woman who actually regards slang as a foreign and unstudied language, and shrinks from being the first to help her to forget the English tongue. "Is there much beauty in Ireland?" she asks, presently.

"Yes, but we are all so different from the English. We have no pretty fair hair in Ireland, or at least very little of it."

"Do you admire our hair? And we are all so heartily tired of it," says the duchess. "Well, tell me more about your own land. Are the women all like you? In style, I mean. I have seen a few, of course, but not enough to describe a whole."

"Like me? Oh, no," says Mrs. Geoffrey. "Some of them are really beautiful, like pictures. When I was staying with Aunt Anastasia—the Provost's wife, you remember—I saw a great many pretty people. I saw a great many students, too," says Mona, brightening, "and liked them very much. They liked me, too."

"How strange!" says the duchess, with an amused smile. "Are you quite sure of that?"

"Oh, quite. They used to take me all over the college, and sometimes to the bands in the squares. They were very good to me."

"They would be, of course," says the duchess.

"But they were troublesome, very troublesome," says Mrs. Geoffrey, with a retrospective sigh, leaning back in her chair and folding her hands together on her lap. "You can't imagine what a worry they were at times,—always ringing the college bell at the wrong hours, and getting tight!"

"Getting what?" asks the duchess, somewhat taken aback.

"Tight,—screwed,—tipsy, you know," replies Mona, innocently. "Tight was the word they taught me. I think they believed it sounded more respectable than the others. And the Divinity boys were the worst. Shall I tell you about them?"

"Do," says the duchess.

"Well, three of them used to come to see Aunt Anastasia; at least they *said* it was auntie, but they never spoke to her if they could help it, and were always so glad when she went to sleep after dinner."

"I think your Aunt Anastasia was very good to them," says the duchess.

"But after a bit they grew very tiresome. When I tell you they all three proposed to me every day for a week, you will understand me. Yet even that we could have borne, though it was very expensive, because they used to go about stealing my gloves and my ribbons, but when they took to punching each other's heads about me auntie said I had better go to Uncle Brian for a while: so I went; and there I met Geoffrey," with a brilliant smile.

"I think Geoffrey owes those Divinity boys more than he can ever pay," says the duchess, very prettily. "You must come and see me soon, child. I am an old woman, and seldom stir from home, except when I am positively ordered out by Malcom, as I was to-night. Come next Thursday. There are some charming trifles at the old Court that may amuse you, though I may fail to do so."

"I sha'n't want any trifles to amuse me, if you will talk to me," says Mona.

"Well, come early. And now go and dance with Mr. Darling. He has been looking at me very angrily for the last three minutes. By the by," putting up her glasses, "is that little girl in the lemon-colored gown his sister?"

"Yes; that is Sir Nicholas's Doatie Darling," returns Mona, with a light laugh. And then Nolly leads her away, and, feeling more confident with him, she is once again dancing as gayly as the best.

"Your foot is plainly 'on your native heath,'" says Nolly, "though your name may not be 'McGregor.' What on earth were you saying to that old woman for the last four hours?"

"It was only twenty minutes," says Mona.

"Twenty minutes! By Jove, she must be more interesting than we thought," says Mr. Darling, "if you can put it at that time. I thought she was going to eat you, she looked so pleased with you. And no wonder, too:" with a loud and a hearty sigh.

"She was very nice to me," says Mona, "and is, I think, a very pleasant old lady. She asked me to go and see her next Thursday."

"Bless my stars!" says Nolly; "you *have* been going it. That is the day on which she will receive no one but her chief pets. The duchess, when she comes down here, reverses the order of things. The rest have an 'at home' day. She has a 'not at home' day."

"Where are people when they are not at home?" asks Mona, simply.

"That's the eighth wonder of the world," says Mr. Darling, mysteriously. "It has never yet been discovered. Don't seek to pry too closely into it; you might meet with a rebuff."

"How sad Nicholas looks!" says Mona, suddenly.

In a doorway, somewhat out of the crush, Sir Nicholas is standing. His eyes are fixed on Dorothy, who is laughing with a gay and gallant plunger in the distance. He is looking depressed and melancholy; a shadow seems to have fallen into his dark eyes.

"Now he is thinking of that horrid lawsuit again," says Nolly, regretfully, who is a really good sort all round. "Let us go to him."

"Yes; let me go to him," says Mona, quickly; "I shall know what to say better than you."

After a little time she succeeds in partially lifting the cloud that has fallen on her brother. He has grown strangely fond of her, and finds comfort in her gentle eyes and sympathetic mouth. Like all the rest, he has gone down before Mona, and found a place for her in his heart. He is laughing at some merry absurdity of hers, and is feeling braver, more hopeful, when a little chill seems to pass over him, and, turning, he confronts a tall dark young man who has come leisurely—but with a purpose—to where he and Mona are standing.

It is Paul Rodney.

Sir Nicholas, just moving his glass from one eye to the other, says "Good evening" to him, bending his head courteously, nay, very civilly, though without a touch, or suspicion of friendliness. He does not put out his hand, however, and Paul Rodney, having acknowledged his salutation by a bow colder and infinitely more distant than his own, turns to Mona.

"You have not quite forgotten me, I hope, Mrs. Rodney. You will give me one dance?"

His eyes, black and faintly savage, seem to burn into hers.

"No; I have not forgotten you," says Mona, shrinking away from him. As she speaks she looks nervously at Nicholas.

"Go and dance, my dear," he says, quickly, in a tone that decides her. It is to please him, for his sake, she must do this thing; and so, without any awkward hesitation, yet without undue haste, she turns and lays her hand on the Australian's arm. A few minutes later she is floating round the room in his arms, and, passing by Geoffrey, though she sees him not, is seen by him.

"Nicholas, what is the meaning of this?" says Geoffrey, a few moments later, coming up with a darkening brow to where Nicholas is leaning against a wall. "What has possessed Mona to give that fellow a dance? She must be mad, or ignorant, or forgetful of everything. She was with you: why did you not prevent it?"

"My dear fellow, let well alone," says Nicholas, with his slow, peculiar smile. "It was I induced Mona to dance with 'that fellow,' as you call him. Forgive me this injury, if indeed you count it one."

"I don't understand you," says Geoffrey, still rather hotly.

"I think I hardly understand myself: yet I know I am possessed of a morbid horror lest the county should think I am uncivil to this man merely because he has expressed a hope that he may be able to turn me out of doors. His hope may be a just one. I rather think it is: so it pleased me that Mona should dance with him, if only to show the room that he is not altogether tabooed by us."

"But I wish it had been any one but Mona," says Geoffrey, still agitated.

"But who? Doatie will not dance with him, and Violet he never asks. I fell back, then, upon the woman who has so little malice in her heart that she could not be ungracious to any one. Against her will she read my desire in my eyes, and has so far sacrificed herself for my sake. I had no right to compel your wife to this satisfying of my vanity, yet I could not resist it. Forget it; the dance will soon be over."

"It seems horrible to me that Mona should be on friendly terms with your enemy," says Geoffrey, passionately.

"He is not my enemy. My dear boy, spare me a three-act drama. What has the man done, beyond wearing a few gaudy rings, and some oppressive neckties, that you should hate him as you do? It is unreasonable. And, besides, he is in all probability your cousin. Parkins and Slow declare they can find no flaw in the certificate of his birth; and—is not every man at liberty to claim his own?"

"If he claims my wife for another dance, I'll——" begins Geoffrey.

"No, you won't," interrupts his brother, smiling. "Though I think the poor child has done her duty now. Let him pass. It is he should hate me, not I him."

At this Geoffrey says something under his breath about Paul Rodney that he ought not to say, looking the while at Nicholas with a certain light in his blue eyes that means not only admiration but affection.

Meantime, Mona, having danced as long as she desires with this enemy in the camp, stops abruptly before a curtained entrance to a small conservatory, into which he leads her before she has time to remonstrate: indeed, there is no apparent reason why she should.

Her companion is singularly silent. Scarce one word has escaped him since she first laid her hand upon his arm, and now again dumbness, or some hidden feeling, seals his lips.

Of this Mona is glad. She has no desire to converse with him, and is just congratulating herself upon her good fortune in that he declines to speak with her, when he breaks the welcome silence.

"Have they taught you to hate me already?" he asks, in a low, compressed tone, that make her nerves assert themselves.

"I have been taught nothing," she says, with a most successful grasp at dignity. "They do not speak of you at the Towers,—at least, not unkindly." She looks at him as she says this, but lowers her eyes as she meets his. This dark, vehement young man almost frightens her.

"Yet, in spite of what you say, you turn from me, you despise me," exclaims he, with some growing excitement.

"Why should I despise you?" asks she, slowly, opening her eyes.

The simple query confounds him more than might a more elaborate one put by a clever worldling. Why indeed?

"I was thinking about this impending lawsuit," he stammers, uneasily. "You know of it, of course? Yet why should I be blamed?"

"No one blames you," says Mona; "yet it is hard that Nicholas should be made unhappy."

"Other people are unhappy, too," says the Australian, gloomily.

"Perhaps they make their own unhappiness," says Mona, at random. "But Nicholas has done nothing. He is good and gentle always. He knows no evil thoughts. He wishes ill to no man."

"Not even to me?" with a sardonic laugh.

"Not even to you," very gravely. There is reproof in her tone. They are standing somewhat apart, and her eyes have been turned from him. Now, as she says this, she changes her position slightly, and looks at him very earnestly. From the distant ballroom the sound of the dying music comes sadly, sweetly; a weeping fountain in a corner mourns bitterly, as it seems to Mona, tear by tear, perhaps for some lost nymph.

"Well, what would you have me do?" demands he, with some passion. "Throw up everything? Lands, title, position? It is more than could be expected of any man."

"Much more," says Mona; but she sighs as she says it, and a little look of hopelessness comes into her face. It is so easy to read Mona's face.

"You are right," he says, with growing vehemence: "no man would do it. It is such a brilliant chance, such a splendid scheme———." He checks himself suddenly. Mona looks at him curiously, but says nothing. In a second he recovers himself, and goes on: "Yet because I will not relinquish my just claim you look upon me with hatred and contempt."

"Oh, no," says Mona, gently; "only I should like you better, of course, if you were not the cause of our undoing."

"'Our'? How you associate yourself with these Rodneys!" he says, scornfully; "yet you are as unlike them as a dove is unlike a hawk. How came you to fall into their nest? And so if I could only consent to efface myself you would like me better,—tolerate me in fact? A poor return for annihilation. And yet," impatiently, "I don't know. If I could be sure that even my memory would be respected by you———." He pauses and pushes back his hair from his brow.

"Why could you not have stayed in Australia?" says Mona, with some excitement. "You are rich; your home is there; you have passed all your life up to this without a title, without the tender associations that cling round Nicholas and that will cost him almost his life to part with. You do not want them, yet you come here to break up our peace and make us all utterly wretched."

"Not you," says Paul, quickly. "What is it to you? It will not take a penny out of your pocket. Your husband," with an evil sneer, "has his income secured. I am not making you wretched."

"You are," says Mona, eagerly. "Do you think," tears gathering in her eyes, "that I could be happy when those I love are reduced to despair?"

"You must have a large heart to include all of them," says Rodney with a shrug. "Whom do you mean by 'those you love?' Not Lady Rodney, surely. She is scarcely a person, I take it to inspire that sentiment in even your tolerant breast. It cannot be for her sake you bear me such illwill?"

"I bear you no illwill; you mistake me," says Mona, quietly: "I am only sorry for Nicholas, because I do love him."

"Do you?" says her companion, staring at her, and drawing his breath a little hard. "Then, even if he should lose to me lands, title, nay, all he possesses, I should still count him a richer man than I am."

"Oh, poor Nicholas!" says Mona sadly, "and poor little Doatie!"

"You speak as if my victory was a foregone conclusion," says Rodney. "How can you tell? He may yet gain the day, and I may be the outcast."

"I hope with all my heart you will," says Mona.

"Thank you," replies he stiffly; "yet, after all, I think I should bet upon my own chance."

"I am afraid you are right," says Mona. "Oh, why did you come over at all?"

"I am very glad I did," replies he, doggedly. "At least I have seen you. They cannot take that from me. I shall always be able to call the remembrance of your face my own."

Mona hardly hears him. She is thinking of Nicholas's face as it was half an hour ago when he had leaned against the deserted doorway and looked at pretty Dorothy.

Yet pretty Dorothy at her very best moments had never looked, nor ever could look, as lovely as Mona appears now, as she stands with her hands loosely clasped before her, and the divine light of pity in her eyes, that are shining softly like twin stars.

Behind her rises a tall shrub of an intense green, against which the soft whiteness of her satin gown gleams with a peculiar richness. Her gaze is fixed upon a distant planet that watches her solemnly through the window from its seat in the far-off heaven, "silent, as if it watch'd the sleeping earth."

She sighs. There is pathos and sweetness and tenderness in every line of her face, and much sadness. Her lips are slightly parted, "her eyes are homes of silent prayer." Paul, watching her, feels as though he is in the presence of some gentle saint, sent for a space to comfort sinful earth.

A passionate admiration for her beauty and purity fills his breast: he could have fallen at her feet and cried aloud to her to take pity upon him, to let some loving thought for him—even him too—enter and find fruitful soil within her heart.

"Try not to hate me," he says, imploringly, in a broken voice, going suddenly up to her and taking one of her hands in his. His grasp is so hard as almost to hurt her. Mona awakening from her reverie, turns to him with a start. Something in his face moves her.

"Indeed, I do not hate you," she says impulsively. "Believe me, I do not. But still I fear you."

Some one is coming quickly towards them. Rodney, dropping Mona's hand, looks hurriedly round, only to see Lady Rodney approaching.

"Your husband is looking for you," she says to Mona, in an icy tone. "You had better go to him. This is no place for you."

Without vouchsafing a glance of recognition to the Australian, she sweeps past, leaving them again alone. Paul laughs aloud.

"'A haughty spirit comes before a fall,'" quotes he contemptuously.

"I must go now. Good-night," says Mona, kindly if coldly. He escorts her to the door of the conservatory There Lauderdale, who is talking with some men, comes forward and offers her his arm to take her to the carriage. And then adieux are said, and the duke accompanies her downstairs, whilst Lady Rodney contents herself with one of her sons.

It is a triumph, if Mona only knew it, but she is full of sad reflections, and is just now wrapped up in mournful thoughts of Nicholas and little Dorothy. Misfortune seems flying towards them on strong swift wings. Can nothing stay its approach, or beat it back in time to effect a rescue? If they fail to find the nephew of the old woman Elspeth in Sydney, whither he is supposed to have gone, or if, on finding him they fail to elicit any information from him on the subject of the lost will, affairs may be counted almost hopeless.

"Mona," says Geoffrey, to her suddenly, in a low whisper, throwing his arm round her (they are driving home, alone in the small night-brougham)— "Mona, do you know what you have done to-night? The whole room went mad about you. They would talk of no one else. Do not let them turn your head."

"Turn it where, darling?" asks she, a little dreamily.

"Away from me," returns he, with some emotion, tightening his clasp around her.

"From you? Was there ever such a dear silly old goose," says Mrs. Geoffrey, with a faint, loving laugh. And then, with a small sigh full of content, she forgets her cares for others for awhile, and, nestling closer to him, lays her head upon his shoulder and rests there happily until they reach the Towers.

CHAPTER XXIV.

HOW THE CLOUD GATHERS—AND HOW NICHOLAS AND DOROTHY HAVE THEIR BAD QUARTER OF AN HOUR.

The blow so long expected, yet so eagerly and hopefully scoffed at with obstinate persistency, falls at last (all too soon) upon the Towers. Perhaps it is not the very final blow that when it comes must shatter to atoms all the old home-ties, and the tender links that youth has forged, but it is certainly a cruel shaft, that touches the heart strings, making them quiver. The first thin edge of the wedge has been inserted: the sword trembles to its fall: *c'est le commencement de la fin.*

It is the morning after Lady Chetwoode's ball. Every one has got down to breakfast. Every one is in excellent spirits, in spite of the fact that the rain is racing down the window-panes in torrents, and that the post is late.

As a rule it always is late, except when it is preternaturally early; sometimes it comes at half-past ten, sometimes with the hot water. There is a blessed uncertainty about its advent that keeps every one on the tiptoe of expectation, and probably benefits circulation.

The postman himself is an institution in the village, being of an unknown age, in fact, the real and original oldest inhabitant, and still with no signs of coming dissolution about him, thereby carrying out Dicken's theory that a dead post-boy or a dead donkey is a thing yet to be seen. He is a hoary-headed old person, decrepit and garrulous, with only one leg worth speaking about, and an ear trumpet. This last is merely for show, as once old Jacob is set fairly talking, no human power could get in a word from any one else.

"I am always so glad when the post doesn't arrive in time for breakfast," Doatie is saying gayly. "Once those horrid papers come, every one gets stupid and engrossed, and thinks it a positive injury to have to say even 'yes' or 'no' to a civil question. Now see how sociable we have been this morning, because that dear Jacob is late again. Ah! I spoke too soon," as the door opens and a servant enters with a most imposing pile of letters and papers.

"Late again, Jermyn," says Sir Nicholas, lazily.

"Yes, Sir Nicholas,—just an hour and a half. He desired me to say he had had another 'dart' in his rheumatic knee this morning, so hoped you would excuse him."

"Poor old soul!" says Sir Nicholas.

"Jolly old bore!" says Captain Rodney, though not unkindly.

"Don't throw me over that blue envelope, Nick," says Nolly: "I don't seem to care about it. I know it, I think it seems familiar. You may have it, with my love. Mrs. Geoffrey, be so good as to tear it in two."

Jack is laughing over a letter written by one of the fellows in India; all are deep in their own correspondence.

Sir Nicholas, having gone leisurely through two of his letters, opens a third, and begins to peruse it rather carelessly. But hardly has he gone half-way down the first page when his face changes; involuntarily his fingers tighten over the luckless letter, crimping it out of all shape. By a supreme effort he suppresses an exclamation. It is all over in a moment. Then he raises his head, and the color comes back to his lips. He smiles faintly, and, saying something about having many things to do this morning, and that therefore he hopes they will forgive his running away from them in such a hurry he rises and walks slowly from the room.

Nobody has noticed that anything is wrong. Only Doatie turns very pale, and glances nervously at Geoffrey, who answers her frightened look with a perplexed one of his own.

Then, as breakfast was virtually over before the letters came, they all rise, and disperse themselves as fancy dictates. But Geoffrey goes alone to where he knows he shall find Nicholas in his own den.

An hour later, coming out of it again, feeling harassed and anxious, he finds Dorothy walking restlessly up and down the corridor outside, as though listening for some sound she pines to hear. Her pretty face, usually so bright and *debonnaire*, is pale and sad. Her lips are trembling.

"May I not see Nicholas, if only for a moment?" she says, plaintively, gazing with entreaty at Geoffrey. At which Nicholas, hearing from within the voice that rings its changes on his heart from morn till eve, calls aloud to her,—

"Come in, Dorothy. I want to speak to you."

So she goes in, and Geoffrey, closing the door behind her, leaves them together.

She would have gone to him then, and tried to console him in her own pretty fashion, but he motions her to stay where she is.

"Do not come any nearer," he says, hastily, "I can tell it all to you better, more easily, when I cannot see you."

So Doatie, nervous and miserable, and with unshed tears in her eyes, stands where he tells her, with her hand resting on the back of an arm-chair, while he, going over to the window, deliberately turns his face from hers. Yet even now he seems to find a difficulty in beginning. There is a long pause; and then——

"They—they have found that fellow,—old Elspeth's nephew," he says in a husky tone.

"Where?" asks Doatie, eagerly.

"In Sydney. In Paul Rodney's employ. In his very house."

"Ah!" says Doatie, clasping her hands. "And——"

"He says he knows nothing about any will."

Another pause, longer than the last.

"He denies all knowledge of it. I suppose he has been bought up by the other side. And now what remains for us to do? That was our last chance, and a splendid one, as there are many reasons for believing that old Elspeth either burned or hid the will drawn up by my grandfather on the night of his death; but it has failed us. Yet I cannot but think this man Warden must know something of it. How did he discover Paul Rodney's home? It has been proved, that old Elspeth was always in communication with my uncle up to the hour of her death; she must have sent Warden to Australia then, probably with this very will she had been so carefully hiding for years. If so, it is beyond all doubt burned or otherwise destroyed by this time. Parkins writes to me in despair."

"This is dreadful!" says Doatie. "But"—brightening—"surely it is not so bad as death or disgrace, is it?"

"It means death to me," replies he, in a low tone. "It means that I shall lose you."

"Nicholas," cries she, a little sharply, "what is it you would say?"

"Nay, hear me," exclaims he, turning for the first time to comfort her; and, as he does, she notices the ravages that the last hour of anxiety and trouble have wrought upon his face. He is looking thin and haggard, and rather tired. All her heart goes out to him, and it is with difficulty she restrains her desire to run to him and encircle him with her soft arms. But something in his expression prevents her.

"Hear me," he says, passionately: "if I am worsted in this fight—and I see no ray of hope anywhere—I am a ruined man. I shall then have literally only five hundred a year that I can call my own. No home; no title. And such an income as that, to people bred as you and I have been, means simply penury. All must be at an end between us, Dorothy. We must try to forget that we have ever been more than ordinary friends."

This tirade has hardly the effect upon Dorothy that might be desired. She still stands firm, utterly unshaken by the storm that has just swept over her (frail child though she is), and, except for a slight touch of indignation that is fast growing within her eyes, appears unmoved.

"You may try just as hard as ever you like," she says, with dignity: "I *sha'n't!*"

"So you think now; but by and by you will find the pressure too great, and you will go with the tide. If I were to work for years and years, I could scarcely at the end achieve a position fit to offer you. And I am thirty-two, remember,—not a boy beginning life, with all the world and time before him,—and you are only twenty. By what right should I sacrifice your youth, your prospects? Some other man, some one more fortunate, may perhaps——"

Here he breaks down ignominiously, considering the amount of sternness he had summoned to his aid when commencing, and, walking to the mantelpiece, lays his arm on it, and his head upon his arms.

"You insult me," says Dorothy, growing even whiter than she was before, "when you speak to me of—of——"

Then she, too, breaks down, and, going to him, deliberately lifts one of his arms and lays it round her neck; after which she places both hers gently round his, and so, having comfortably arranged herself, proceeds to indulge in a hearty burst of tears. This is, without exception, the very wisest course she could have taken, as it frightens the life out of Nicholas, and brings him to a more proper frame of mind in no time.

"Oh, Dorothy, don't do that! Don't, my dearest, my pet!" he entreats. "I won't say another word, not one, if you will only stop."

"You have said too much already, and there *sha'n't* be an end of it, as you declared just now," protests Doatie, vehemently, who declines to be comforted just yet, and is perhaps finding some sorrowful enjoyment in the situation. "I'll take very good care there sha'n't! And I won't let you give me up. I don't care how poor you are. And I must say I think it is very rude and heartless of you, Nicholas, to want to hand me over to 'some other man,' as if I was a book or a parcel! 'Some other man,' indeed!" winds up Miss Darling, with a final sob and a heavy increase of righteous wrath.

"But what is to be done?" asks Nicholas, distractedly, though inexpressibly cheered by these professions of loyalty and devotion. "Your people won't hear of it."

"Oh, yes, they will," returns Doatie, emphatically, "They will probably hear a great deal of it! I shall speak of it morning, noon, and night, until out of sheer vexation of spirit they will come in a body and entreat you to remove me.

Ah!" regretfully, "if only I had a fortune now, how sweet it would be! I never missed it before. We are really very unfortunate."

"We are, indeed. But I think your having a fortune would only make matters worse." Then he grows despairing once more. "Dorothy, it is madness to think of it. I am speaking only wisdom, though you are angry with me for it. Why encourage hope where there is none?"

"Because 'the miserable hath no other medicine but only hope,'" quotes she, very sadly.

"Yet what does Feltham say? 'He that hopes too much shall deceive himself at last' Your medicine is dangerous, darling. It will kill you in the end. Just think, Dorothy, how could you live on five hundred a year!"

"Other people have done it,—do it every day," says Dorothy, stoutly. She has dried her eyes, and is looking almost as pretty as ever. "We might find a dear nice little house somewhere, Nicholas," this rather vaguely, "might we not? with some furniture in Queen Anne's style. Queen Anne, or what looks like her, is not so very expensive now, is she?"

"No," says Nicholas, "she isn't; though I should consider her dear at any price." He is a depraved young man who declines to see beauty in ebony and gloom. "But," with a sigh, "I don't think you quite understand, darling."

"Oh, yes, I do," says Dorothy, with a wise shake of her blonde head; "you mean that probably we shall not be able to order any furniture at all. Well, even if it comes to sitting on one horrid kitchen deal chair with you, Nicholas, I sha'n't mind it a scrap." She smiles divinely, and with the utmost cheerfulness, as she says this. But then she has never tried to sit on a deal chair, and it is a simple matter to conjure up a smile when woes are imaginary.

"You are an angel," says Nicholas. And, indeed, considering all things, it is the least he could have said. "If we weather this storm, Dorothy," he goes on, earnestly,—"if, by any chance, Fate should reinstate me once more firmly in the position I have always held,—it shall be my proudest remembrance that in my adversity you were faithful to me, and were content to share my fortune, evil though it showed itself to be."

They are both silent for a little while, and then Dorothy says, softly,—

"Perhaps it will all come right at last. Oh! if some kind good fairy would but come to our aid and help us to confound our enemies!"

"I am afraid there is only one fairy on earth just now, and that is you," says Nicholas, with a faint smile, smoothing back her pretty hair with loving fingers, and gazing fondly into the blue eyes that have grown so big and earnest during their discussion.

"I mean a real fairy," says Dorothy, shaking her head "If she were to come now this moment and say, 'Dorothy'——"

"Dorothy," says a voice outside at this very instant, so exactly as Doatie pauses that both she and Nicholas start simultaneously.

"That is Mona's voice," says Doatie. "I must go. Finish your letters, and come for me then, and we can go into the garden and talk it all over again. Come in, Mona; I am here."

She opens the door, and runs almost into Mona's arms, who is evidently searching for her everywhere.

"Ah! now, I have disturbed you," says Mrs. Geoffrey, pathetically, to whom lovers are a rare delight and a sacred study. "How stupid of me! Sure you needn't have come out, when you knew it was only me. And of course he wants you, poor dear fellow. I thought you were in the small drawing-room, or I shouldn't have called you at all."

"It doesn't matter. Come upstairs with me, Mona. I want to tell you all about it," says Doatie. The reaction has set in, and she is again tearful, and reduced almost to despair.

"Alas! Geoffrey has told me everything," says Mona, "That is why I am now seeking for you. I thought, I *knew*, you were unhappy, and I wanted to tell you how I suffer with you."

By this time they have reached Dorothy's room, and now, sitting down, gaze mournfully at each other. Mona is so truly grieved that any one might well imagine this misfortune, that is rendering the very air heavy, in her own, rather than another's. And this wholesale sympathy, this surrendering of her body and mind to a grief that does not touch herself, is inexpressibly sweet to her poor little friend.

Kneeling down by her, Dorothy lays her head upon Mona's knee, and bursts out crying afresh.

"Don't now," says Mona, in a low, soothing tone folding her in a close embrace; "this is wrong, foolish. And when things come to the worst they mend."

"Not always," sobs Doatie. "I know how it will be. We shall be separated,— torn asunder, and then after a while they will make me marry somebody else; and in a weak moment I shall do it! And then I shall be utterly wretched for ever and ever."

"You malign yourself," says Mona. "It is all impossible. You will have no such weak moment, or I do not know you. You will be faithful always, until he can marry you, and, if he never can, why, then you can be faithful too, and go to your grave with his image only in your heart That is not so bad a thought, is it?"

"N—ot very," says Doatie, dolefully.

"And, besides, you can always see him, you know," goes on Mona, cheerfully. "It is not as if death had stolen him from you. He will be always somewhere; and you can look into his eyes, and read how his love for you has survived everything. And perhaps, after some time, he may distinguish himself in some way and gain a position far grander than mere money or rank can afford, because you know he is wonderfully clever."

"He is," says Dorothy, with growing animation.

"And perhaps, too, the law may be on his side: there is plenty of time yet for a missing will or a—a—useful witness to turn up. That will," says Mona, musingly, "must be somewhere. I cannot tell you why I think so, but I am quite sure it is still in existence, that no harm has come to it. It may be discovered yet."

She looks so full of belief in her own fancy that she inspires Doatie on the spot with a similar faith.

"Mona! There is no one so sweet or comforting as you are," she cries, giving her a grateful hug. "I really think I do feel a little better now."

"That's right, then," says Mona, quite pleased at her success.

Violet, coming in a few moments later, finds them still discussing the all-important theme.

"It is unfortunate for every one," says Violet, disconsolately, sinking in a low chair. "Such a dear house, and to have it broken up and given into the possession of such a creature as that." She shrugs her shoulders with genuine disgust.

"You mean the Australian?" says Dorothy. "Oh, as for him, he is perfectly utter!—such a man to follow in Nicholas's footsteps!"

"I don't suppose any one will take the slightest notice of him," says Violet: "that is one comfort."

"I don't know that: Lilian Chetwoode made him welcome in her house last night," says Doatie, a little bitterly.

"That is because Nicholas will insist on proving to every one he bears him no malice, and speaks of him persistently as his cousin. Well, he may be his cousin; but there is a limit to everything," says Violet, with a slight frown.

"That is just what is so noble about Nicholas," returns Doatie, quickly. "He supports him, simply because it is his own quarrel. After all, it matters to nobody but Nicholas himself: no one else will suffer if that odious black man conquers."

"Yes, many will. Lady Rodney,—and—and Jack too. He also must lose by it," says Violet, with suppressed warmth.

"He may; but how little in comparison! Nobody need be thought of but my poor Nicholas," persists Doatie, who has not read between the lines, and fails therefore in putting a proper construction upon the faint delicate blush that is warming Violet's cheek.

But Mona has read, and understands perfectly.

"I think every one is to be pitied; and Jack more than most,—after dear Nicholas," she says, gently, with such a kindly glance at Violet as goes straight to that young woman's heart, and grows and blossoms there forever after.

CHAPTER XXV.

HOW DISCUSSION WAXES RIFE—AND HOW NICHOLAS, HAVING MADE A SUGGESTION THAT IS BITTER TO THE EARS OF HIS AUDIENCE, YET CARRIES HIS POINT AGAINST ALL OPPOSITION.

"The day is done, and the darkness falls from the wings of night." The dusk is slowly creeping up over all the land, the twilight is coming on apace. As the day was, so is the gathering eve, sad and mournful, with sounds of rain and sobbings of swift winds as they rush through the barren beeches in the grove. The harbor bar is moaning many miles away, yet its voice is borne by rude Boreas up from the bay to the walls of the stately Towers, that neither rock nor shiver before the charges of this violent son of "imperial Æolus."

There is a ghostly tapping (as of some departed spirit who would fain enter once again into the old halls so long forgotten) against the window pane. Doubtless it is some waving branch flung hither and thither by the cruel tempest that rages without. Shadows come and go; and eerie thoughts oppress the breast:—

"Whilst the scritch-owl, scritching loud,Puts the wretch that lies in woeIn remembrance of a shroud."

"What a wretched evening!" says Violet, with a little shiver. "Geoffrey, draw the curtains closer."

"A fit ending to a miserable day," says Lady Rodney, gloomily.

"Night has always the effect of making bad look worse," says Doatie with a sad attempt at cheerfulness. "Never mind; morning will soon be here again."

"But why should night produce melancholy?" says Nicholas, dreamily. "It is but a reflection of the greater light, after all. What does Richter call it? 'The great shadow and profile of day.' It is our own morbid fancies that make us dread it."

"Nevertheless, close the curtains, Geoffrey, and ask Lady Rodney if she would not like tea now," says Violet, *sotto voce.*

Somebody pokes the fire, until a crimson light streams through the room. The huge logs are good-naturedly inclined, and burst their great sides in an endeavor to promote more soothing thought.

"As things are so unsettled, Nicholas, perhaps we had better put off our dance," says Lady Rodney, presently. "It may only worry you, and distress us all."

"No. It will not worry me. Let us have our dance by all means," says Nicholas, recklessly. "Why should we cave in, in such hot haste? It will give us all something to think about. Why not get up tableaux? Our last were rather a success. And to represent Nero fiddling, whilst Rome was on fire, would be a very appropriate one for the present occasion."

He laughs a little as he says this, but there is no mirth in his laugh.

"Nicholas, come here," says Doatie, anxiously, from out the shadow in which she is sitting, somewhat away from the rest. And Nicholas, going to her finds comfort and grows calm again beneath the touch of the slim little fingers she slips into his beneath the cover of the friendly darkness, "I don't see why we shouldn't launch out into reckless extravagance now our time threatens to be so short," says Jack, moodily. "Let's us entertain our neighbors right royally before the end comes. Why not wind up like the pantomimes, with showers of gold and rockets and the gladsome noise of ye festive cracker?"

"What nonsense some people are capable of talking!" says Violet, with a little shrug.

"Well, why not?" says Captain Rodney, undaunted by this small snub. "It is far more difficult to talk than sense. Any fellow can do that. If I were to tell you that Nolly is sound asleep, and that if he lurches even half a degree more to the right he will presently be lost to sight among the glowing embers" (Nolly rouses himself with a start), "you would probably tell me I was a very silly fellow to waste breath over such a palpable fact, but it would be sense nevertheless. I hope I haven't disturbed you, Nolly? On such a night as this a severe scorching would perhaps be a thing to be desired."

"Thanks. I'll put it off for a night or two," says Nolly, sleepily.

"Besides, I don't believe I *was* talking nonsense," goes on Jack in an aggrieved tone. "My last speech had very little folly in it. I feel the time is fast approaching when we sha'n't have money even to meet our tailors' bills."

"'In the midst of life we are in debt,'" says Nolly, solemnly. Which is the best thing he could have said, as it makes them all laugh in spite of their pending misfortunes.

"Nolly is waking up. I am afraid we sha'n't have that *auto da fe*, after all," says Jack in a tone of rich disappointment. "I feel as if we are going to be done out of a good thing."

"What a day we're avin'," says Mr. Darling, disdaining to notice this puerile remark. "It's been pouring since early dawn. I feel right down cheap,—very nearly as depressed as when last night Nicholas stuck me down to dance with the Æsthetic."

"Lady Lilias Eaton, you mean?" asks Lady Rodney. "That reminds me we are bound to go over there to-morrow. At least, some of us."

"Mona must go," says Nicholas, quickly. "Lady Lilias made a point of it. You will go, Mona?"

"I should very much like to go," says Mona, gently, and with some eagerness. She has been sitting very quietly with her hands before her, hardly hearing what is passing around her,—lost, buried in thought.

"Poor infant! It is her first essay," says Nolly, pitifully.

"Wait till to-morrow evening, and see if you will feel as you do now. Your cheerful complaisance in this matter is much to be admired. And Nicholas should be grateful But I think you will find one dose of Lady Lilias and her ancient Briton sufficient for your lifetime."

"You used to be tremendous friends there at one time," says Geoffrey; "never out of the house."

"I used to stay there occasionally when old Lord Daintree was alive, if you mean that," says Nolly, meekly. "As far as I can recollect, I was always shipped there when naughty, or troublesome, or in the way at home; and as a rule I was always in the way. There is a connection between the Eatons and my mother, and Anadale saw a good deal of me off and on during the holidays. It was a sort of rod in pickle, or dark closet, that used to be held over my head when in disgrace."

"Lilias must have been quite a child then," says Lady Rodney.

"She was never a child: she was born quite grown up. But the ancient Britons had not come into favor at that time: so she was a degree more tolerable. Bless me," says Mr. Darling, with sudden animation, "what horrid times I put in there. The rooms were ghastly enough to freeze the blood in one's veins, and no candles would light 'em. The beds were all four-posters, with heavy curtains round them, so high that one had to get a small ladder to mount into bed. I remember one time—it was during harvest, and the mowers were about—I suggested to Lord Daintree he should get the men in to mow down the beds; but no one took any notice of my proposal, so it fell to the ground. I was frightened to death, and indeed was more in awe of the four-posters than of the old man, who wasn't perhaps half bad."

Dorothy from her corner laughs gayly. "Poor old Noll," she says: "it was his unhappy childhood that blighted his later years and made him the melancholy object he is."

"Well, you know, it was much too much,—it was really," says Mr. Darling, very earnestly. "Mrs. Geoffrey, won't you come to my rescue?".

Mrs. Geoffrey, thus addressed, rouses herself, and says, "What can I do for you?" in a far-away tone that proves she has been in thought-land miles away from every one. Through her brain some words are surging. Her mind has gone back to that scene in the conservatory last night when she and Paul Rodney had been together. What was it he had said? What were the exact words he had used? She lays two fingers on her smooth white brow, and lets a little frown—born only of bewildered thought—contract its fairness.

"A scheme," he had said; and then in a moment the right words flash across her brain. "A brilliant chance, a splendid scheme." What words for an honest man to use! Could he be honest? Was there any flaw, any damning clause anywhere in all this careful plot, so cleverly constructed to bring ruin upon the heads of these people who have crept into her tender heart?

"Where are you now, Mona?" asks Geoffrey, suddenly, laying his hand with a loving pressure on her shoulder. "In Afghanistan or Timbuctoo? Far from us, at least." There is a little vague reproach and uneasiness in his tone.

"No; very near you,—nearer than you think," says Mona, quick to notice any variation in his tone, awaking from her reverie with a start, and laying one of her hands over his. "Geoffrey," earnestly, "what is the exact meaning of the word 'scheme'? Would an honest man (surely he would not) talk of scheming?" Which absurd question only shows how unlearned she yet is in the great lessons of life.

"Well, that is rather a difficult question to answer," says Geoffrey. "Monsieur de Lesseps, when dreaming out the Suez Canal, called it a scheme; and he, I presume, is an honest man. Whereas, on the other side, if a burglar were arranging to steal all your old silver, I suppose he would call that a scheme too. What have you on the brain now, darling? You are not going to defraud your neighbor, I hope."

"It is very strange," says Mona, with a dissatisfied sigh, "but I'll tell you all about it by and by."

Instinct warns her of treachery; common sense belies the warning. To which shall she give ear?

"Shall we ask the Carsons to our dance, Nicholas?" asks his mother, at this moment.

"Ask any one you like,—any one, I mean, that is not quite impossible," says Nicholas.

"Edith Carson is very nearly so, I think."

"Is that the girl who spoke to you, Geoffrey, at the tea room door?" asks Mona, with some animation.

"Yes. Girl with light, frizzy hair and green eye."

"A strange girl, I thought, but very pretty. Yes—was it English she talked?"

"Of the purest," says Geoffrey.

"What did she say, Mona?" inquired Doatie.

"I am not sure that I can tell you,—at least not exactly as she said it," says Mona, with hesitation. "I didn't quite understand her; but Geoffrey asked her how she was enjoying herself, and she said it was 'fun all through;' and that she was amusing herself just then by hiding from her partner, Captain Dunscombe, who was hunting for her 'all over the shop,'—it was 'shop,' she said, wasn't it, Geoff? And that it did her good to see him in a tearing rage, in fact on a regular 'champ,' because it vexed Tricksy Newcombe, whose own particular he was in the way of 'pals.'"

Everybody laughs. In fact, Nolly roars.

"Did she stop there?" he says: "that was unworthy of her. Breath for once must have failed her, as nothing so trivial as want of words could have influenced Miss Carson."

"You should have seen Mona," says Geoffrey. "She opened her eyes and her lips, and gazed fixedly upon the lively Edith. Curiosity largely mingled with awe depicted itself upon her expressive countenance. She was wondering whether she should have to conquer that extraordinary jargon before being pronounced fit for polite society."

"No, indeed," says Mona, laughing. "But it surely wasn't English, was it? That is not the way everybody talks, surely."

"Everybody," says Geoffrey; "that is, all specially nice people. You won't be in the swim at all, unless you take to that sort of thing."

"Then you are not a nice person yourself."

"I am far from it, I regret to say; but time cures all things, and I trust to that and careful observation to reform me."

"And I am to say 'pals' for friends, and call it pure English?"

"It is not more extraordinary, surely, than calling a drunken young man 'tight,'" says Lady Rodney, with calm but cruel meaning.

Mona blushes painfully.

"Well, no; but that is pure Irish," says Geoffrey, unmoved. Mona, with lowered head, turns her wedding-ring round and round upon her finger, and repents bitterly that little slip of hers when talking with the duchess last night.

"If I must ask Edith Carson, I shall feel I am doing something against my will," says Lady Rodney.

"We have all to do that at times," says Sir Nicholas. "And there is another person, mother, I shall be glad if you will send a card to."

"Certainly dear. Who is it?"

"Paul Rodney," replies he, very distinctly.

"Nicholas!" cries his mother, faintly: "this is too much!"

"Nevertheless, to oblige me," entreats he, hastily.

"But this is morbid,—a foolish pride," protests she, passionately, while all the others are struck dumb at this suggestion from Nicholas. Is his brain failing? Is his intellect growing weak, that he should propose such a thing? Even Doatie, who as a rule supports Nicholas through evil report and good, sits silent and aghast at his proposition.

"What has he done that he should be excluded?" demands Nicholas, a little excitedly. "If he can prove a first right to claim this property, is that a crime? He is our cousin: why should we be the only people in the whole countryside to treat him with contempt? He has committed no violation of the law, no vile sin has been laid to his charge beyond this fatal one of wanting his own— and—and———"

He pauses. In the darkness a loving, clinging hand has again crept into his, full of sweet entreaty, and by a gentle pressure has reduced him to calmness.

"Ask him, if only to please me," he says, wearily.

"Everything shall be just as you wish it, dearest," says his mother, with unwonted tenderness, and then silence falls upon them all.

The fire blazes up fiercely, and anon drops its flame and sinks into insignificance once more. Again the words that bear some vague but as yet undiscovered meaning haunt Mona's brain. "A splendid scheme." A vile conspiracy, perhaps. Oh, that she might be instrumental in saving these people from ruin, among whom her lot had been cast! But how weak her arm! How insufficient her mind to cope with an emergency like this!

CHAPTER XXVI.

HOW MONA GOES TO ANADALE—AND HOW SHE THERE SEES MANY THINGS AS YET TO HER UNKNOWN.

About half-past two next day they start for Anadale. Not Violet, or Captain Rodney, who have elected to go on a mission of their own, nor Nicholas, who has gone up to London.

The frost lies heavy on the ground; the whole road, and every bush and tree, sparkle brilliantly, as though during the hours when darkness lay upon the earth the dread daughter of Chaos, as she traversed the expanse of the firmament in her ebony chariot, had dropped heaven's diamonds upon the land. The wintry sunshine lighting them up makes soft and glorious the midday.

The hour is enchanting, the air almost mild; and every one feels half aggrieved when the carriage, entering the lodge-gates, bears them swiftly towards the massive entrance that will lead them into the house and out of the cold.

But before they reach the hall door Geoffrey feels it his duty to bestow upon them a word or two of warning.

"Now, look here," he says, impressively: "I hope nobody is going to indulge in so much as a covert smile to-day." He glances severely at Nolly, who is already wreathed in smiles. "Because the Æsthetic won't have it. She wouldn't hear of it at any price. We must all be in tense! If you don't understand what that means, Mona, you had better learn at once. You are to be silent, rapt, lifted far above all the vulgar commonplaces of life. You may, if you like, go into a rapture over a colorless pebble, or shed tears of joy above a sickly lily; but avoid ordinary admiration."

"The only time I shed tears," says Mr. Darling, irrelevantly, "for many years, was when I heard of the old chap's death. And they were drops of rich content. Do you know I think unconsciously he impregnated her with her present notions; because he was as like an 'ancient Briton' himself before he died as if he had posed for it."

"He was very eccentric, but quite correct," says Lady Rodney, reprovingly.

"He was a man who never took off his hat," begins Geoffrey.

"But why?" asks Mona, in amaze. "Didn't he wear one?"

"Yes, but he always doffed it; and he never put one on like ordinary mortals, he always donned it. You can't think what a difference it makes."

"What a silly boy you are, Geoff!" says his wife, laughing.

"Thank you, darling," replies he, meekly.

"But what is Lady Lilias like? I did not notice her the other night," says Mona.

"She has got one nose and two eyes, just like every one else," says Nolly. "That is rather disappointing, is it not? And she attitudinizes a good deal. Sometimes she reclines full length upon the grass, with her bony elbow well squared and her chin buried in her palm. Sometimes she stands beside a sundial, with her head to one side, and a carefully educated and very much superannuated peacock beside her. But I dare say she will do the greyhound pose to-day. In summer she goes abroad with a huge wooden fan with which she kills the bumble-bee as it floats by her. And she gowns herself in colors that make one's teeth on edge. I am sure it is her one lifelong regret that she must clothe herself at all, as she has dreams of savage nakedness and a liberal use of the fetching woad."

"My dear Oliver!" protests Lady Rodney, mildly.

"If she presses refreshments on you, Mona, say, 'No, thank you,' without hesitation," says Geoffrey, with anxious haste, seeing they are drawing near their journey's end. "Because if you don't she will compel you to partake of metheglin and unleavened bread, which means sudden death. Forewarned is forearmed. Nolly and I have done what we can for you."

"Is she by herself? Is there nobody living with her?" asks Mona, somewhat nervously.

"Well, practically speaking, no. But I believe she has a sister somewhere."

"'Sister Anne,' you mean?" says Nolly. "Oh, ay! I have seen her, though as a rule she is suppressed. She is quite all she ought to be, and irreproachable in every respect—unapproachable, according to some. She is a very good girl, and never misses a Saint's Day by any chance, never eats meat on Friday, or butter in Lent, and always confesses. But she is not of much account in the household, being averse to 'ye goode olde times.'"

At this point the house comes in view, and conversation languishes. The women give a small touch to their furs and laces, the men indulge in a final yawn that is to last them until the gates of Anadale close behind them again.

"There is no moat, and no drawbridge, and no eyelet-hole through which to spy upon the advance of the enemy," says Darling, in an impressive whisper, just as they turn the curve that leads into the big gravel sweep before the hall door. "A drawback, I own; but even the very greatest are not infallible."

It is a lovely old castle, ancient and timeworn, with turrets rising in unexpected places, and walls covered with drooping ivy, and gables dark with age.

A terrace runs all along one side of the house, which is exposed to view from the avenue. And here, with a gaunt but handsome greyhound beside her, stands a girl tall and slim, yet beautifully moulded. Her eyes are gray, yet might at certain moments be termed blue. Her mouth is large, but not unpleasing. Her hair is quite dark, and drawn back into a loose and artistic coil behind. She is clad in an impossible gown of sage green, that clings closely to her slight figure, nay, almost desperately, as though afraid to lose her.

One hand is resting lightly with a faintly theatrical touch upon the head of the lean greyhound, the other is raised to her forehead as though to shield her eyes from the bright sun.

Altogether she is a picture, which, if slightly suggestive of artificiality, is yet very nearly perfection. Mona is therefore agreeably surprised, and, being— as all her nation is—susceptible to outward beauty, feels drawn towards this odd young woman in sickly green, with her canine friend beside her.

Lady Lilias, slowly descending the stone steps with the hound Egbert behind her, advances to meet Lady Rodney. She greets them all with a solemn cordiality that impresses everybody but Mona, who is gazing dreamily into the gray eyes of her hostess and wondering vaguely if her lips have ever smiled. Her hostess in return is gazing at her, perhaps in silent admiration of her soft loveliness.

"You will come first and see Philippa?" she says, in a slow peculiar tone that sounds as if it had been dug up and is quite an antique in its own way. It savors of dust and feudal days. Every one says he or she will be delighted, and all try to look as if the entire hope of their existence is centred in the thought that they shall soon lay longing eyes on Philippa,—whose name in reality is Anne, but who has been rechristened by her enterprising sister. Anne is all very well for everyday life, or for Bluebeard's sister-in-law; but Philippa is art of the very highest description. So Philippa she is, poor soul, whether she likes it or not.

She has sprained her ancle, and is now lying on a couch in a small drawing room as the Rodneys are ushered in. She is rather glad to see them, as life with an "intense" sister is at times trying, and the ritualistic curate is from home. So she smiles upon them, and manages to look as amiable as plain people ever can look.

The drawing-room is very much the same as the ordinary run of drawing-rooms, at which Mona feels distinct disappointment, until, glancing at Lady Lilias, she notices a shudder of disgust run through her frame.

"I really cannot help it," she explains to Mona, in her usual slow voice, "it all offends me so. But Philippa must be humored. All these glaring colors and hideous pieces of furniture take my breath away. And the light——By and by you must come to some of my rooms; but first, if you are not tired, I should like you to look at my garden; that is, if you can endure the cold."

They don't want to endure the cold; but what can they say? Politeness forbids secession of any kind, and, after a few words with the saintly Philippa, they follow their guide in all meekness through halls and corridors out into the garden she most affects.

And truly it is a very desirable garden, and well worth a visit. It is like a thought from another age.

Yew-trees—grown till they form high walls—are cut and shaped in prim and perfect order, some like the walls of ancient Troy, some like steps of stairs. Little doors are opened through them, and passing in and out one walks on for a mile almost, until one loses one's way and grows puzzled how to extricate one's self from so charming a maze.

Here and there are basins of water on which lilies can lie and sleep dreamily through a warm and sunny day. A sundial, old and green with honorable age, uprears itself upon a chilly bit of sward. Near it lie two gaudy peacocks sound asleep. All seems far from the world, drowsy, careless, indifferent to the weals and woes of suffering humanity.

"It is like the garden of the palace where the Sleeping Beauty dwelt," whispers Mona to Nolly; she is delighted, charmed, lost in admiration.

"You are doing it beautifully: keep it up," whispers he back: "she'll give you something nice if you sustain that look for five minutes longer. Now!—she is looking; hurry—make haste—put it on again!"

"I am not pretending," says Mona, indignantly; "I am delighted: it is the most enchanting place I ever saw. Really lovely."

"I didn't think it was in you," declares Mr. Darling, with wild but suppressed admiration. "You would make your fortune on the stage. Keep it up, I tell you; it couldn't be better."

"Is it possible you see nothing to admire?" says Mona, with intense disgust.

"I do. More than I can express. I see you," retorts he; at which they both give way to merriment, causing Geoffrey, who is walking with Lady Lilias, to dodge behind her back and bestow upon them an annihilating glance that Nolly afterwards describes as a "lurid glare."

The hound stalks on before them; the peacocks wake up and rend the air with a discordant scream. Lady Lilias, coming to the sundial, leans her arm upon it, and puts her head in the right position. A snail slowly travelling across a broad ivy-leaf attracts her attention; she lifts it slowly, leaf and all, and directs attention to the silvery trail it has left behind it.

"How tender! how touching!" she says, with a pensive smile, raising her luminous eyes to Geoffrey: whether it is the snail, or the leaf, or the slime, that is tender and touching, nobody knows; and nobody dares ask, lest he shall betray his ignorance. Nolly, I regret to say, gives way to emotion of a frivolous kind, and to cover it blows his nose sonorously. Whereupon Geoffrey, who is super-naturally grave, asks Lady Lilias if she will walk with him as far as the grotto.

"How could you laugh?" says Mona, reproachfully.

"How couldn't I?" replies he. "Come; let us follow it up to the bitter end."

"I never saw anything so clean as the walks," says Mona, presently: "there is not a leaf or a weed to be seen, yet we have gone through so many of them. How does she manage it?"

"Don't you know?" says Mr. Darling, mysteriously. "It is a secret, but I know you can be trusted. Every morning early she has them carefully swept, with tea-leaves to keep down the dust, and if the tea is strong it kills the weeds."

Then they do the grotto, and then Lady Lilias once more leads the way indoors.

"I want you to see my own work," she says, going up markedly to Mona. "I am glad my garden has pleased you. I could see by your eyes how well you appreciated it. To see the beautiful in everything, that is the only true religion." She smiles her careful absent smile again as she says this, and gazes earnestly at Mona. Perhaps, being true to her religion, she is noting "the beautiful" in her Irish guest.

With Philippa they have some tea, and then again follow their indefatigable hostess to a distant apartment that seems more or less to jut out from the house, and was in olden days a tiny chapel or oratory.

It has an octagon chamber of the most uncomfortable description, but no doubt artistic, and above all praise, according to some lights. To outsiders it presents a curious appearance, and might by the unlearned be regarded as a jumble of all ages, a make-up of objectionable bits from different centuries; but to Lady Lilias and her sympathizers it is simply perfection.

The furniture is composed of oak of the hardest and most severe. To sit down would be a labor of anything but love. The chairs are strictly Gothic. The table is a marvel in itself for ugliness and in utility.

There are no windows; but in their place are four unpleasant slits about two yards in length, let into the thick walls at studiously unequal distances. These are filled up with an opaque substance that perhaps in the Middle Ages was called glass.

There is no grate, and the fire, which has plainly made up its mind not to light, is composed of Yule-logs. The floor is shining with sand, rushes having palled on Lady Lilias.

Mona is quite pleased. All is new, which in itself is a pleasure to her, and the sanded floor carries her back on the instant to the old parlor at home, which was their "best" at the Farm.

"This is nicer than anything," she says, turning in a state of childish enthusiasm to Lady Lilias. "It is just like the floor in my uncle's house at home."

"Ah! indeed! How interesting!" says Lady Lilias, rousing into something that very nearly borders on animation. "I did not think there was in England another room like this."

"Not in England, perhaps. When I spoke I was thinking of Ireland," says Mona.

"Yes?" with calm surprise. "I—I have heard of Ireland, of course. Indeed, I regard the older accounts of it as very deserving of thought; but I had no idea the more elevated aspirations of modern times had spread so far. So this room reminds you of—your uncle's?"

"Partly," says Mona. "Not altogether: there was always a faint odor of pipes about Uncle Brian's room that does not belong to this."

"Ah! Tobacco! First introduced by Sir Walter Raleigh," murmurs Lady Lilias, musingly. "Too modern, but no doubt correct and in keeping. Your uncle, then,"—looking at Mona,—"is beyond question an earnest student of our faith."

"A—student?" says Mona, in a degree puzzled.

Doatie and Geoffrey have walked to a distant slit. Nolly is gazing vacantly through another, trying feebly to discern the landscape beyond. Lady Rodney is on thorns. They are all listening to what Mona is going to say next.

"Yes. A disciple, a searcher after truth," goes on Lady Lilias, in her Noah's Ark tone. "By a student I mean one who studies, and arrives at perfection—in time."

"I don't quite know," says Mona, slowly, "but what Uncle Brian principally studies is—pigs!"

"Pigs!" repeats Lady Lilias, plainly taken aback.

"Yes; pigs!" says Mona, sweetly.

There is a faint pause,—so faint that Lady Rodney is unable to edge in the saving clause she would fain have uttered. Lady Lilias, recovering with wonderful spirit from so severe a blow, comes once more boldly to the front. She taps her white taper fingers lightly on the table near her, and says, apologetically,—the apology being meant for herself,—

"Forgive me that I showed surprise. Your uncle is more advanced than I had supposed. He is right. Why should a pig be esteemed less lovely than a stag? Nature in its entirety can know no blemish. The fault lies with us. We are creatures of habit: we have chosen to regard the innocent pig as a type of ugliness for generations, and now find it difficult to see any beauty in it."

"Well; there isn't much, is there?" says Mona, pleasantly.

"No doubt education, and a careful study of the animal in question, might betray much to us," says Lady Lilias. "We object to the uncovered hide of the pig, and to his small eyes; but can they not see as well as those of the fawn, or the delicate lapdog we fondle all day on our knees? It is unjust that one animal should be treated with less regard than another."

"But you couldn't fondle a pig on your knees," says Mona, who is growing every minute more and more mixed.

"No, no; but it should be treated with courtesy. We were speaking of the size of its eyes. Why should they be despised? Do we not often in our ignorance and narrow mindedness cling to paltry things and ignore the truly great? The tiny diamond that lies in the hollow of our hands is dear and precious in our sight, whilst we fail to find beauty in the huge boulder that is after all far more worthy of regard, with its lights and shades, its grand ruggedness, and the soft vegetable matter that decks its aged sides, rendering their roughness beautiful."

Here she gets completely out of her depths, and stops to consider from whence this train of thought sprung. The pig is forgotten,—indeed, to get from pigs to diamonds and back again is not an easy matter,—and has to be searched for again amidst the dim recesses of her brain, and if possible brought to the surface.

She draws up her tall figure to its utmost height, and gazes at the raftered ceiling to see if inspiration can be drawn from thence. But it fails her.

"You were talking of pigs," says Mona, gently.

"Ah! so I was," says Lady Lilias, with a sigh of relief: she is quite too intense to feel any of the petty vexations of ordinary mortals, and takes Mona's help in excellent part. "Yes, I really think there is loveliness in a pig when surrounded by its offspring. I have seen them once or twice, and I think the little pigs—the—the——"

"Bonuvs," says Mona, mildly, going back naturally to the Irish term for those interesting babies.

"Eh?" says Lady Lilias.

"Bonuvs," repeats Mona, a little louder, at which Lady Rodney sinks into a chair, as though utterly overcome. Nolly and Geoffrey are convulsed with laughter. Doatie is vainly endeavoring to keep them in order.

"Oh, is that their name?—a pretty one too—if—er—somewhat difficult," says Lady Lilias, courteously. "Well as I was saying, in spite of their tails, they really are quite pretty."

At this Mona laughs unrestrainedly; and Lady Rodney, rising hurriedly, says,—

"Dear Lady Lilias, I think we have at last nearly taken in all the beauties of your charming room. I fear," with much suavity, "we must be going."

"Oh, not yet," says Lady Lilias, with the nearest attempt at youthfulness she has yet made. "Mrs. Rodney has not half seen all my treasures."

Mrs. Rodney, however, has been foraging on her own account during this brief interlude, and now brings triumphantly to light a little basin filled with early snowdrops.

"Snowdrops,—and so soon," she says, going up to Lady Lilias, and looking quite happy over her discovery. "We have none yet at the Towers."

"Yes, they are pretty, but insignificant," says the Æsthete, contemptuously. "Paltry children of the earth, not to be compared with the lenten or the tiger lily, or the fiercer beauty of the sunflower, or the hues of the unsurpassable thistle!"

"I am very ignorant I know," says Mrs. Geoffrey, with her sunny smile, "but I think I should prefer a snowdrop to a thistle."

"You have not gone into it," says Lady Lilias, regretfully. "To you Nature is as yet a blank. The exquisite purple of the stately thistle, that by the scoffer is called dull, is not understood by you. Nor does your heart swell beneath the influence of the rare and perfect green of its leaves, which doubtless the untaught deemed soiled. To fully appreciate the yieldings and gifts of earth is a power given only to some." She bows her head, feeling a modest pride in the thought that she belongs to the happy "some." "Ignorance," she says, sorrowfully, "is the greatest enemy of our cause."

"I am afraid you must class me with the ignorant," says Mona, shaking her pretty head. "I know nothing at all about thistles, except that donkeys love them!"

Is this, *can* this be premeditated, or is it a fatal slip of the tongue? Lady Rodney turns pale, and even Geoffrey and Nolly stand aghast. Mona alone is smiling unconcernedly into Lady Lilias's eyes, and Lady Lilias, after a brief second, smiles back at her. It is plain the severe young woman in the sage-green gown has not even noticed the dangerous remark.

"You must come again very soon to see me," she says to Mona, and then goes with her all along the halls and passages, and actually stands upon the door-steps until they drive away. And Mona kisses hands gayly to her as they turn the corner of the avenue, and then tells Geoffrey that she thinks he has been very hard on Lady Lilias, because, though she is plainly quite mad, poor thing, there is certainly nothing to be disliked about her.

CHAPTER XXVII.

HOW MONA TAKES A WALK ABROAD—AND HOW SHE ASKS CROSS-QUESTIONS AND RECEIVES CROOKED ANSWERS.

It is ten days later,—ten dreary, interminable days, that have struggled into light, and sunk back again into darkness, leaving no trace worthy of remembrance in their train. "Swift as swallows' wings" they have flown, scarce breaking the air in their flight, so silently, so evenly they have departed, as days will, when dull monotony marks them for its own.

To-day is cool, and calm, and bright. Almost one fancies the first faint breath of spring has touched one's cheek, though as yet January has not wended to its weary close, and no smallest sign of growth or vegetation makes itself felt.

The grass is still brown, the trees barren, no ambitious floweret thrusts its head above the bosom of its mother earth,—except, indeed, those "floures white and rede, such as men callen daisies," that always seem to beam upon the world, no matter how the wind blows.

Just now it is blowing softly, delicately, as though its fury of the night before had been an hallucination of the brain. It is "a sweet and passionate wooer," says Longfellow, and lays siege to "the blushing leaf." There are no leaves for it to kiss to-day: so it bestows its caresses upon Mona as she wanders forth, close guarded by her two stanch hounds that follow at her heels.

There is a strange hush and silence everywhere. The very clouds are motionless in their distant homes.

"There has not been a sound to-dayTo break the calm of Nature:Nor motion, I might almost say,Of life, or living creature,Of waving bough, or warbling bird,Or cattle faintly lowing:I could have half believed I heardThe leaves and blossoms growing."

Indeed, no sound disturbs the sacred silence save the crisp rustle of the dead leaves, as they are trodden into the ground.

Over the meadows and into the wood goes Mona, to where a streamlet runs, that is her special joy,—being of the garrulous and babbling order, which is, perhaps, the nearest approach to divine music that nature can make. But to-day the stream is swollen, is enlarged beyond all recognition, and, being filled with pride at its own promotion, has forgotten its little loving song, and is rushing onward with a passionate roar to the ocean.

Down from the cataract in the rocks above the water comes with a mighty will, foaming, glistening, shouting a loud triumphant paen as it flings itself into the arms of the vain brook beneath, that only yesterday-eve was a stream, but to-day may well be deemed a river.

Up high the rocks are overgrown with ferns, and drooping things, all green and feathery, that hide small caves and picturesque crannies, through which the bright-eyed Naiads might peep whilst holding back with bare uplifted arms their amber hair, the better to gaze upon the unconscious earth outside.

A loose stone that has fallen from its home in the mountain-side above uprears itself in the middle of this turbulent stream. But it is too far from the edge, and Mona, standing irresolutely on the brink, pauses, as though half afraid to take the step that must either land her safely on the other side or else precipitate her into the angry little river.

As she thus ponders within herself, Spice and Allspice, the two dogs, set up a simultaneous howl, and immediately afterwards a voice says, eagerly,—

"Wait, Mrs. Rodney. Let me help you across."

Mona starts, and, looking up, sees the Australian coming quickly towards her.

"You are very kind. The river is greatly swollen," she says, to gain time. Geoffrey, perhaps, will not like her to accept any civility at the hands of this common enemy.

"Not so much so that I cannot help you to cross over in safety, if you will only trust yourself to me," replies he.

Still she hesitates, and he is not slow to notice the eloquent pause.

"Is it worth so much thought?" he says, bitterly. "It surely will not injure you fatally to lay your hand in mine for one instant."

"You mistake me," says Mona, shocked at her own want of courtesy; and then she extends to him her hand, and, setting her foot upon the huge stone, springs lightly to his side.

Once there she has to go with him down the narrow woodland path, there being no other, and so paces on, silently, and sorely against her will.

"Sir Nicholas has sent me an invitation for the 19th," he says, presently, when the silence has become unendurable.

"Yes," says Mona, devoutly hoping he is going to say he means to refuse it. But such devout hope is wasted.

"I shall go," he says, doggedly, as though divining her secret wish.

"I am sure we shall all be very glad," she says, faintly, feeling herself bound to make some remark.

"Thanks!" returns he, with an ironical laugh. "How excellently your tone agrees with your words?"

Another pause. Mona is on thorns. Will the branching path, that may give her a chance of escaping a further *tete-a-tete* with him, never be reached?

"So Warden failed you?" he says, presently, alluding to old Elspeth's nephew.

"Yes,—so far," returns she, coldly.

"It was a feeble effort," declares he, contemptuously striking with his cane the trunks of the trees as he goes by them.

"Yet I think Warden knows more than he cares to tell," says Mona, at a venture. Why, she herself hardly knows.

He turns, as though by an irrepressible impulse, to look keenly at her. His scrutiny endures only for an instant. Then he says, with admirable indifference,—

"You have grounds for saying so, of course?"

"Perhaps I have. Do you deny I am in the right?" asks she, returning his gaze undauntedly.

He drops his eyes, and the low, sneering laugh she has learned to know and to hate so much comes again to his lips.

"It would be rude to deny that," he says, with a slight shrug. "I am sure you are always in the right."

"If I am, Warden surely knows more about the will than he has sworn to."

"It is very probable,—if there ever was such a will. How should I know? I have not cross-examined Warden on this or any other subject. He is an overseer over my estate, a mere servant, nothing more."

"Has he the will?" asks Mona, foolishly, but impulsively.

"He may have, and a stocking full of gold, and the roc's egg, or anything else, for aught I know. I never saw it. They tell me there was an iniquitous and most unjust will drawn up some years ago by old Sir George: that is all I know."

"By your grandfather!" corrects Mona, in a peculiar tone.

"Well, by my grandfather, if you so prefer it," repeats he, with much unconcern. "It got itself, if it ever existed, irretrievably lost, and that is all any one knows about it."

Mona is watching him intently.

"Yet I feel sure—I know," she says, tremulously, "you are hiding something from me. Why do you not look at me when you answer my questions?"

At this his dark face flames, and his eyes instinctively, yet almost against his will, seek hers.

"Why?" he says, with suppressed passion. "Because, each time I do, I know myself to be—what I am! Your truthful eyes are mirrors in which my heart lies bare." With an effort he recovers himself, and, drawing his breath quickly, grows calm again. "If I were to gaze at you as often as I should desire, you would probably deem me impertinent," he says, with a lapse into his former half-insolent tone.

"Answer me," persists Mona, not heeding—nay, scarcely hearing—his last speech. "You said once it would be difficult to lie to me. Do you know anything of this missing will?"

"A great deal. I should. I have heard of almost nothing else since my arrival in England," replies he, slowly.

"Ah! Then you refuse to answer me," says Mona, hastily, if somewhat wearily.

He makes no reply. And for a full minute no word is spoken between them.

Then Mona goes on quietly,—

"That night at Chetwoode you made use of some words that I have never forgotten since."

He is plainly surprised. He is indeed glad. His face changes, as if by magic, from sullen gloom to pleasurable anticipation.

"You have remembered something that I said, for eleven days?" he says, quickly.

"Yes. When talking then of supplanting Sir Nicholas at the Towers, you spoke of your project as a 'splendid scheme.' What did you mean by it? I cannot get the words out of my head since. Is 'scheme' an honest word?"

Her tone is only too significant. His face has grown black again. A heavy frown sits on his brow.

"You are not perhaps aware of it, but your tone is insulting," he begins, huskily. "Were you a man I could give you an answer, now, here; but as it is I am of course tied hand and foot. You can say to me what you please. And I shall bear it. Think as badly of me as you will. I am a schemer, a swindler, what you will!"

"Even in my thoughts I never applied those words to you," says Mona, earnestly. "Yet some feeling here"—laying her hand upon her heart—

"compels me to believe you are not dealing fairly by us." To her there is untruth in every line of his face, in every tone of his voice.

"You condemn me without a hearing, swayed by the influence of a carefully educated dislike," retorts he:

"'Alas for the rarityOf Christian charityUnder the sun!'

But I blame the people you have fallen among,—not you."

"Blame no one," says Mona. "But if there is anything in your own heart to condemn you, then pause before you go further in this matter of the Towers."

"I wonder *you* are not afraid of going too far," he puts in, warningly, his dark eyes flashing.

"I am afraid of nothing," says Mona, simply. "I am not half so much afraid as you were a few moments since, when you could not let your eyes meet mine, and when you shrank from answering me a simple question. In my turn I tell you to pause before going too far."

"Your advice is excellent," says he, sneeringly. Then suddenly he stops short before her, and breaks out vehemently,——

"Were I to fling up this whole business and resign my chance, and leave these people in possession, what would I gain by it?" demands he. "They have treated me from the beginning with ignominy and contempt. You alone have treated me with common civility; and even you they have tutored to regard me with averted eyes."

"You are wrong," says Mona, coldly. "They seldom trouble themselves to speak of you at all." This is crueller than she knows.

"Why don't I hate you?" he says, with some emotion. "How bitterly unkind even the softest, sweetest women can be! Yet there is something about you that subdues me and renders hatred impossible. If I had never met you, I should be a happier man."

"How can you be happy with a weight upon your heart?" says Mona, following out her own thoughts irrespective of his. "Give up this project, and peace will return to you."

"No, I shall pursue it to its end," returns, he, with slow malice, that makes her heart grow cold, "until the day comes that shall enable me to plant my heel upon these aristocrats and crush them out of recognition."

"And after that what will remain to you?" asks she, pale but collected. "It is bare comfort when hatred alone reigns in the heart. With such thoughts in your breast what can you hope for?—what can life give you?"

"Something," replies he, with a short laugh. "I shall at least see you again on the 19th."

He raises his hat, and, turning abruptly away, is soon lost to sight round a curve in the winding pathway. He walks steadily and with an unflinching air, but when the curve has hidden him from her eyes he stops short, and sighs heavily.

"To love such a woman as that, and be beloved by her, how it would change a man's whole nature, no matter how low he may have sunk," he says, slowly. "It would mean salvation! But as it is—No, I cannot draw back now: it is too late."

Meantime Mona has gone quickly back to the Towers her mind disturbed and unsettled. Has she misjudged him? is it possible that his claim is a just one after all, and that she has been wrong in deeming him one who might defraud his neighbor?

She is sad and depressed before she reaches the hall door, where she is unfortunate enough to find a carriage just arrived, well filled with occupants eager to obtain admission.

They are the Carsons, mustered in force, and, if anything, a trifle more noisy and oppressive than usual.

"How d'ye do, Mrs. Rodney? Is Lady Rodney at home? I hope so," says Mrs. Carson, a fat, florid, smiling, impossible person of fifty.

Now, Lady Rodney *is* at home, but, having given strict orders to the servants to say she is anywhere else they like,—that is, to tell as many lies as will save her from intrusion,—is just now reposing calmly in the small drawing-room, sleeping the sleep of the just, unmindful of coming evil.

Of all this Mona is unaware; though even were it otherwise I doubt if a lie could come trippingly to her lips, or a nice evasion be balanced there at a moment's notice. Such foul things as untruths are unknown to her, and have no refuge in her heart. It is indeed fortunate that on this occasion she knows no reason why her reply should differ from the truth, because in that case I think she would stand still, and stammer sadly, and grow uncomfortably red, and otherwise betray the fact that she would lie if she knew how.

As things are, however, she is able to smile pleasantly at Mrs. Carson, and tell her in her soft voice that Lady Rodney is at home.

"How fortunate!" says that fat woman, with her broad expansive grin that leaves her all mouth, with no eyes or nose to speak of. "We hardly dared hope for such good luck this charming day."

She doesn't put any *g* into her "charming," which, however, is neither here or there, and is perhaps a shabby thing to take notice of at all.

Then she and her two daughters quit the "coach," as Carson *pere* insist on calling the landau, and flutter through the halls, and across the corridors, after Mona, until they reach the room that contains Lady Rodney.

Mona throws open the door, and the visitors sail in, all open-eyed and smiling, with their very best company manners hung out for the day.

But almost on the threshold they come to a full stop to gaze irresolutely at one another, and then over their shoulders at Mona. She, marking their surprise, comes hastily to the front, and so makes herself acquainted with the cause of their delay.

Overcome by the heat of the fire, her luncheon, and the blessed certainty that for this one day at least no one is to be admitted to her presence, Lady Rodney has given herself up a willing victim to the child Somnus. Her book—that amiable assistant of all those that court siestas—has fallen to the ground. Her cap is somewhat awry. Her mouth is partly open, and a snore—gentle, indeed, but distinct and unmistakable—comes from her patrician throat.

It is a moment never to be forgotten!

Mona, horror-stricken, goes quickly over to her, and touches her lightly on the shoulder.

"Mrs. Carson has come to see you," she says, in an agony of fear, giving her a little shake.

"Eh? What?" asks Lady Rodney, in a dazed fashion, yet coming back to life with amazing rapidity. She sits up. Then in an instant the situation explains itself to her; she collects herself, bestows one glance of passionate anger upon Mona, and then rises to welcome Mrs. Carson with her usual suave manner and bland smile, throwing into the former an air meant to convey the flattering idea that for the past week she has been living on the hope of seeing her soon again.

She excuses her unwonted drowsiness with a little laugh, natural and friendly, and begs them "not to betray her." Clothed in all this sweetness she drops a word or two meant to crush Mona; but that hapless young woman hears her not, being bent on explaining to Mrs. Carson that, as a rule, the Irish peasantry do not go about dressed only in glass beads, like the gay and festive Zulus, and that petticoats and breeches are not utterly unknown.

This is tough work, and takes her all her time, as Mrs. Carson, having made up her mind to the beads, accepts it rather badly being undeceived, and goes nearly so far as telling Mona that she knows little or nothing about her own people.

Then Violet and Doatie drop in, and conversation becomes general, and presently the visit comes to an end, and the Carsons fade away, and Mona is left to be bear the brunt of Lady Rodney's anger, which has been steadily growing, instead of decreasing, during the past half-hour.

"Are there no servants in my house," demands she, in a terrible tone, addressing Mona a steely light coming into her blue eyes that Mona knows and hates so well, "that you must feel it your duty to guide my visitors to my presence?"

"If I made a mistake I am sorry for it."

"It was unfortunate Mona should have met them at the hall door,—Edith Carson told me about it,—but it could not be helped," says Violet calmly.

"No, it couldn't be helped," says little Doatie. But their intervention only appears to add fuel to the fire of Lady Rodney's wrath.

"It *shall* be helped," she says, in a low, but condensed tone. "For the future I forbid any one in my house to take it upon them to say whether I am in or out. I am the one to decide that. On what principle did you show them in here?" she asks, turning to Mona, her anger increasing as she remembers the rakish cap: "why did you not say, when you were unlucky enough to find yourself face to face with them, that I was not at home?"

"Because you were at home," replies Mona, quietly, though in deep distress.

"That doesn't matter," says Lady Rodney: "it is a mere formula. If it suited your purpose you could have said so—I don't doubt—readily enough."

"I regret that I met them," says Mona, who will not say she regrets she told the truth.

"And to usher them in here! Into one of my most private rooms! Unlikely people, like the Carsons, whom you have heard me speak of in disparaging terms a hundred times! I don't know what you could have been thinking about. Perhaps next time you will be kind enough to bring them to my bedroom."

"You misunderstand me," says Mona, with tears in her eyes.

"I hardly think so. You can refuse to see people yourself when it suits you. Only yesterday, when Mr. Boer, our rector, called, and I sent for you, you would not come."

"I don't like Mr. Boer," says Mona, "and it was not me he came to see."

"Still, there was no necessity to insult him with such a message as you sent. Perhaps," with unpleasant meaning, "you do not understand that to say you are busy is rather more a rudeness than an excuse for one's non-appearance."

"It was true," says Mona: "I was writing letters for Geoffrey."

"Nevertheless, you might have waived that fact, and sent down word you had a headache."

"But I hadn't a headache," says Mona, bending her large truthful eyes with embarrassing earnestness upon Lady Rodney.

"Oh, if you were determined—" returns she, with a shrug.

"I was not determined: you mistake me," exclaims Mona, miserably. "I simply hadn't a headache: I never had one in my life,—and I shouldn't know how to get one!"

At this point, Geoffrey—who has been hunting all the morning—enters the room with Captain Rodney.

"Why, what is the matter?" he says, seeing signs of the lively storm on all their faces. Doatie explains hurriedly.

"Look here," says Geoffrey. "I won't have Mona spoiled. If she hadn't a headache, she hadn't, you know, and if you were at home, why, you were, and that's all about it. Why should she tell a lie about it?"

"What do you mean, Geoffrey?" demands his mother, with suppressed indignation.

"I mean that she shall remain just as she is. The world may be 'given to lying,' as Shakspeare tells us, but I will not have Mona tutored into telling fashionable falsehoods," says this intrepid young man facing his mother without a qualm of a passing dread. "A lie of any sort is base, and a prevarication is only a mean lie. She is truthful, let her stay so. Why should she learn it is the correct thing to say she is not at home when she is, or that she is suffering from a foolish megrim when she isn't? I don't suppose there is much harm in saying either of these things, as nobody ever believes them; but—let her remain as she is."

"Is she also to learn that you are at liberty to lecture your own mother?" asks Lady Rodney, pale with anger.

"I am not lecturing anyone," replies he, looking very like her, now that his face has whitened a little and a quick fire has lit itself within his eyes. "I am merely speaking against a general practice. 'Dare to be true: nothing can need a lie,' is a line that always returns to me. And, as I love Mona better than anything on earth, I shall make it the business of my life to see she is not made unhappy by any one."

At this Mona lifts her head, and turns upon him eyes full of the tenderest love and trust. She would have dearly liked to go to him, and place her arms round his neck, and thank him with a fond caress for this dear speech, but some innate sense of breeding restrains her.

Any demonstration on her part just now may make a scene, and scenes are ever abhorrent. And might she not yet further widen the breach between mother and son by an ill-timed show of affection for the latter?

"Still, sometimes, you know, it is awkward to adhere to the very letter of the law," says Jack Rodney, easily. "Is there no compromise? I have heard of women who have made a point of running into the kitchen-garden when unwelcome visitors were announced, and so saved themselves and their principles. Couldn't Mona do that?"

This speech is made much of, and laughed at for no reason whatever except that Violet and Doatie are determined to end the unpleasant discussion by any means, even though it may be at the risk of being deemed silly. After some careful management they get Mona out of the room, and carry her away with them to a little den off the eastern hall, that is very dear to them.

"It is the most unhappy thing I ever heard of," begins Doatie, desperately. "What Lady Rodney can see to dislike in you, Mona, I can't imagine. But the fact is, she is hateful to you. Now, we," glancing at Violet, "who are not particularly amiable, are beloved by her, whilst you, who are all 'sweetness and light,' she detests most heartily."

"It is true," says Violet, evenly. "Yet, dear Mona, I wish you could try to be a little more like the rest of the world."

"I want to very much," says poor Mona, her eyes filling with tears. "But," hopelessly, "must I begin by learning to tell lies?" All this teaching is very bitter to her.

"Lies! Oh, fie!" says Doatie. "Who tells lies? Nobody, except the naughty little boys in tracts, and they always break their legs off apple-trees, or else get drowned on a Sunday morning. Now, we are not drowned, and our legs are uninjured. No, a lie is a horrid thing,—so low, and in such wretched taste. But there are little social fibs that may be uttered,—little taradiddles,—that do no harm to anybody, and that nobody believes in, but all pretend to, just for the sake of politeness."

Thus Doatie, looking preternaturally wise, but faintly puzzled at her own view of the question.

"It doesn't sound right," says Mona, shaking her head.

"She doesn't understand," puts in Violet, quickly. "Mona, are you going to see everybody that may choose to call upon you, good, bad, and indifferent, from this till you die?"

"I suppose so," says Mona lifting her brows.

"Then I can only say I pity you," says Miss Mansergh, leaning back in her chair, with the air of one who would say, "Argument here is in vain."

"I sha'n't want to see them, perhaps," says Mona, apologetically, "but how shall I avoid it?"

"Ah, now, that is more reasonable; now we are coming to it," says Doatie, briskly. "We 'return to our muttons.' As Lady Rodney, in a very rude manner, tried to explain to you, you will either say you are not at home, or that you have a headache. The latter is not so good; it carries more offence with it, but it comes in pretty well sometimes."

"But, as I said to Lady Rodney, suppose I haven't a headache," retorts Mona, triumphantly.

"Oh, you are incorrigible!" says Doatie, leaning back in her chair in turn, and tilting backward her little flower-like face, that looks as if even the most harmless falsehood must be unknown to it.

"Could you not imagine you had one?" she says, presently as a last resource.

"I could not," says Mona. "I am always quite well." She is standing before them like a culprit called to the bar of justice. "I never had a headache, or a toothache, or a nightmare, in my life."

"Or an umbrella, you should add. I once knew a woman like that, but she was not like you," says Doatie. "Well, if you are going to be as literal as you now are, until you call for your shroud, I must say I don't envy you."

"Be virtuous and you'll be happy, but you won't have a good time," quotes Violet; "you should take to heart that latest of copy-book texts."

"Oh, fancy receiving the Boers whenever they call!" says Doatie, faintly, with a deep sigh that is almost a groan.

"I sha'n't mind it very much," says Mona, earnestly. "It will be after all, only one half hour out of my whole day."

"You don't know what you are talking about," says Doatie, vehemently. "Every one of those interminable half-hours will be a year off your life. Mr. Boer is obnoxious, but Florence is simply insupportable. Wait till she begins about the choir, and those hateful school-children, and the parish subsidies; then you perhaps will learn wisdom, and grow headaches if you have them not. Violet, what is it Jack calls Mr. Boer?"

"Better not remember it," says Violet, but she smiles as she calls to mind Jack's apt quotation.

"Why not? it just suits him: 'A little, round, fat, oily man of——'"

"Hush, Dorothy! It was very wrong of Jack," interrupts Violet. But Mona laughs for the first time for many hours—which delights Doatie.

"You and I appreciate Jack, if she doesn't, don't we, Mona?" she says, with pretty malice, echoing Mona's merriment. After which the would-be lecture comes to an end, and the three girls, clothing themselves in furs, go for a short walk before the day quite closes in.

CHAPTER XXVIII.

HOW THE TOWERS WAKES INTO LIFE—AND HOW MONA SHOWS THE LIBRARY TO PAUL RODNEY.

Lights are blazing, fiddles are sounding; all the world is abroad to-night. Even still, though the ball at the Towers has been opened long since by Mona and the Duke of Lauderdale, the flickering light of carriage-lamps is making the roads bright, by casting tiny rays upon the frosted ground.

The fourth dance has come to an end; cards are full; every one is settling down to work in earnest; already the first touch of satisfaction or of carefully-suppressed disappointment is making itself felt.

Mona, who has again been dancing with the duke, stopping near where the duchess is sitting, the latter beckons her to her side by a slight wave of her fan. To the duchess "a thing of beauty is a joy forever," and to gaze on Mona's lovely face and admire her tranquil but brilliant smile gives her a strange pleasure.

"Come and sit by me. You can spare me a few minutes," she says, drawing her ample skirts to one side. Mona, taking her hand from Lauderdale's arm, drops into the proffered seat beside his mother, much to that young man's chagrin, who, having inherited the material hankering after that "delightful prejudice," as Theocritus terms beauty, is decidedly *epris* with Mrs. Geoffrey, and takes it badly being done out of his *tete-a-tete* with her.

"Mrs. Rodney would perhaps prefer to dance, mother," he says, with some irritation.

"Mrs. Rodney will not mind wasting a quarter of an hour on an old woman," says the duchess, equably.

"I am not so sure of that," says Mona, with admirable tact and an exquisite smile, "but I shouldn't mind spending an *hour* with you."

Lauderdale makes a little face, and tells himself secretly "all women are liars," but the duchess is very pleased, and bends her friendliest glance upon the pretty creature at her side, who possesses that greatest of all charms, inability to notice the ravages of time.

Perhaps another reason for Mona's having found such favor in the eyes of "the biggest woman in our shire, sir," lies in the fact that she is in many ways so totally unlike all the other young women with whom the duchess is in the habit of associating. She is *naive* to an extraordinary degree, and says and does things that might appear *outre* in others, but are so much a part of Mona that it neither startles nor offends one when she gives way to them.

Just now, for example, a pause occurring in the conversation, Mona, fastening her eyes upon her Grace's neck, says, with genuine admiration,—

"What a lovely necklace you are wearing!"

To make personal remarks, we all know, is essentially vulgar, is indeed a breach of the commonest show of good breeding; yet somehow Mrs. Geoffrey's tone does not touch on vulgarity, does not even belong to the outermost skirts of ill-breeding. She has an inborn gentleness of her own, that carries her safely over all social difficulties.

The duchess is amused.

"It is pretty, I think," she says. "The duke," with a grave look, "gave it to me just two years after my son was born."

"Did he?" says Mona. "Geoffrey gave me these pearls," pointing to a pretty string round her own white neck, "a month after we were married. It seems quite a long time ago now," with a sigh and a little smile. "But your opals are perfect. Just like the moonlight. By the by," as if it has suddenly occurred to her, "did you ever see the lake by moonlight? I mean from the mullioned window in the north gallery?"

"The lake here? No," says the duchess.

"Haven't you?" in surprise. "Why it is the most enchanting thing in the world. Oh, you must see it: you will be delighted with it. Come with me, and I will show it to you," says Mona, eagerly, rising from her seat in her impulsive fashion.

She is plainly very much in earnest, and has fixed her large expressive eyes— lovely as loving—with calm expectancy upon the duchess. She has altogether forgotten that she is a duchess (perhaps, indeed, has never quite grasped the fact), and that she is an imposing and portly person not accustomed to exercise of any description.

For a moment her Grace hesitates, then is lost. It is to her a new sensation to be taken about by a young woman to see things. Up to this, it has been she who has taken the young women about to see things. But Mona is so openly and genuinely anxious to bestow a favor upon her to do her, in fact, a good turn, that she is subdued, sweetened, nay, almost flattered, by this artless desire to please her for "love's sake" alone.

She too rises, lays her hand on Mona's arm, and walks through the long room, and past the county generally, to "see the lake by moonlight." Yet it is not for the sake of gazing upon almost unrivalled scenery she goes, but to please this Irish girl, whom so very few can resist.

"Where has Mona taken the duchess?" asks Lady Rodney of Sir Nicholas half an hour later.

"She took her to see the lake. Mona, you know, raves about it, when the moon lights it up.

"She is very absurd, and more troublesome and unpleasant than anybody I ever had in my house. Of course the duchess did not want to see the water. She was talking to old Lord Dering about the drainage question, and seemed quite happy, when that girl interfered. Common courtesy compelled her, I suppose, to say yes to—Mona's—proposition."

"I hardly think the duchess is the sort of woman to say yes when she meant no," says Nicholas, with a half smile. "She went because it so pleased her, and for no other reason. I begin to think, indeed, that Lilian Chetwoode is rather out of it, and that Mona is the first favorite at present. She has evidently taken the duchess by storm."

"Why not say the duke too?" says his mother, with a cold glance, to whom praise of Mona is anything but "cakes and ale." "Her flirtation with him is very apparent. It is disgraceful. Every one is noticing and talking about it. Geoffrey alone seems determined to see nothing! Like all under-bred people, she cannot know satisfaction unless perched upon the topmost rung of the ladder."

"You are slightly nonsensical when on the subject of Mona," says Sir Nicholas, with a shrug. "Intrigue and she could not exist in the same atmosphere. She is to Lauderdale what she is to everyone else,—gay, bright, and utterly wanting in self-conceit. I cannot understand how it is that you alone refuse to acknowledge her charms. To me she is like a little soft sunbeam floating here and there and falling into the hearts of those around her, carrying light, and joy, and laughter, and merry music with her as she goes."

"You speak like a lover," says Lady Rodney, with an artificial laugh. "Do you repeat all this to Dorothy? She must find it very interesting."

"Dorothy and I are quite agreed about Mona," replies he, calmly. "She likes her as much as I do. As to what you say about her encouraging Lauderdale's attentions, it is absurd. No such evil thought could enter her head."

At this instant a soft ringing laugh, that once heard is not easily forgotten, comes from an inner room, that is carefully curtained and delicately lighted, and smites upon their ears.

It is Mona's laugh. Raising their eyes, both mother and son turn their heads hastily (and quite involuntarily) and gaze upon the scene beyond. They are so situated that they can see into the curtained chamber and mark the picture it contains. The duke is bending over Mona in a manner that might perhaps be termed by an outsider slightly *empresse*, and Mona is looking up at him, and both are laughing gayly,—Mona with all the freshness of unchecked youth, the duke with such a thorough and wholesome sense of enjoyment as he has not known for years.

Then Mona rises, and they both come to the entrance of the small room, and stand where Lady Rodney can overhear what they are saying.

"Oh! so you can ride, then," says Lauderdale, alluding probably to the cause of his late merriment.

"Sure of course," says Mona. "Why, I used to ride the colts barebacked at home."

Lady Rodney shudders.

"Sometimes I long again for a mad, wild gallop straight across country, where nobody can see me,—such as I used to have," goes on Mona, half regretfully.

"And who allowed you to risk your life like that?" asks the duke, with simple amazement. His sister before she married was not permitted to cross the threshold without a guardian at her side. This girl is a revelation.

"No one," says Mona. "I had no need to ask permission for anything. I was free to do what I wished."

She looks up at him again with some fire in her eyes and a flush upon her cheeks. Perhaps some of the natural lawlessness of her kindred is making her blood warm. So standing, however, she is the very embodiment of youth and love and sweetness, and so the duke admits.

"Have you any sisters?" he asks, vaguely.

"No. Nor brothers. Only myself.

"'I am all the daughters of my father's house,And all the brothers too!'"

She nods her head gayly as she says this, being pleased at her apt quotation from the one book she has studied very closely.

The duke loses his head a little.

"Do you know," he says, slowly, staring at her the while, "you are the most beautiful woman I ever saw?"

"Ah! so Geoffrey says," returns she, with a perfectly unembarrassed and pleased little laugh, while a great gleam of tender love comes into her eyes as she makes mention of her husband's name. "But I really am not you know."

This answer, being so full of thorough unconsciousness and childish *naivete*, has the effect of reducing the duke to common sense once more, and of making him very properly ashamed of himself. He feels, however, rather out of it for a minute or two, which feeling renders him silent and somewhat *distrait*. So Mona, flung upon her own resources, looks round the room seeking for inspiration, and presently finds it.

"What a disagreeable-looking man that is over there!" she says: "the man with the shaggy beard, I mean, and the long hair."

She doesn't want in the very least to know who he is, but thinks it her duty to say something, as the silence being protracted grows embarrassing.

"The man with the mane? that is Griffith Blount. The most objectionable person any one could meet, but tolerated because his tongue is so awful. Do you know Colonel Graves? No! Well, he has a wife calculated to terrify the bravest man into submission, and last year when he was going abroad Blount met him, and asked him before a roomful 'if he was going for pleasure, or if he was going to take his wife with him.' Neat, wasn't it? But I don't remember hearing that Graves liked it."

"It was very unkind," says Mona; "and he has a hateful face."

"He has," says the duke. "But he has his reward, you know: nobody likes him. By the by, what horrid bad times they are having in your land!—ricks of hay burning nightly, cattle killed, everybody boycotted, and small children speared!"

"Oh, no, not that," says Mona. "Poor Ireland! Every one either laughs at her or hates her. Though I like my adopted country, still I shall always feel for old Erin what I could never feel for another land."

"And quite right too," says Lauderdale. "You remember what Scott says:

"'Breathes there the man, with soul so dead,Who never to himself hath said,This is my own, my native land!'"

"Oh, yes, lots of 'em," says Mr. Darling, who has come suddenly up beside them: "for instance, I don't believe I ever said it in all my life, either to myself or to any one else. Are you engaged, Mrs. Geoffrey? And if not, may I have this dance?"

"With pleasure," says Mona.

Paul Rodney, true to his word, has put in an appearance, much to the amazement of many in the room. Almost as Mona's dance with Nolly is at an end, he makes his way to her, and asks her to give him the next. Unfortunately, she is not engaged for it, and, being unversed in polite evasions, she says yes, quietly, and is soon floating round the room with him.

After one turn she stops abruptly, near an entrance.

"Tired?" says Rodney, fixing his black, gloomy eyes upon her.

"A little," says Mona. It is perhaps the nearest approach to a falsehood she has ever made.

"Perhaps you would rather rest for a while. Do you know this is the first time I have ever been inside the Towers?" He says this as one might who is desirous of making conversation, yet there is a covert meaning in his tone. Mona is silent. To her it seems a base thing that he should have accepted the invitation at all.

"I have heard the library is a room well worth seeing," goes on the Australian, seeing she will not speak.

"Yes; every one admires it. It is very old. You know one part of the Towers is older than all the rest."

"I have heard so. I should like to see the library," says Paul, looking at her expectantly.

"You can see it now if you wish," says Mona, quickly, the thought that she may be able to entertain him in some fashion that will not require conversation is dear to her. She therefore takes his arm, and leads him out of the ballroom, and across the halls into the library, which is brilliantly lighted, but just at this moment empty.

I forget if I described it before, but it is a room quite perfect in every respect, a beautiful room, oak-panelled from floor to ceiling, with this peculiarity about it, that whereas three of the walls have their panels quite long, without a break from top to bottom, the fourth—that is, the one in which the fireplace has been inserted—has the panels of a smaller size, cut up into pieces from about one foot broad to two feet long.

The Australian seems particularly struck with this fact. He stares in a thoughtful fashion at the wall with the small panels, seeming blind to the other beauties of the room.

"Yes, it is strange why that wall should be different from the others," Mona says, rather glad that he appears interested in something besides herself. "But it is altogether quite a nice old room, is it not?"

"It is," replies he, absently. Then, below his breath, "and well worth fighting for."

But Mona does not hear this last addition; she is moving a chair a little to one side, and the faint noise it makes drowns the sound of his voice. This perhaps is as well.

She turns up one of the lamps, whilst Rodney still continues his contemplation of the wall before him. Conversation languishes, then dies. Mona, raising her hand to her lips, suppresses valiantly a yawn.

"I hope you are enjoying yourself," she says, presently, hardly knowing what else to say.

"Enjoying myself?—No, I never do that," says Rodney, with unexpected frankness.

"You can hardly mean that?" says Mona, with some surprise.

"I do. Just now," looking at her, "I am perhaps as near enjoyment as I can be. But I have not danced before to-night. Nor should I have danced at all had you been engaged. I have forgotten what it is to be light-hearted."

"But surely there must be moments when——"

"I never have such moments," interrupts he moodily.

"Dear me! what a terribly unpleasant young man!" thinks Mona, at her wits' end to know what to say next. Tapping her fingers in a perplexed fashion on the table nearest her, she wonders when he will cease his exhaustive survey of the walls and give her an opportunity of leaving the room.

"But this is very sad for you, isn't it?" she says, feeling herself in duty bound to say something.

"I dare say it is; but the fact remains. I don't know what is the matter with me. It is a barren feeling,—a longing, it may be, for something I can never obtain."

"All that is morbid," says Mona: "you should try to conquer it. It is not healthy."

"You speak like a book," says Rodney, with an unlovely laugh; "but advice seldom cures. I only know that I have learned what stagnation means. I may alter in time, of course, but just at present I feel that

'My night has no eve,And my day has no morning.'

At home—in Sydney, I mean—the life was different. It was free, unfettered, and in a degree lawless. It suited me better."

"Then why don't you go back?" suggests Mona, simply.

"Because I have work to do here," retorts he, grimly. "Yet ever since I first set foot on this soil, contentment has gone from me. Abroad a man lives, here he exists. There, he carries his life in his hand, and trusts to his revolver rather than to the most learned of counsels, but here all is on another footing."

"It is to be regretted you cannot like England, as you have made up your mind to live in it; and yet I think——" She pauses.

"Yes—you think; go on," says Rodney, gazing at her attentively.

"Well, then, I think it is only *just* you should be unhappy," says Mona, with some vehemence. "Those who seek to scatter misery broadcast among their fellows should learn to taste of it themselves."

"Why do you accuse me of such a desire?" asks he, paling beneath her indignation, and losing courage because of the unshed tears that are gleaming in her eyes.

"When you gain your point and find yourself master here, you will know you have made not only one, but many people miserable."

"You seem to take my success in this case as a certainty," he says, with a frown. "I may fail."

"Oh, that I could believe so!" says Mona, forgetful of manners, courtesy, everything, but the desire to see those she loves restored to peace.

"You are candor itself," returns he, with a short laugh, shrugging his shoulders. "Of course I am bound to hope your wish may be fulfilled. And yet I doubt it. I am nearer my object to-night than I have ever been before; and," with a sardonic smile, "yours has been the hand to help me forward."

Mona starts, and regards him fixedly in a puzzled, uncertain manner. What he can possibly mean is unknown to her; but yet she is aware of some inward feeling, some instinct such as animals possess, that warns her to beware of him. She shrinks from him, and in doing so a slight fold of her dress catches in the handle of a writing-table, and detains her.

Paul, dropping on his knees before her, releases her gown; the fold is in his grasp, and still holding it he looks up at her, his face pale and almost haggard.

"If I were to resign all hope of gaining the Towers, if I were to consent to leave your people still in possession," he says, passionately, but in a low tone, "should I earn one tender thought in your heart? Speak, Mona! speak!"

I am sure at even this supreme moment it never enters Mona's brain that the man is actually making love to her. A deep pity for him fills her mind. He is unhappy, justly so, no doubt, but yet unhappy. A sure passport to her heart.

"I do not think unkindly of you," she says, gently, but coldly. "And do as your conscience dictates, and you will gain not only my respect, but that of all men."

"Bah!" he says, impatiently, rising from the ground and turning away. Her answer has frozen him again, has dried up the momentary desire for her approbation above all others that only a minute ago had agitated his breast.

At this moment Geoffrey comes into the room and up to Mona. He takes no notice whatever of her companion, "Mona, will you come and sing us something?" he says, as naturally as though the room is empty. "Nolly has been telling the duchess about your voice, and she wants to hear you. Anything simple, darling,"—seeing she looks a little distressed at the idea: "you sing that sort of thing best."

"I hardly think our dance is ended yet, Mrs. Rodney," says the Australian, defiantly, coming leisurely forward, his eyes bent somewhat insolently upon Geoffrey.

"You will come, Mona, to oblige the duchess," says Geoffrey, in exactly as even a tone as if the other had never spoken. Not that he cares in the very least about the duchess; but he is determined to conquer here, and is also desirous that all the world should appreciate and admire the woman he loves.

"I will come, of course," says Mona, nervously, "but I am afraid she will be disappointed. You will excuse me, Mr. Rodney, I am sure," turning graciously to Paul, who is standing with folded arms in the background.

"Yes, I excuse _you_," he says, with a curious stress upon the pronoun, and a rather strained smile. The room is filling with other people, the last dance having plainly come to an end. Geoffrey, taking Mona's arm, leads her into the hall.

"Dance no more to-night with that fellow," he says quickly, as they get outside.

"No?" Then, "Not if you dislike it of course. But Nicholas made a point of my being nice to him. I did not know you would object to my dancing with him."

"Well, you know it now. I do object," says Geoffrey, in a tone he has never used to her before. Not that it is unkind or rude, but cold and unlover-like.

"Yes, I know it now!" returns she, softly, yet with the gentle dignity that always belongs to her. Her lips quiver, but she draws herself up to her fullest height, and, throwing up her head, walks with a gait that is almost stately into the presence of the duchess.

"You wish me to sing to you," she says, gently, yet so unsmilingly that the duchess wonders what has come to the child. "It will give me pleasure if I can give *you* pleasure, but my voice is not worth thinking about."

"Nevertheless, let me hear it," says the duchess. "I cannot forget that your face is musical."

Mona, sitting down to the piano, plays a few chords in a slow, plaintive fashion, and then begins. Paul Rodney has come to the doorway, and is standing there gazing at her, though she knows it not. The ballroom is far distant, so far that the sound of the band does not break upon the silence of the room in which they are assembled. A hush falls upon the listeners as Mona's fresh, pathetic, tender voice rises into the air.

It is an old song she chooses, and simple as old, and sweet as simple. I almost forget the words now, but I know it runs in this wise:

Oh, hame, hame—hame fain wad I be,Hame, hame to my ain countrie,

and so on.

It touches the hearts of all who hear it as she sings it and brings tears to the eyes of the duchess. So used the little fragile daughter to sing who is now chanting in heaven!

There is no vehement applause as Mona takes her fingers from the keys, but every one says, "Thank you," in a low tone. Geoffrey, going up to her, leans over her chair and whispers, with some agitation,—

"You did not mean it, Mona, did you? You are content here with me?—you have no regret?"

At which Mona turns round to him a face very pale, but full of such love as should rejoice the heart of any man, and says, tremulously,—

"Darling, do you need an answer?"

"Then why did you choose that song?"

"I hardly know."

"I was hateful to you just now, and most unjust."

"Were you? I have forgotten it," replies she, smiling happily, the color coming back to her cheeks. Whereupon Paul Rodney's brows contract, and with a muttered curse he turns aside and leaves the room, and then the house, without another word or backward glance.

CHAPTER XXIX.

HOW GEOFFREY DINES OUT, AND HOW MONA FARES DURING HIS ABSENCE.

"Must you really go, Geoffrey?—really?" asks Mona, miserably, looking the very personification of despair. She has asked the same question in the same tone ever since early dawn, and it is now four o'clock.

"Yes, really. Horrid bore, isn't it?—but county dinners must be attended, and Nicholas will do nothing. Besides, it isn't fair to ask him just now, dear old fellow, when he has so much upon his mind."

"But *you* have something on your mind, too. You have *me*. Why doesn't Jack go?"

"Well, I rather think he has Violet on his mind. Did you ever see anything so spooney as they looked all through dinner yesterday and luncheon to-day? I didn't think it was in Violet."

"Did she never look at you like that?" asks Mona, maliciously; "in the early days, I mean, before—before——"

"I fell a victim to your charms? No. Jack has it all to himself as far as I'm concerned. Well, I must be off, you know. It is a tremendous drive, and I'll barely do it in time. I shall be back about two in the morning."

"Not until two?" says Mona, growing miserable again.

"I can't well get away before that, you know, as Wigley is a good way off. But I'll try all I know. And, after all," says Geoffrey, with a view to cheering her, "it isn't as bad as if I was ordered off somewhere for a week, is it?"

"A week? I should be *dead* when you came back," declares Mrs. Geoffrey, with some vehemence, and a glance that shows she can dissolve into tears at a moment's notice.

"Some fellows go away for months," says Geoffrey, still honestly bent on cheering her, but unfortunately going the wrong way to work.

"Then they ought to be ashamed of themselves," says Mona, with much indignation. "Months indeed!"

"Why, they can't help it," explains he. "They are sent half the time."

"Then the people who send them should be ashamed! But what about the other half of their time that they spend from home?"

"Oh, I don't know: that was a mere figure of speech," says Mr. Rodney, who is afraid to say such absences are caused by an innate love of freedom and a vile desire for liberty at any cost, and has nothing else handy. "Now don't stay moping up here when I go, but run downstairs and find the girls and make yourself happy with them."

"Happy?" reproachfully. "I shan't know a happy moment until I see you again!"

"Nor I, till I see you," says Geoffrey, earnestly, actually believing what he says himself.

"I shall do nothing but look at the clock and listen for the sound of the horse's feet."

"Mona, you musn't do that. Now, I shall be really annoyed if you insist on sitting up for me and so lose a good night's rest. Now, don't, darling. It will only take it out of you, and make you pale and languid next day."

"But I shall be more content so; and even if I went to bed I could not sleep. Besides, I shall not be companionless when the small hours begin to creep upon me."

"Eh?" says Geoffrey.

"No; I shall have him with me: but, hush! It is quite a secret," placing her finger on her lips.

"'Him'?—whom?"—demands her husband, with pardonable vivacity.

"My own old pet," says Mrs. Geoffrey, still mysteriously, and with the fondest smile imaginable.

"Good gracious, Mona, whom do you mean?" asks he, aghast both at her look and tone.

"Why, Spice, of course," opening her eyes. "Didn't you know. Why, what else could I mean?"

"I don't know, I'm sure; but really the way you expressed yourself, and——Yes, of course, Spice will be company, the very best company for you."

"I think I shall have Allspice too," goes on Mona. "But say nothing. Lady Rodney, if she knew it, would not allow it for a moment. But Jenkins" (the old butler) "has promised to manage it all for me, and to smuggle my dear dogs up to my room without any one being in the least the wiser."

"If you have Jenkins on your side you are pretty safe," says Geoffrey. "My mother is more afraid of Jenkins than you would be of a land-leaguer. Well, good-by again. I must be off."

"What horse are you taking?" asks she, holding him.

"Black Bess."

"Oh, Geoffrey, do you want to break my heart? Sure you know he is the most vicious animal in the whole stables. Take any horse but that."

"Well, if only to oblige you, I'll take Truant."

"What! the horrid brute that puts back his ears and shows the white of his eyes! Geoffrey, once for all, I desire you to have nothing to do with him."

"Anything to please you," says Geoffrey, who is laughing by this time. "May I trust my precious bones to Mazerin? He is quite fifteen, has only one eye, and a shameless disregard for the whip."

"Ye—es; he will do," says Mona, after a second's careful thought, and even now reluctantly.

"I think I see myself behind Mazerin, at this time of day," says Mr. Rodney, heartlessly. "You don't catch me at it, if I know it. I'm not sure what horse I shall have, but I trust to Thomas to give me a good one. For the last time, good-by, you amiable young goose, and don't expect me till I come."

So saying, he embraces her warmly, and, running downstairs, jumps into the dog-cart, and drives away behind the "vicious Black Bess."

Mona watches him from her window, as far as the curve in the avenue will permit, and, having received and returned his farewell wave of the hand, sits down, and taking out her handkerchief, indulges in a good cry.

It is the first time since their marriage that she and Geoffrey have been parted, and it seems to her a hard thing that such partings should be. A sense of desolation creeps over her,—a sense of loneliness she has never known before.

Then she remembers her promise to go down to the girls and abstain from fretting, and, rising bravely, she bathes her eyes, and goes down the marble staircase through the curtained alcove towards the small drawing-room, where one of the servants tells her, the family is assembled.

The door of the room she is approaching is wide open, and inside, as Mona draws nearer, it becomes apparent that some one is talking very loudly, and with much emphasis, and as though determined not to be silenced. Argument is plainly the order of the hour.

As Mona comes still nearer, the words of the speaker reach her, and sink into her brain. It is Lady Rodney who is holding forth, and what she says floats lightly to Mona's ears. She is still advancing, unmindful of anything but the fact that she cannot see Geoffrey again for more hours than she cares to count, when the following words become clear to her, and drive the color from her cheeks,—

"And those dogs forever at her heels!—positively, she is half a savage. The whole thing is in keeping, and quite detestable. How can you expect me to welcome a girl who is without family and absolutely penniless? Why, I am convinced that misguided boy bought her even her trousseau!"

Mona has no time to hear more; pale, but collected, she walks deliberately into the room and up to Lady Rodney.

"You are mistaken in one point," she says, slowly. "I may be savage, penniless, without family,—but I bought my own trousseau. I do not say this to excuse myself, because I should not mind taking anything from Geoffrey; but I think it a pity you should not know the truth. I had some money of my own,—very little, I allow, but enough to furnish me with wedding garments."

Her coming is a thunderbolt, her speech lightning. Lady Rodney changes color, and is for once utterly disconcerted.

"I beg your pardon," she manages to say. "Of course had I known you were listening at the door I should not have said what I did,"—this last with a desire to offend.

"I was not listening at the door," says Mona, with dignity, yet with extreme difficulty: some hand seems clutching at her heart-strings, and he who should have been near to succor her is far away. "I never," haughtily, "listened at a door in all my life. *I* should not understand how to do it." Her Irish blood is up, and there is a distinct emphasis upon the pronoun. "You have wronged me twice!"

Her voice falters. Instinctively she looks round for help. She feels deserted,— alone. No one speaks. Sir Nicholas and Violet, who are in the room, are as yet almost too shocked to have command of words; and presently the silence becomes unbearable.

Two tears gather, and roll slowly down Mona's white cheeks. And then somehow her thoughts wander back to the old farmhouse at the side of the hill, with the spreading trees behind it, and to the sanded floor and the cool dairy, and the warmth of the love that abounded there, and the uncle, who, if rough, was at least ready to believe her latest action—whatever it might be—only one degree more perfect than the one that went before it.

She turns away in a desolate fashion, and moves towards the door; but Sir Nicholas, having recovered from his stupefaction by this time, follows her, and placing his arm round her, bends over her tenderly, and presses her face against his shoulder.

"My dearest child, do not take things so dreadfully to heart," he says, entreatingly and soothingly: "it is all a mistake; and my mother will, I know, be the first to acknowledge herself in error."

"I regret—" begins Lady Rodney, stonily; but Mona by a gesture stays her.

"No, no," she says, drawing herself up and speaking with a touch of pride that sits very sweetly on her; "I beg you will say nothing. Mere words could not cure the wound you have inflicted."

She lays her hand upon her heart, as though she would say, "The wound lies here," and once more turns to the door.

Violet, rising, flings from her the work she has been amusing herself with, and, with a gesture of impatience very foreign to her usual reserve goes up to Mona, and, slipping her arm round her, takes her quietly out of the room.

Up the stairs she takes her and into her own room, without saying a word. Then she carefully turns the key in the door, and, placing Mona in a large and cosey arm-chair, stands opposite to her, and thus begins,—

"Now listen, Mona," she says, in her low voice, that even now, when she is somewhat excited, shows no trace of heat or haste, "for I shall speak to you plainly. You must make up your mind to Lady Rodney. It is the common belief that mere birth will refine most people; but those who cling to that theory will surely find themselves mistaken. Something more is required: I mean the nobility of soul that Nature gives to the peasant as well as the peer. This, Lady Rodney lacks; and at heart, in sentiment, she is—at times—coarse. May I say what I like to you?"

"You may," says Mona, bracing herself for the ordeal.

"Well, then, I would ask you to harden your heart, because she will say many unpleasant things to you, and will be uncivil to you, simply because she has taken it into her head that you have done her an injury in that you have married Geoffrey! But do you take no notice of her rudeness; ignore her, think always of the time that is coming when your own home will be ready for you, and where you can live with Geoffrey forever, without fear of a harsh word or an unkind glance. There must be comfort in this thought."

She glances anxiously at Mona, who is gazing into the fire with a slight frown upon her brow, that looks sadly out of place on that smooth white surface. At Violet's last words it flies away, not to return.

"Comfort? I think of nothing else," she says, dreamily.

"On no account quarrel with Lady Rodney. Bear for the next few weeks (they will quickly pass) anything she may say, rather than create a breach between mother and son. You hear me, Mona?"

"Yes, I hear you. But must you say this? Have I ever sought a quarrel with— Geoffrey's mother?"

"No, no, indeed. You have behaved admirably where most women would have ignominiously failed. Let that thought console you. To have a perfect temper, such as yours, should be in itself a source of satisfaction. And now bathe your eyes, and make yourself look even prettier than usual. A difficult matter, isn't it?" with a friendly smile.

Mona smiles too in return, though still heavy at heart.

"Have you any rose-water?" goes on Miss Mansergh in her matter-of-fact manner. "No? A good sign that tears and you are enemies. Well, I have, and so I shall send it to you in a moment. You will use it?"

"Oh, yes, thank you," says Mona, who is both surprised and carried away by the other's unexpected eloquence.

"And now a last word, Mona. When you come down to dinner to-night (and take care you are a little late), be gay, merry, wild with spirits, anything but depressed, whatever it may cost you. And if in the drawing-room, later on, Lady Rodney should chance to drop her handkerchief, or that eternal knitting, do not stoop to pick it up. If her spectacles are on a distant table, forget to see them. A nature such as hers could not understand a nature such as yours. The more anxious you may seem to please, the more determined she will be not to be pleased."

"But you like Lady Rodney?" says Mona, in a puzzled tone.

"Very much indeed. But her faults are obvious, and I like you too. I have said more to you of her than I have ever yet said to human being; why, I know not, because you are (comparatively speaking) a stranger to me, whilst she is my very good friend. Yet so it rests. You will, I know, keep faith with me."

"I am glad you know that," says Mona. Then, going nearer to Violet, she lays her hand upon her arm and regards her earnestly. The tears are still glistening in her eyes.

"I don't think I should mind it if I did not feel so much alone. If I had a place in your hearts," she says. "You all like me, I know, but I want to be loved." Then, tremulously, "Will you *try* to love me?"

Violet looks at her criticizingly, then she smiles, and, placing her hand beneath Mrs. Geoffrey's chin, turns her face more to the fading light.

"Yes, that is just your greatest misfortune," she says, meditatively. "Love at any price. You would die out of the sunshine, or spoil, which would be worse. You will never be quite happy, I think; and yet perhaps," with a faint sigh, "you get your own good out of your life, after all,—happiness more intense, if briefer, than we more material people can know. There, shall I tell you something? I think you have gained more love in a short time than any other person I ever knew. You have conquered me, at least; and, to tell you the truth," with a slight grimace, "I was quite determined not to like you. Now lie down, and in a minute or two I shall send Halkett to you with the rose-water."

For the first time she stoops forward and presses her lips to Mona's warmly, graciously. Then she leaves her, and, having told her maid to take the rose-water to Mrs. Rodney, goes downstairs again to the drawing-room.

Sir Nicholas is there, silent, but angry, as Violet knows by the frown upon his brow. With his mother he never quarrels, merely expressing disapproval by such signs as an unwillingness to speak, and a stern grave line that grows upon his lips.

"Of course you are all against me," Lady Rodney is saying, in a rather hysterical tone. "Even you, Violet, have taken up that girl's cause!" She says this expectantly, as though calling on her ally for support. But for once the ally fails her. Miss Mansergh maintains an unflinching silence, and seats herself in her low wicker chair before the fire with all the air of one who has made up her mind to the course she intends to pursue, and is not be enticed from it.

"Oh, yes, no doubt I am in the wrong, because I cannot bring myself to adore a vulgar girl who all day long shocks me with her Irishisms," goes on Lady Rodney, almost in tears, born of vexation. "A girl who says, 'Sure you know I didn't' or 'Ah, did ye, now,' or 'Indeed I won't, then!' every other minute. It is too much. What you all see in her I can't imagine. And you too, Violet, you condemn me, I can see."

"Yes, I think you are quite and altogether in the wrong," says Miss Mansergh, in her cool manner, and without any show of hesitation, selecting carefully from the basket near her the exact shade of peacock blue she will require for the cornflower she is working.

Lady Rodney, rising hurriedly, sails with offended dignity from the room.

CHAPTER XXX.

HOW MONA, GHOST-LIKE, FLITS THROUGH THE OLD TOWERS AT MIDNIGHT—HOW THE MOON LIGHTS HER WAY—AND HOW SHE MEETS ANOTHER GHOST MORE FORMIDABLE THAN HERSELF.

Jenkins, the antediluvian butler, proves himself a man of his word. There are, evidently, "no two ways" about Jenkins. "Seeking the seclusion that her chamber grants" about ten o'clock to-night, after a somewhat breezy evening with her mother-in-law, Mona descries upon her hearthrug, dozing blissfully, two huge hounds, that raise their sleepy tails and heads to welcome her, with the utmost condescension, as she enters her room.

Spice and Allspice are having a real good time opposite her bedroom fire, and, though perhaps inwardly astonished at their promotion from a distant kennel to the sleeping-apartment of their fair mistress, are far too well-bred to betray any vulgar exaltation at the fact.

Indeed, it is probably a fear lest she shall deem them unduly elated that causes them to hesitate before running to greet her with their usual demonstrative joy. Then politeness gets the better of pride, and, rising with a mighty effort, they stretch themselves, yawn, and, going up to her, thrust their soft muzzles into her hands and look up at her with their great, liquid, loving eyes. They rub themselves against her skirts, and wag their tails, and give all other signs of loyalty and devotion.

Mona, stooping, caresses them fondly. They are a part of her old life, and dear, therefore, to her own faithful heart. Having partly undressed, she sits down upon the hearthrug with them, and, with both their big heads upon her lap, sits staring into the fire, trying to while away with thought the hours that must elapse before Geoffrey can return to her again.

It is dreary waiting. No sleep comes to her eyes; she barely moves; the dogs slumber drowsily, and moan and start in their sleep, "fighting their battles o'er again," it may be, or anticipating future warfare. Slowly, ominously, the clock strikes twelve. Two hours have slipped into eternity; midnight is at hand!

At the sound of the twelfth stroke the hounds stir uneasily, and sigh, and, opening wide their huge jaws, yawn again. Mona pats them reassuringly: and, flinging some fresh logs upon the fire, goes back once more to her old position, with her chin in the palm of one hand, whilst the other rests on the sleek head of Spice.

Castles within the fire grow grand and tall, and then crumble into dust; castles in Mona's brain fare likewise. The shadows dance upon the walls; silently imperceptibly, the minutes flit away.

One o'clock chimes the tiny timepiece on the mantelshelf; outside the sound is repeated somewhere in the distance in graver, deeper tones.

Mona shivers. Getting up from her lowly position, she draws back the curtains of her window and looks out upon the night. It is brilliant with moonlight, clear as day, full of that hallowed softness, that peaceful serenity, that belongs alone to night.

She is enchanted, and stands there for a minute or two spellbound by the glory of the scene before her. Then a desire to see her beloved lake from the great windows in the northern gallery takes possession of her. She will go and look at it, and afterwards creep on tiptoe to the library, seize the book she had been reading before dinner, and make her way back again to her room without any one being in the least the wiser. Anything will be better than sitting here any longer, dreaming dismal day-dreams.

She beckons to the dogs, and they, coming up to her, follow her out of the room and along the corridor outside their soft velvet paws making no sound upon the polished floor. She has brought with her no lamp. Just now, indeed, it would be useless, such "a wide and tender light," does heaven's lamp fling upon floor and ceiling, chamber and corridor.

The whole of the long north gallery is flooded with its splendor. The oriel window at its farther end is lighted up, and from it can be seen a picture, living, real, that resembles fairy-land.

Sinking into the cushioned embrasure of the window, Mona sits entranced, drinking in the beauty that is balm to her imaginative mind. The two dogs, with a heavy sigh, shake themselves, and then drop with a soft thud upon the ground at her feet,—her pretty arched feet that are half naked and white as snow: their blue slippers being all too loose for them.

Below is the lake, bathed in moonshine. A gentle wind has arisen, and little wavelets silver-tinged are rolling inward, breaking themselves with tender sobs upon the shore.

"The floor of heavenIs thick inlaid with patines of bright gold."

The floor itself is pale, nay, almost blue. A little snow is sifted lightly on branch, and grass, and ivied wall. Each object in the sleeping world is quite distinct.

"All things are calm, and fair, and passive; earthLooks as if lulled upon an angel's lapInto a breathless, dewy sleep; so stillThat we can only say of things, they be."

The cold seems hardly to touch Mona, so wrapped she is in the beauties of the night. There is at times a solemn indefinable pleasure in the thought that we are awake whilst all the world sleepeth; that we alone are thinking, feeling, holding high communion with our own hearts and our God.

The breeze is so light that hardly a trembling of the leafless branches breaks the deadly silence that reigns all round:

"A lone owl's hoot,The waterfall's faint drip,Alone disturb the stillness of the scene,"

Tired at length, and feeling somewhat chilled, Mona rouses herself from her reverie, and, followed by her two faithful guardians, moves towards the staircase. Passing the armored men that stand in niches along the walls, a little sensation of fear, a certain belief in the uncanny, runs through her. She looks in a terrified fashion over her left shoulder, and shudders perceptibly. Do dark fiery eyes look upon her in very truth from those ghastly visors?— surely a clank of supernatural armor smote upon her ear just then!

She hastens her steps, and runs down hurriedly into the hall below, which is almost as light as day. Turning aside, she makes for the library, and now (and not till now) remembers she has no light, and that the library, its shutters carefully closed every night by the invaluable Jenkins himself, is of necessity in perfect darkness.

Must she go back for a candle? Must she pass again all those belted knights upon the staircase and in the upper gallery? No! rather will she brave the darkness of the more congenial library, and—but soft—what is that? Surely a tiny gleam of light is creeping to her feet from beneath the door of the room towards which she wends her way.

It is a light, not of stars or of moonbeams, but of a *bona fide* lamp, and as such is hailed by Mona, with joy. Evidently the thoughtful Jenkins has left it lighted there for Geoffrey's benefit when he returns. And very thoughtful, too, it is of him.

All the servants have received orders to go to bed, and on no account to sit up for Mr. Rodney, as he can let himself in in his own way,—a habit of his for many years. Doubtless, then, one of them had placed this lamp in the library with some refreshments for him, should he require them.

So thinks Mona, and goes steadily on to the library, dreading nothing, and inexpressibly cheered by the thought that gloom at least does not await her there.

Pushing open the door very gently, she enters the room, the two dogs at her heels.

At first the light of the lamp—so unlike the pale transparent purity of the moonbeams—puzzles her sight; she advances a few steps unconsciously, treading lightly, as she has done all along, lest she shall wake some member of the household, and then, passing her hand over her eyes, looks leisurely up. The fire is nearly out. She turns her head to the right, and then—*then*—she utters a faint scream, and grasps the back of a chair to steady herself.

Standing with his back to her (being unaware of her entrance), looking at the wall with the smaller panels that had so attracted him the night of the dance, is Paul Rodney!

Starting convulsively at the sound of her cry, he turns, and, drawing with lightning rapidity a tiny pistol from his pocket, raises his arm, and deliberately covers her.

CHAPTER XXXI.

HOW MONA STANDS HER GROUND—HOW PAUL RODNEY BECOMES HER PRISONER—AND HOW GEOFFREY ON HIS RETURN HOME MEETS WITH A WARM RECEPTION.

For a second Mona's courage fails her, and then it returns with threefold force. In truth, she is nearer death at this moment than she herself quite knows.

"Put down your pistol, sir," she says, hastily. "Would you fire on a woman?" Her tone, though hurried, is not oppressed with fear. She even advances a few steps in his direction. Her words, her whole manner, fill him with admiration. The extreme courage she betrays is, indeed worthy of any man's laudation, but the implied trust in his chivalry touches Paul Rodney more than anything has ever had power to touch him before.

He lowers the weapon at her command, but says nothing. Indeed, what is there to say?

"Place it on the table," says Mona, who, though rich in presence of mind, has yet all a woman's wholesome horror of anything that may go off.

Again he obeys her.

"Now, perhaps, you will explain why you are here?" says Mrs. Geoffrey, speaking as sternly as her soft voice will permit. "How did you get in?"

"Through the window. I was passing, and found it open." There is some note in his voice that might well be termed mocking.

"Open at this hour of the morning?"

"Wide open."

"And the lamp, did you find it burning?"

"Brilliantly."

He lifts his head here, and laughs aloud, a short, unmirthful laugh.

"You are lying, sir," says Mona, contemptuously.

"Yes, deliberately," returns he, with wilful recklessness.

He moves as though to take up the pistol again; but Mona is beforehand with him, and, closing her fingers round it, holds it firmly.

"Do you think you are stronger than I am?" he says, amusement blended with the old admiration in his eyes.

"No, but they are," she says, pointing to her two faithful companions, who are staring hungrily at Rodney and evidently only awaiting the word from Mona to fling themselves upon him.

She beckons to them, and, rising slowly, they advance towards Rodney, who involuntarily moves back a little. And in truth they are formidable foes, with their bloodshot eyes, and bristling coats, and huge jaws that, being now parted, show the gleaming teeth within.

"On guard," says Mona, whereupon both the brutes crouch upon the ground right before Rodney, and fix him seriously and menacingly with their eyes.

"You are certainly too strong for me," says Rodney, with a frown and a peculiar smile.

"As you have refused to explain your presence here to me, you shall remain where you now are until help arrives," says Mona, with evident determination.

"I am content to stay here until the day dawns, if you keep me company," replies he, easily.

"Insolence, sir, is perhaps another part of your *role*," returns she, with cold but excessive anger.

She is clad in a long white dressing-gown, loose, yet clinging, that betrays each curve of her *svelte*, lissom figure. It is bordered with swansdown, and some rich white lace, that sits high to her neck and falls over her small hands. Her hair is drawn back into a loose knot, that looks as if it would tumble down her back should she shake her head. She is pale, and her eyes are peculiarly large and dark from excitement. They are fixed upon Rodney with a gaze that belies all idea of fear, and her lips are compressed and somewhat dangerous.

"Is truth insolence?" asks Rodney. "If so, I demand your pardon. My speech, no doubt, was a *betise*, yet it came from my heart."

"Do not trouble yourself to make any further excuse," says Mona, icily.

"Pray sit down," says Rodney, politely: "if you insist on spending your evening with me, let me at least know that you are comfortable." Again the comicality of the whole proceeding strikes him, and he laughs aloud. He takes, too, a step forward, as if to get her a chair.

"Do not stir," says Mona, hastily, pointing to the bloodhounds. Allspice has risen—so has the hair on his back—and is looking thunder-claps at Paul. A low growl breaks from him. He is plainly bent upon reducing to reason whosoever shall dispute the will of his beloved mistress. "The dogs know their orders, and will obey me. Down, Allspice, down. You will do well, sir, to remain exactly where you are," continues Mona.

"Then get a chair for yourself, at least, as you will not permit me to go to your aid," he entreats. "I am your prisoner,—perhaps," in a low tone, "the most willing captive that ever yet was made."

He hardly realizes the extent of his subjection,—is blind to the extreme awkwardness of the situation. Of Geoffrey's absence, and the chance that he may return at any moment, he is altogether ignorant.

Mona takes no notice of his words, but still stands by the table, with her hands folded, her long white robes clinging to her, her eyes lowered, her whole demeanor like that of some mediæval saint. So thinks Rodney, who is gazing at her as though he would forever imprint upon his brain the remembrance of a vision as pure as it is perfect.

The moments come and go. The fire is dying out. No sound but that of the falling cinders comes to disturb the stillness that reigns within the library. Mona is vaguely, wondering what the end of it all will be. And then at last the silence is broken. A noise upon the gravel outside, a quick rush up the balcony steps; some one emerges from the gloom of the night, and comes into the room through the open window. Mona utters a passionate cry of relief and joy. It is Geoffrey!

Perhaps, just at first, surprise is too great to permit of his feeling either astonishment or indignation. He looks from Paul Rodney to Mona, and then from Mona back to Rodney. After that his gaze does not wander again. Mona, running to him, throws herself into his arms, and there he holds her closely, but always with his eyes fixed upon the man he deems his enemy.

As for the Australian, he has grown pale indeed, but is quite self-possessed, and the usual insolent line round his mouth has deepened. The dogs have by no means relaxed their vigil, but still crouch before him, ready for their deadly spring at any moment. It is a picture, almost a lifeless one, so motionless are all those that help to form it. The fading fire, the brilliant lamp, the open window with the sullen night beyond, Paul Rodney standing upon the hearthrug with folded arms, his dark insolent face lighted up with the excitement of what is yet to come, gazing defiantly at his cousin, who is staring back at him, pale but determined. And then Mona, in her soft white gown, somewhat in the foreground, with one arm (from which the loose sleeve of the dressing-gown has fallen back, leaving the fair rounded flesh to be seen) thrown around her husband's neck, is watching Rodney with an expression on her face that is half haughtiness, half nervous dread. Her hair has loosened, and is rippling over her shoulders, and down far below her waist; with her disengaged hand she is holding it back from her ear, hardly knowing how picturesque and striking is her attitude, and how it betrays each perfect curve of her lovely figure.

"Now, sir speak," she says, at length in rather tremulous tones growing fearful of the lengthened silence. There is a dangerous vibration in the arm that Geoffrey has round her, that gives her warning to make some change in the scene as soon as possible.

For an instant Rodney turns his eyes on her, and then goes back to his sneering examination of Geoffrey. Between them the two dogs still lie, quiet but eager.

"Call off the dogs," says Geoffrey to Mona, in a low tone; "there is no longer any necessity for them. And tell me how you come to be here, at this hour, with this—fellow."

Mona calls off the dogs. They rise unwillingly, and, walking into a distant corner, sit there, as though still awaiting a chance of taking some active part in the coming fray. After which Mona, in a few words, explains the situation to Geoffrey.

"You will give me an explanation at once," says Geoffrey, slowly, addressing his cousin. "What brought you here?"

"Curiosity, as I have already told Mrs. Rodney," returns he, lightly. "The window was open, the lamp burning. I walked in to see the old room."

"Who is your accomplice?" asks Geoffrey, still with studied calmness.

"You are pleased to talk conundrums," says Rodney, with a shrug. "I confess my self sufficiently dull to have never guessed one."

"I shall make myself plainer. What servant did you bribe to leave the window open for you at this hour?"

For a brief instant the Australian's eyes flash fire; then he lowers his lids, and laughs quite easily.

"You would turn a farce into a tragedy," he says, mockingly, "Why should I bribe a servant to let me see an old room by midnight?"

"Why, indeed, unless you wished to possess yourself of something in the old room?"

"Again I fail to understand," says Paul; but his very lips grow livid. "Perhaps for the second time, and with the same delicacy you used at first, you will condescend to explain."

"Is it necessary?" says Geoffrey, very insolently in his turn. "I think not. By the by, is it your usual practice to prowl round people's houses at two o'clock in the morning? I thought all such festive habits were confined to burglars, and blackguards of that order."

"We are none of us infallible," says Rodney, in a curious tone, and speaking as if with difficulty. "You see, even you erred. Though I am neither burglar nor blackguard, I, too enjoy a walk at midnight."

"Liar!" says Geoffrey between his teeth, his eyes fixed with deadly hatred upon his cousin. "Liar—and thief!" He goes a few steps nearer him, and then waits.

"Thief!" echoes Paul in a terrible tone. His whole face quivers, A murderous light creeps into his eyes.

Mona, seeing it, moves away from Geoffrey, and, going stealthily up to the table, lays her hand upon the pistol, that is still lying where last she left it. With a quick gesture, and unseen she covers it with a paper, and then turns her attention once more upon the two men.

"Ay, thief!" repeats Geoffrey, in a voice low but fierce, "It was not without a purpose you entered this house to-night, alone and uninvited. Tell your story to any one foolish enough to believe you. I do not. What did you hope to find? What help towards the gaining of your unlawful cause?"

"Thief!" interrupts Rodney, repeating the vile word again, as though deaf to everything but this degrading accusation. Then there is a faint pause, and then——

Mona never afterwards could say which man was the first to make the attack, but in a second they are locked in each other's arms in a deadly embrace. A desire to cry aloud, to summon help, takes hold of her, but she beats it down, some inward feeling, clear, yet undefined, telling her that publicity on such a matter as this will be eminently undesirable.

Geoffrey is the taller man of the two, but Paul the more lithe and sinewy. For a moment they sway to and fro; then Geoffrey, getting his fingers upon his cousin's throat, forces him backward.

The Australian struggles for a moment. Then, finding Geoffrey too many for him, he looses one of his hands, and, thrusting it between his shirt and waistcoat, brings to light a tiny dagger, very flat, and lightly sheathed.

Fortunately this dagger refuses to be shaken from its hold. Mona, feeling that fair play is at an end, and that treachery is asserting itself, turns instinctively to her faithful allies the bloodhounds, who have risen, and, with their hair standing straight on their backs, are growling ominously.

Cold, and half wild with horror, she yet retains her presence of mind, and, beckoning to one of the dogs, says imperiously, "At him, Spice!" pointing to Paul Rodney.

Like a flash of lightning, the brute springs forward, and, flinging himself upon Rodney, fastens his teeth upon the arm of the hand that holds the dagger.

The extreme pain, and the pressure—the actual weight—of the powerful animal, tell. Rodney falls back, and with an oath staggers against the mantelpiece.

"Call off that dog," cries Geoffrey, turning savagely to Mona. Whereupon, having gained her purpose, Mona bids the dog lie down, and the faithful brute, exquisitely trained, and unequal to disobedience, drops off his foe at her command and falls crouching to the ground, yet with his eyes red and bloodshot, and his breath coming in parting gasps that betray the wrath he would gladly gratify.

The dagger has fallen to the carpet in the struggle, and Mona, picking it up, flings it far from her into the darksome night through the window. Then she goes up to Geoffrey, and laying her hand upon his breast, turns to confront their cousin.

Her hair is falling like a veil all round her; through it she looks out at Rodney with eyes frightened and imploring.

"Go, Paul!" she says, with vehement entreaty, the word passing her lips involuntarily.

Geoffrey does not hear her. Paul does. And as his own name, coming from her lips, falls upon his ear, a great change passes over his face. It is ashy pale; his lips are bloodless; his eyes are full of rage and undying hatred: but at her voice it softens, and something that is quite indescribable, but is perhaps pain and grief and tenderness and despair combined, comes into it. Her lips—the purest and sweetest under heaven—have deigned to address him as one not altogether outside the pale of friendship,—of common fellowship. In her own divine charity and tenderness she can see good in others who are not (as he acknowledges to himself with terrible remorse) worthy to touch the very hem of her white skirts.

"Go," she says, again, entreatingly, still with her hand on Geoffrey's breast, as though to keep him back, but with her eyes on Paul.

It is a command. With a last lingering glance at the woman who has enthralled him, he steps out through the window on to the balcony, and in another moment is lost to sight.

Mona, with a beating heart, but with a courage that gives calmness to her outward actions, closes the window, draws the shutters together, bars them, and then goes back to Geoffrey, who has not moved since Rodney's departure.

"Tell me again how it all happened," he says, laying his hands on her shoulders. And then she goes through it again, slowly, carefully.

"He was standing just there," she says, pointing to the spot where first she had seen Paul when she entered the library, "with his face turned to the panels, and his hand up like this," suiting the action to the word. "When I came in, he turned abruptly. Can he be eccentric?—odd? Sometimes I have thought that——"

"No; eccentricity is farther from him than villainy. But, my darling, what a terrible ordeal for you to come in and find him here! Enough to frighten you to death, if you were any one but my own brave girl."

"The dogs gave me courage. And was it not well I did bring them? How strange that I should have wished for them so strongly to-night! That time when he drew out the dagger!—my heart failed me then, and but for Spice what would have been the end of it?" She shudders. "And yet," she says, with sudden passion, "even then I knew what I should have done. I had his pistol. I myself would have shot him, if the worst came to the worst. Oh, to think that that man may yet reign here in this dear old house, and supplant Nicholas!"

Her eyes fill with tears.

"He may not,—there is a faint chance,—but of course the title is gone, as he has proved his birth beyond dispute."

"What could he have wanted? When I came in, he turned pale and levelled the pistol at me. I was frightened, but not much. When I desired him, he laid down the pistol directly, and then I seized it. And then——"

Her eyes fall upon the hearthrug. Half under the fender a small piece of crumpled paper attracts her notice. Still talking, she stoops mechanically and picks it up, smooths it, and opens it.

"Why, what is this?" she says, a moment later; "and what a curious hand! Not a gentleman's surely."

"One of Thomas's *billet-doux*, no doubt," says Geoffrey, dreamily, alluding to the under-footman, but thinking of something else.

"No, no; I think not. Come here, Geoffrey; do. It is the queerest thing,—like a riddle. See!"

He comes to her and looks over her shoulder at the paper she holds. In an ugly unformed hand the following figures and words are written upon it,—

"7—4. Press top corner,—right hand."

This is all. The paper is old, soiled, and has apparently made large acquaintance with pockets. It looks, indeed, as if much travel and tobacco are not foreign to it. Geoffrey, taking it from Mona, holds it from him at full length, with amiable superciliousness, between his first finger and thumb.

"Thomas has plainly taken to hieroglyphics,—if it be Thomas," he says. "I can fancy his pressing his young woman's right hand, but her 'top corner' baffles me. If I were Thomas, I shouldn't hanker after a girl with a 'top corner;' but there is no accounting for tastes. It really is curious, though, isn't it?" As he speaks he looks at Mona; but Mona, though seemingly returning his gaze, is for the first time in her life absolutely unmindful of his presence.

Slowly she turns her head away from him, and, as though following out a train of thought, fixes her eyes upon the panelled wall in front of her.

"It is illiterate writing, certainly; and the whole concern dilapidated to the last degree," goes on Rodney, still regarding the soiled paper with curiosity mingled with aversion. "Any objection to my putting it in the fire?"

"'7—4,'" murmurs she, absently, still staring intently at the wall.

"It looks like the production of a lunatic,—a very dangerous lunatic,—an *habitue* of Colney Hatch," muses Geoffrey, who is growing more and more puzzled with the paper's contents the oftener he reads it.

"'Top corner,—right hand,'" goes on Mona, taking no heed of him, and speaking in the same low, mysterious, far-off tone.

"Yes, exactly; you have it by heart; but what does it mean, and what are you staring at that wall for?" asks he, hopelessly, going to her side.

"It means—the missing will," returns she, in a voice that would have done credit to a priestess of Delphi. As she delivers this oracular sentence, she points almost tragically towards the wall in question.

"Eh!" says Geoffrey, starting, not so much at the meaning of her words as at the words themselves. Have the worry and excitement of the last hour unsettled her brain!

"My dear child, don't talk like that," he says, nervously: "you're done up, you know. Come to bed."

"I sha'n't go to bed at all," declares Mrs. Geoffrey, excitedly. "I shall never go to bed again, I think, until all this is cleared up. Geoffrey, bring me over that chair."

She motions impatiently with her hand, and Geoffrey, being compelled to it by her vehemence, draws a high chair close to that part of the wall that seems to have claimed her greatest attention.

Springing up on it, she selects a certain panel, and, laying one hand on it as if to make sure it is the one she wants, counts carefully six more from it to the next wall, and three from it to the floor. I think I have described these panels before as being one foot broad and two feet long.

Having assured herself that the panel selected is the one she requires, she presses her fingers steadily against the upper corner on the side farthest from the fire. Expectation lies in every line of her face, yet she is doomed to disappointment. No result attends her nervous pressure, but distinct defeat. The panel is inexorable. Nothing daunted, she moves her hand lower down, and tries again. Again failure crushes her; after which she makes one last attempt, and, touching the very uppermost corner, presses hard.

Success at last rests with her. Slowly the panel moves, and, sliding to one side, displays to view a tiny cupboard that for many years has been lost sight of by the Rodney family. It is very small, about half a foot in depth, with three small shelves inside. But, alas! these shelves are empty.

Geoffrey utters an exclamation, and Mona, after one swift comprehensive glance at the rifled cupboard, bursts into tears. The bitter disappointment is more than she can bear.

"Oh! it isn't here! He has stolen it!" cries she, as one who can admit of no comfort. "And I felt so sure I should find it myself. That was what he was doing when I came into the room. Ah, Geoffrey, sure you didn't malign him when you called him a thief."

"What has he done?" asks Geoffrey, somewhat bewildered and greatly distressed at her apparent grief.

"He has stolen the will. Taken it away. That paper you hold must have fallen from him, and contains the directions about finding the right panel. Ah! what shall we do now?"

"You are right: I see it now," says Geoffrey, whitening a little, "Warden wrote that paper, no doubt," glancing at the dirty bit of writing that has led to the discovery. "He evidently had his knowledge from old Elspeth, who must have known of this secret hiding-place from my great-grandfather. My father, I am convinced, knew nothing of it. Here, on the night of my grandfather's death, the old woman must have hidden the will, and here it has remained ever since until to-night. Yet, after all, this is mere supposition," says Geoffrey. "We are taking for granted what may prove a myth. The will may never been placed here, and he himself——"

"It *was* placed here; I feel it, I know it," says Mona, solemnly, laying her hand upon the panel. Her earnestness impresses him. He wakes into life.

"Then that villain, that scoundrel, has it now in his possession," he says, quickly. "If I go after him, even yet I may come up with him before he reaches his home, and compel him to give it up."

As he finishes he moves towards the window, as though bent upon putting his words into execution at once, but Mona hastily stepping before him, gets between it and him, and, raising her hand, forbids his approach.

"You may compel him to murder you," she says, feverishly, "or, in your present mood, you may murder him. No, you shall not stir from this to-night."

"But——" begins he, impatiently, trying gently to put her to one side.

"I will not listen," she interrupts, passionately. "I know how you both looked a while ago. I shall never forget it; and to meet again now, with fresh cause for hatred in your hearts, would be——No. There is crime in the very air of to-night."

She winds her arms, around him, seeing he is still determined to go, and, throwing back her head, looks into his face.

"Besides, you are going on a fool's errand," she says, speaking rapidly, as though to gain time. "He has reached his own place long ago. Wait until the morning, I entreat you, Geoffrey. I——" her lips tremble, her breath comes fitfully—"I can bear no more just now."

A sob escapes her, and falls heavily on Geoffrey's heart. He is not proof against a woman's tears,—as no true man ever is,—especially *her* tears, and so he gives in at once.

"There, don't cry, and you shall have it all your own way," he says, with a sigh. "To-morrow we will decide what is to be done."

"To-day, you mean: you will only have to wait a few short hours," she says, gratefully. "Let us leave this hateful room," with a shudder. "I shall never be able to enter it again without thinking of this night and all its horrors."

CHAPTER XXXII.

HOW MONA KEEPS HER OWN COUNSEL—AND HOW AT MIDDAY SHE RECEIVES A NOTE.

Sleep, even when she does get to bed, refuses to settle upon Mona's eyelids. During the rest of the long hours that mark the darkness she lies wide awake, staring upon vacancy, and thinking ceaselessly until

"Morn, in the white wake of the morning star,Comes furrowing all the Orient into gold."

Then she rises upon her elbow, and notices how the light comes through the chinks of the shutters. It must be day indeed. The dreary night has fled affrighted; the stars hide their diminished rays. Surely

"Yon gray linesThat fret the clouds are messengers of day."

There is relief in the thought. She springs from her bed, clothes herself rapidly, and descends to the breakfast room. Yet the day thus begun appears to her singularly unattractive. Her mind is full of care. She has persuaded Geoffrey to keep silence about all that last night produced, and wait, before taking further steps. But wait for what? She herself hardly knows what it is she hopes for.

She makes various attempts at thinking it out. She places her pretty hands upon her prettier brows, under the mistaken impression common to most people that this attitude is conducive to the solution of mysteries; but with no result. Things will not arrange themselves.

To demand the will from Paul Rodney without further proof that it is in his possession than the fact of having discovered by chance a secret cupboard is absurd; yet not to demand it seems madness. To see him, to reason with him, to accuse him of it, is her one desire; yet she can promise herself no good from such an interview. She sighs as she thus seeks aimlessly to see a satisfactory termination to all her meditations.

She is *distraite* and silent all the morning, taking small notice of what goes on around her. Geoffrey, perplexed too, in spirit, wanders vaguely from pillar to post, unable to settle to anything,—bound by Mona to betray no hint of what happened in the library some hours ago, yet dying to reveal the secret of the panel-cupboard to somebody.

Nolly is especially and oppressively cheerful. He is blind to the depression that marks Mona and Geoffrey for its own, and quite outdoes himself in geniality and all-round amiability.

Violet has gone to the stables to bestow upon her bonny brown mare her usual morning offering of bread; Jack, of course, has gone with her.

Geoffrey is nowhere just at this moment. Doatie and Nicholas are sitting hand in hand and side by side in the library, discussing their own cruel case, and wondering for the thousandth time whether—if the worst comes to the worst (of which, alas! there now seems little doubt)—her father will still give his consent to their marriage, and, if so, how they shall manage to live on five hundred pounds a year, and whether it may not be possible for Nicholas to get something or other to do (on this subject they are vague) that may help "to make the crown a pound."

Mona is sitting in the morning-room, the faithful and ever lively Nolly at her side. According to his lights, she is "worth a ship-load of the whole lot," and as such he haunts her. But to-day she fails him. She is absent, depressed, weighed down with thought,—anything but congenial. She forgets to smile in the right place, says, "Yes" when courtesy requires "No," and is deaf to his gayest sallies.

When he has told her a really good story.—quite true, and all about the æsthetic, Lady Lilias, who has declared her intention of calling this afternoon, and against whose wearing society he is strenuously warning her,—and when she has shown no appreciation of the wit contained therein, he knows there is something—as he himself describes it—"rotten in the state of Denmark."

"You are not well, are you, Mrs. Geoffrey?" he says, sympathetically, getting up from his own chair to lean tenderly over the back of hers. Nolly is nothing if not affectionate, where women are concerned. It gives him no thought or trouble to be attentive to them, as in his soul he loves them all,—in the abstract,—from the dairymaid to the duchess, always provided they are pretty.

"You are wrong: I am quite well," says Mona, smiling, and rousing herself.

"Then you have something on your mind. You have not been your usual perfect self all the morning."

"I slept badly last night; I hardly slept at all," she says, plaintively, evading direct reply.

"Oh, well, that's it," says Mr. Darling, somewhat relieved. "I'm an awful duffer not to have guessed that Geoffrey's being out would keep you awake."

"Yes, I could not sleep. Watching and waiting destroy all chance of slumber."

"Lucky he," says Nolly, fervently, "to know there is somebody who longs for his return when he is abroad; to feel that there are eyes that will mark his coming, and look brighter when he comes, and all that sort of thing. Nobody ever cares about *my* coming," says Mr. Darling, with deep regret, "except to lament it."

"How melancholy!" says Mona, with a nearer approach to brightness than she has shown all day.

"Yes. I'm not much," confesses Mr. Darling, blandly. "Others are more fortunate. I'm like 'the man in the street,' subject to all the winds of heaven. Why, it would almost tempt a man to stay away from home occasionally to know there was some one longing for his return. It would positively encourage him to dine out whenever he got the chance."

"I pity your wife," says Mona, almost severely.

"Oh, now, Mrs. Geoffrey, come—I say—how cruel yon can be!"

"Well, do not preach such doctrine to Geoffrey," she says, with repentance mixed with pathos.

"I shall do only what you wish," returns he, chivalrously, arranging the cushion that adorns the back of her chair.

The morning wanes, and luncheon declares itself. When it has come to an end, Mona going slowly up the stairs to her own room is met there by one of the maids,—not her own,—who hands her a sealed note.

"From whom?" demands Mona, lazily, seeing the writing is unknown to her.

"I really don't know, ma'am. Mitchell gave it to me," says the girl, in an injured tone. Now, Mitchell is Lady Rodney's maid.

"Very good," says Mona, indifferently, after which the woman, having straightened a cushion or two, takes her departure.

Mona, sinking languidly into a chair, turns the note over and over between her fingers, whilst wondering in a disjointed fashion as to whom it can be from. She guesses vaguely at the writer of it, as people will when they know a touch of the hand and a single glance can solve the mystery.

Then she opens the letter, and reads as follows:

"In spite of all that has passed, I do entreat you to meet me at three o'clock this afternoon at the river, beneath the chestnut-tree. Do not refuse. Let no shrinking from the society of such as I am deter you from granting me this first and last interview, as what I have to say concerns not you, but those you love. I feel the more sure you will accede to this request because of the heavenly pity in your eyes last night, and the grace that moved you to address me as you did. I shall wait for you until four o'clock. But let me not wait in vain.—P. R."

So runs the letter.

"The man is eccentric, no matter what Geoffrey may say," is Mona's first thought, when she has perused it carefully for the second time. Then the belief that it may have something to do with the restoration of the lost will takes possession of her, and makes her heart beat wildly. Yes, she will go; she will keep this appointment whatever comes of it.

She glances at her watch. It is now a quarter past three; so there is no time to be lost. She must hasten.

Hurriedly she gets into her furs, and, twisting some soft black lace around her throat, runs down the stairs, and, opening the hall door without seeing any one, makes her way towards the appointed spot.

It is the 20th of February; already winter is dying out of mind, and little flowers are springing everywhere.

"Daisies pied, and violets blue,And lady-smocks all silver white,And cuckoo-buds of yellow hueDo paint the meadows with delight."

Each bank and root of mossy tree is studded with pale primroses that gleam like stars when the morning rises to dim their lustre. My lady's straw-bed spreads its white carpet here and there; the faint twitter of birds is in the air, with "liquid lapse of murmuring streams;" every leaf seems bursting into life, the air is keen but soft, the clouds rest lightly on a ground of spotless blue; the world is awake, and mad with youthful glee as

"Spring comes slowly up this way"

Every flower has opened wide its pretty eye, because the sun, that so long has been a stranger, has returned to them, and is gazing down upon them with ardent love. They—fond nurslings of an hour—accept his tardy attentions, and, though, still chilled and *desolee* because of the sad touches of winter that still remain, gaze with rapt admiration at the great Ph[oe]bus, as he sits enthroned above.

Mona, in spite of her haste, stoops to pluck a bunch of violets and place them in her breast, as she goes upon her way. Up to this the beauty of the early spring day has drawn her out of herself, and compelled her to forget her errand. But as she comes near to the place appointed for the interview, a strange repugnance to go forward and face Paul Rodney makes her steps slower and her eyes heavy. And even as she comprehends how strongly she shrinks from the meeting with him, she looks up and sees the chestnut-tree in front of her, and the stream rushing merrily to the ocean, and Paul Rodney standing in his favorite attitude with his arms folded and his sombre eyes fixed eagerly upon her.

"I have come," she says, simply, feeling herself growing pale, yet quite self-possessed, and strong in a determination not to offer him her hand.

"Yes. I thank you for your goodness," returns he, slowly.

Then follows an uncomfortable silence.

"You have something important to say to me," says Mona, presently, seeing he will not speak: "at least, so your letter led me to believe."

"It is true; I have." Then some other train of thought seems to rush upon him; and he goes on in a curious tone that is half mocking, yet wretched above every other feeling; "You had the best of me last night, had you not? And yet," with a sardonic laugh. "I'm not so sure, either. See here."

Slowly he draws from his pocket a paper, folded neatly, that looks like some old parchment. Mona draws her breath quickly, and turns first crimson with emotion, then pale as death. Opening it at a certain page, he points out to her the signature of George Rodney, the old baronet.

"Give it to me!" cries she, impulsively, her voice, trembling. "It is the missing will. You found it last night. It belongs to Nicholas. You must—nay," softly, beseechingly, "you *will* give it to me."

"Do you know all you ask? By relinquishing this iniquitous deed I give up all hope of ever gaining this place,—this old house that even to me seems priceless. You demand much. Yet on one condition it shall be yours."

"And the condition?" asks she, eagerly, going closer to him. What is it that she would not do to restore happiness to those she has learned to love so well?

"A simple one."

"Name it!" exclaims she, seeing he still hesitates.

He lays his hands lightly on her arm, yet his touch seems to burn through her gown into her very flesh. He stoops towards her.

"For one kiss this deed shall be yours," he whispers, "to do what you like with it."

Mona starts violently, and draws back; shame and indignation cover her. Her breath comes in little gasps.

"Are you a man, to make me such a speech?" she says, passionately, fixing her eyes upon him with withering contempt.

"You have heard me," retorts he, coldly, angered to the last degree by the extreme horror and disgust she has evinced at his proposal. He deliberately replaces the precious paper in his pocket, and turns as if to go.

"Oh, stay?" she says, faintly, detaining him both by word and gesture.

He turns to her again.

She covers her eyes with her hands, and tries vainly to decide on what is best for her to do. In all the books she has ever read the young woman placed in her position would not have hesitated at all. As if reared to the situation, she would have thrown up her head, and breathing defiance upon the tempter, would have murmured to the sympathetic air, "Honor above everything," and so, full of dignity, would have moved away from her discomfited companion, her nose high in the air. She would think it a righteous thing that all the world should suffer rather than one tarnish, however slight, should sully the brightness of her fame.

For the first time Mona learns she is not like this well-regulated young woman. She falls lamentably short of such excellence. She cannot bring herself to think the world of those she loves well lost for any consideration whatever. And after all—this horrid condition—it would be over in a moment. And she could run home with the coveted paper, and bathe her face in sweet cold water. And then again she shudders. Could she bathe the remembrance of the insult from her heart?

She presses her hands still closer against her eyes, as though to shut out from her own mind the hatefulness of such a thought. And then, with a fresh effort, she brings herself back once more to the question that lies before her.

Oh, if by this one act of self-sacrifice she could restore the Towers with all its beauty and richness to Nicholas, and—and his mother,—how good a thing it would be! But will Geoffrey ever forgive her? Ah, sure when she explains the matter to him, and tells him how and why she did it, and how her heart bled in the doing of it, he will put his arms round her and pardon her sin. Nay, more, he may see how tender is the longing that compels her to the deed.

She uncovers her eyes, and glances for a bare instant at Rodney. Then once more the heavily-fringed lids close upon the dark-blue eyes, as if to hide the anguish in them, and in a smothered voice she says, with clenched teeth and a face like marble, "Yes, you may kiss me,—if you will."

There is a pause. In shrinking doubt she awaits the moment that shall make him take advantage of her words. But that moment never comes. In vain she waits. At length she lifts her eyes, and he, flinging the parchment at her feet, cries, roughly,—

"There! take it. *I* can be generous too."

"But," begins Mona, feebly, hardly sure of her blessed release.

"Keep your kiss," exclaims he, savagely, "since it cost you such an effort to give it, and keep the parchment too. It is yours because of my love for you."

Ashamed of his vehemence, he stoops, and, raising the will from the ground, presents it to her courteously. "Take it: it is yours," he says. Mona closes her fingers on it vigorously, and by a last effort of grace suppresses the sigh of relief that rises from her heart.

Instinctively she lowers her hand as though to place the document in the inside pocket of her coat, and in doing so comes against something that plainly startles her.

"I quite forgot it," she says, coloring with sudden fear, and then slowly, cautiously, she draws up to view the hated pistol he had left in the library the night before. She holds it out to him at arm's length, as though it is some noisome reptile, as doubtless indeed she considers it. "Take it," she says; "take it quickly. I brought it to you, meaning to return it. Good gracious! fancy my forgetting it! Why, it might have gone off and killed me, and I should have been none the wiser."

"Well, I think you would, for a moment or two at least," returns he, smiling grimly, and dropping the dangerous little toy with some carelessness into his own pocket.

"Oh, do take care!" cries Mona, in an agony: "it is loaded. If you throw it about in that rough fashion, it will certainly go off and do you some injury."

"Blow me to atoms, perhaps, or into some region unknown," says he, recklessly. "A good thing, too. Is life so sweet a possession that one need quail before the thought of resigning it?"

"You speak as one might who has no aim in life, says Mona, looking at him with sincere pity. When Mona looks piteous she is at her best. Her eyes grow large, her sweet lips tremulous, her whole face pathetic. The *role* suits her. Rodney's heart begins to beat with dangerous rapidity. It is quite on the cards that a man of his reckless, untrained, dare-devil disposition should fall madly in love with a woman *sans peur et sans reproche.*

"An aim!" he says, bitterly. "I think I have found an end to my life where most fellows find a beginning."

"By and you will think differently," says Mona, believing he alludes to his surrender of the Rodney property "You will get over this disappointment."

"I shall,—when death claims me," replies he.

"Nay, now," says Mona, sweetly, "do not talk like that. It grieves me. When you have formed a purpose worth living for, the whole world will undergo a change for you. What is dark now will seem light then; and death will be an enemy, a thing to battle with, to fight with desperately until one's latest breath. In the meantime," nervously, "*do* be cautious about that horrid weapon: won't you, now?"

"You ask me no questions about last night," he says, suddenly; "and there is something I must say to you. Get rid of that fellow Ridgway, the under-gardener. It was he opened the library window for me. He is untrustworthy, and too fond of filthy lucre ever to come to good. I bribed him."

He is now speaking with some difficulty, and is looking, not at her, but at the pattern he is drawing on the soft loam at his feet.

"Bribed him?" says Mona, in an indescribable tone.

"Yes. I knew about the secret panel from Warden, old Elspeth's nephew, who alone, I think, knew of its existence. I was determined to get the will. It seemed to me," cries he, with sudden excitement, "no such great crime to do away with an unrighteous deed that took from an elder son (without just cause) his honest rights, to bestow them upon the younger. What had my father done? Nothing! His brother, by treachery and base subterfuge, supplanted him, and obtained his birthright, while he, my father, was cast out, disinherited, without a hearing."

His passion carries Mona along with it.

"It was unjust, no doubt; it sounds so," she says, faintly. Yet even as she speaks she closes her little slender fingers resolutely upon the parchment that shall restore happiness to Nicholas and dear pretty Dorothy.

"To return to Ridgway," says Paul Rodney, pulling himself up abruptly. "See him yourself, I beg of you, as a last favor, and dismiss him. Send him over to me: I will take him back with me to Australia and give him a fresh start in life. I owe him so much, as I was the first to tempt him into the wrong path; yet I doubt whether he would have kept straight even had he not met me. He is *mauvais sujet* all through."

"Surely," thinks Mona to herself, "this strange young man is not altogether bad. He has his divine touches as well as another."

"I will do as you ask," she says, wondering when the interview will come to an end.

"After all, I am half glad Nicholas is not to be routed," he says, presently, with some weariness in his tone. "The game wasn't worth the candle; I should never have been able to do the *grand seigneur* as he does it. I suppose I am not to the manner born. Besides, I bear *him* no malice."

His tone, his emphasis on the pronoun, is significant.

"Why should you bear malice to any one?" says Mona uneasily.

"Your husband called me 'thief.' I have not forgotten that," replies he, gloomily, the dark blood of his mother's race rushing to his cheek. "I shall remember that insult to my dying day. And let him remember *this*, that if ever I meet him again, alone, and face to face, I shall kill him for that word only."

"Oh, no! no!" says Mona, shrinking from him. "Why cherish such revenge in your heart? Would you kill me too, that you speak like this? Fling such thoughts far from you, and strive after good. Revenge is the food of fools."

"Well, at least I sha'n't have many more opportunities of meeting him," says Rodney. "I shall leave this country as soon as I can. Tell Nicholas to keep the title with the rest. I shall never use it. And now," growing very pale, "it only remains to say good-by."

"Good-by," says Mona, softly, giving him her hand. He keeps it fast in both his own. Just at this moment it dawns upon her for the first time that this man loves her with a love surpassing that of most. The knowledge does not raise within her breast—as of course it should do—feelings of virtuous indignation: indeed, I regret to say that my heroine feels nothing but a deep and earnest pity, that betrays itself in her expressive face.

"Last night you called me Paul. Do you remember? Call me it again, for the last time," he entreats, in a low tone. "I shall never forget what I felt then. If ever in the future you hear good of me, believe it was through you it sprung to life. Till my dying day your image will remain with me. Say now, 'Good-by, Paul,' before I go."

"Good by, dear Paul," says Mona, very gently, impressed by his evident grief and earnestness.

"Good-by, my—my beloved—cousin," he says, in a choked voice. I think the last word is an afterthought. He is tearing himself from all he holds most sacred upon earth, and the strain is terrible. He moves resolutely a a few yards away from her, as though determined to put space between him and her; yet then he pauses, and, as though powerless to withdraw from her presence, returns again, and, flinging himself on his knees before her, presses a fold of her gown to his lips with passionate despair.

"It is forever!" he says, incoherently. "Oh, Mona, at least—*at least* promise you will always think kindly of me."

"Always—indeed, always!" says Mona, with tears in her eyes; after which, with a last miserable glance, he strides away, and is lost to sight among the trees.

Then Mrs. Geoffrey turns quickly, and runs home at the top of her speed. She is half sad, yet half exultant, being filled to the very heart with the knowledge that life, joy, and emancipation from present evil lie in her pocket. This thought crowns all others.

As she comes to the gravel walk that leads from the shrubberies to the sweep before the hall door, she encounters the disgraced Ridgway, doing something or other to one of the shrubs that has come to grief during the late bad weather.

He touches his hat to her, and bids her a respectful "good afternoon," but for once she is blind to his salutation. Nevertheless, she stops before him, and, in a clear voice, says, coldly,—

"For the future your services will not be required here. Your new master, Mr. Paul Rodney, whom you have chosen to obey in preference to those in whose employ you have been, will give you your commands from this day. Go to him, and after this try to be faithful."

The boy—he is little more—cowers beneath her glance. He changes color, and drops the branch he holds. No excuse rises to his lips. To attempt a lie with those clear eyes upon him would be worse than useless. He turns abruptly away, and is dead to the Towers from this moment.

CHAPTER XXXIII.

HOW CONVERSATION GROWS RIFE AT THE TOWERS— AND HOW MONA ASSERTS HERSELF—AND HOW LADY RODNEY LICKS THE DUST.

"Where can Mona be?" says Doatie, suddenly.

We must go back one hour. Lady Lilias Eaton has come and gone. It is now a quarter to five, and Violet is pouring out tea in the library.

"Yes; where is Mona?" says Jack, looking up from the cup she has just given him.

"I expect I know more than most about her," says Nolly, who is enjoying himself immensely among the sponge, and the plum-cakes. "I told her the Æsthetic was likely to call this afternoon, and advised her strongly to make her escape while she could."

"She evidently took your advice," says Nicholas.

"Well, I went rather minutely into it, you know. I explained to her how Lady Lilias was probably going to discuss the new curfew-bell in all its bearings; and I hinted gloomily at the 'Domesday Book.' *That* fetched her. She vamoosed on the spot."

"Nothing makes me so hungry as Lady Lilias," says Doatie, comfortably. She is lying back in a huge arm-chair that is capable of holding three like her, and is devouring bread and butter like a dainty but starved little fairy. Nicholas, sitting beside her, is holding her tea-cup, her own special tea-cup of gaudy Sèvres. "She is very trying, isn't she, Nicholas? What a dazzling skin she has!—the very whitest I ever saw."

"Well, that is in her favor, I really think," says Violet, in her most unprejudiced manner. "If she were to leave off her rococo toilettes, and take to Elise or Worth like other people, and give up posing, and try to behave like a rational being, she might almost be called handsome."

No one seconds this rash opinion. There is a profound silence. Miss Mansergh looks mildly round for support, and, meeting Jack's eyes, stops there.

"Well, really, you know, yes. I think there *is* something special about her," he says, feeling himself in duty bound to say something.

"So there is; something specially awful," responds Nolly, pensively. "She frightens me to death. She has an 'eye like a gimlet.' When I call to mind the day my father inveigled me into the library and sort of told me I couldn't do better than go in for Lilias, my knees give way beneath me and smite each other with fear. I shudder to think what part in her mediæval programme would have been allotted to me."

"You would have been her henchman,—is that right, Nicholas?—or her *varlet*," says Dorothy, with conviction, "And you would have had to stain your skin, and go round with a cross-bow, and with your mouth widened from ear to ear to give you the correct look. All æsthetic people have wide mouths, have they not, Nicholas?"

"Bless me, what an enthralling picture!" says Mr. Darling. "You make me regret all I have lost. But perhaps it is not yet too late. I say, Dolly, you are eating nothing. Have some more bread-and-butter or cake, old girl. You don't half take care of yourself."

"Well, do you know, I think I will take another bit of cake," says Doatie, totally unabashed. "And—cut it thick. After all, Noll, I don't believe Lilias would ever marry you, or any other man: she wouldn't know what to do with you."

"It is very good of you to say that," says Nolly, meekly but gratefully. "It gives me great support. You honestly believe, then, that I may escape?"

"Just fancy the Æsthetic with a husband, and a baby on her knee."

"Like 'Loraine Loraine Loree,'" says Violet, laughing.

"Did she have both together on her knee?" asks Dorothy, vaguely. "She must have found it heavy."

"Oh, one at a time," says Nolly. "She couldn't do it all at once. Such a stretch of fancy requires thought."

At this moment, Geoffrey—who has been absent—saunters into the room, and, after a careless glance around, says, lightly, as if missing something,—

"Where is Mona?"

"Well, we thought you would know," says Lady Rodney, speaking for the first time.

"Yes. Where is she?" says Doatie: "that is just what we all want to know. She won't get any tea if she doesn't come presently, because Nolly is bent on finishing it. Nolly," with plaintive protest, "don't be greedy."

"We thought she was with you," says Captain Rodney, idly.

"She is out," says Lady Rodney, in a compressed tone.

"Is she? It is too late for her to be out," returns Geoffrey, thinking of the chill evening air.

"Quite too late," acquiesces his mother, meaningly. "It is, to say the least of it, very strange, very unseemly. Out at this hour, and alone,—if, indeed, she is alone!"

Her tone is so unpleasant and so significant that silence falls upon the room. Geoffrey says nothing. Perhaps he alone among them fails to understand the meaning of her words. He seems lost in thought. So lost, that the others, watching him, wonder secretly what the end of his meditations will bring forth: yet, one and all, they mistake him: no doubt of Mona ever has, or ever will, I think, cross his mind.

Lady Rodney regards him curiously, trying to read his downcast face. Has the foolish boy at last been brought to see a flaw in his idol of clay?

Nicholas is looking angry. Jack, sinking into a chair near Violet, says, in a whisper, that "it is a beastly shame his mother cannot let Mona alone. She seems, by Jove! bent on turning Geoffrey against her."

"It is cruel," says Violet, with suppressed but ardent ire.

"If—if *you* loved a fellow, would anything turn you against him?" asks he, suddenly, looking her full in the face.

And she answers,—

"Nothing. Not all the talking in the wide world," with a brilliant blush, but with steady earnest eyes.

Nolly, mistrustful of Geoffrey's silence, goes up to him, and, laying his hands upon his shoulders, says, quietly,—

"Mrs. Geoffrey is incapable of making any mistake. How silent you are, old fellow!"

"Eh?" says Geoffrey, rousing himself and smiling genially. "A mistake? Oh, no. She never makes mistakes. I was thinking of something else. But she really ought to be in now, you know; she will catch her death of cold."

The utter want of suspicion in his tone drives Lady Rodney to open action. To do her justice, dislike to Mona has so warped her judgment that she almost believes in the evil she seeks to disseminate about her.

"You are wilfully blind," she says, flushing hotly, and smoothing with nervous fingers an imaginary wrinkle from her gown. "Of course I explained matters as well as I could to Mitchell, but it was very awkward, and very unpleasant, and servants are never deceived."

"I hardly think I follow you," says Geoffrey, in a frozen tone. "In regard to what would you wish your servants deceived?"

"Of course it is quite the correct thing your taking it in this way," goes on his mother, refusing to be warned, and speaking with irritation,—"the only course left open; but it is rather absurd with *me*. We have all noticed your wife's extraordinary civility to that shocking young man. Such bad taste on her part, considering how he stands with regard to us, and the unfortunate circumstances connected with him. But no good ever comes of unequal marriages."

"Now, once for all, mother—" begins Nicholas, vehemently, but Geoffrey, with a gesture, silences him.

"I am perfectly content, nay more than content, with the match I have made," he says, haughtily; "and if you are alluding to Paul Rodney, I can only say I have noticed nothing reprehensible in Mona's treatment of him."

"You are very much to be admired," says his mother, in an abominable tone.

"I see no reason why she should not talk to any man she pleases. I know her well enough to trust her anywhere, and am deeply thankful for such knowledge. In fact," with some passion, sudden but subdued, "I feel as though in discussing her in this cold-blooded fashion I am doing her some grievous wrong."

"It almost amounts to it," says Nicholas, with a frown.

"Besides, I do not understand what you mean," says Geoffrey, still regarding his mother with angry eyes "Why connect Mona's absence with Paul Rodney?"

"I shall tell you," exclaims she, in a higher tone, her pale-blue eyes flashing. "Two hours ago my own maid received a note from Paul Rodney's man directed to your wife. When she read it she dressed herself and went from this house in the direction of the wood. If you cannot draw your own conclusions from these two facts, you must be duller or more obstinate than I give you credit for."

She ceases, her work accomplished. The others in the room grow weak with fear, as they tell themselves that things are growing too dreadful to be borne much longer. When the silence is quite insupportable, poor little Dorothy struggles to the front.

"Dear Lady Rodney," she says, in a tremulous tone, "are you quite sure the note was from that—that man?"

"Quite sure," returns her future mother-in law, grimly. "I never speak, Dorothy, without foundation for what I say."

Dorothy, feeling snubbed, subsides into silence and the shadow that envelopes the lounge on which she is sitting.

To the surprise of everybody, Geoffrey takes no open notice of his mother's speech. He does not give way to wrath, nor does he open his lips on any subject. His face is innocent of anger, horror, or distrust. It changes, indeed, beneath the glow of the burning logs but in a manner totally unexpected. An expression that might even be termed hope lights it up. Like this do his thoughts run: "Can it be possible that the Australian has caved in, and, fearing publicity after last night's *fiasco*, surrendered the will to Mona?"

Possessed with this thought,—which drowns all others,—he clasps his hands behind his back and saunters to the window. "Shall he go and meet Mona and learn the truth at once? Better not, perhaps; she is such a clever child that it is as well to let her achieve victory without succor of any sort."

He leans against the window and looks out anxiously upon the darkening twilight. His mother watches him with curious eyes. Suddenly he electrifies the whole room by whistling in a light and airy fashion his favorite song from "Madame Favart." It is the "Artless Thing," and nothing less, and he whistles it deliberately and dreamily from start to finish.

It seems such a direct running commentary on Mona's supposed ill deed that every one—as by a single impulse—looks up. Nolly and Jack Rodney exchange covert glances. But for the depression that reigns all round, I think these two would have given way to frivolous merriment.

"By Jove, you know, it is odd," says Geoffrey, presently, speaking as one might who has for long been following out a train of thought by no means unpleasant, "his sending for her, and that: there must be something in it. Rodney didn't write to her for nothing. It must have been to——" Here he checks himself abruptly, remembering his promise to Mona to say nothing about the scene in the library. "It certainly means something," he winds up, a little tamely.

"No doubt," returns his mother, sneeringly.

"My dear mother," says Geoffrey, coming back to the firelight, "what you would insinuate is too ridiculous to be taken any notice of." Every particle of his former passion has died from his voice, and he is now quite calm, nay cheerful.

"But at the same time I must ask you to remember you are speaking of my wife."

"I do remember it," replies she, bitterly.

Just at this moment a light step running up the stairs outside and across the veranda makes itself heard. Every one looks expectant, and the slight displeasure dies out of Geoffrey's face. A slender, graceful figure appears at the window, and taps lightly.

"Open the window, Geoff," cries Mona, eagerly, and as he obeys her commands she steps into the room with a certain touch of haste about her movements, and looks round upon them earnestly,—some peculiar expression, born of a glad thought, rendering her lovely face even more perfect than usual.

There is a smile upon her lips; her hands are clasped behind her.

"I am so glad you have come, darling," says little Dorothy, taking off her hat, and laying it on a chair near her.

Geoffrey removes the heavy lace that lies round her throat, and then leads her up to the hearthrug nearly opposite to his mother's arm-chair.

"Where have you been, Mona?" he asks, quietly, gazing into the great honest liquid eyes raised so willingly to his own.

"You shall guess," says Mrs. Geoffrey, gayly, with a little laugh. "Now, where do you think?"

Geoffrey says nothing. But Sir Nicholas, as though impulsively, says,—

"In the wood?"

Perhaps he is afraid for her. Perhaps it is a gentle hint to her that the truth will be best. Whatever it may be, Mona understands him not at all. His mother glances up sharply.

"Why, so I was," says Mona, opening her eyes with some surprise, and with an amused smile. "What a good guess, and considering how late the hour is, too!"

She smiles again. Lady Rodney, watching her intently, tells herself if this is acting it is the most perfectly done thing she ever saw in her life, either on the stage or off it.

Geoffrey's arm slips from his wife's shoulders to her rounded waist.

"Perhaps, as you have been so good at your first guess you will try again," says Mona, still addressing Nicholas, and speaking in a tone of unusual light-heartedness, but so standing that no one can see why her hands are so persistently clasped behind her back. "Now tell me who I was with."

This is a thunderbolt. They all start guiltily, and regard Mona with wonder. What is she going to say next?

"So," she says, mockingly, laughing at Nicholas, "you cannot play the seer any longer? Well, I shall tell you. I was with Paul Rodney!"

She is plainly quite enchanted with the sensation she is creating, though she is far from comprehending how complete that sensation is. Something in her expression appeals to Doatie's heart and makes her involuntarily go closer to her. Her face is transfigured. It is full of love and unselfish joy and happy exultation: always lovely, there is at this moment something divine about her beauty.

"What have you got behind your back?" says Geoffrey, suddenly, going up to her.

She flushes, opens her lips as if to speak, and yet is dumb,—perhaps through excess of emotion.

"Mona, it is not—it cannot be—but is it?" asks he incoherently.

"The missing will? Yes—yes—*yes!*" cries she, raising the hand that is behind her, and holding it high above her head with the will held tightly in it.

It is a supreme moment. A deadly silence falls upon the room, and then Dorothy bursts into tears. In my heart I believe she feels as much relief at Mona's exculpation as at the discovery of the desired deed.

Mona, turning not to Nicholas or to Doatie or to Geoffrey but to Lady Rodney, throws the paper into her lap.

"The will—but are you sure—sure?" says Lady Rodney, feebly. She tries to rise, but sinks back again in her chair, feeling faint and overcome.

"Quite sure," says Mona, and then she laughs aloud—a sweet, joyous laugh,—and clasps her hands together with undisguised delight and satisfaction.

Geoffrey, who has tears in his eyes, takes her in his arms and kisses her once softly, before them all.

"My best beloved," he says, with passionate fondness, beneath his breath; but she hears him, and wonders vaguely but gladly at his tone, not understanding the rush of tenderness that almost overcomes him as he remembers how his mother—whom she has been striving with all her power to benefit—has been grossly maligning and misjudging her. Truly she is too good for those among whom her lot has been cast.

"It is like a fairy-tale," says Violet, with unwonted excitement. "Oh, Mona, tell us how you managed it."

"Well, just after luncheon Letitia, your maid, brought me a note. I opened it. It was from Paul Rodney, asking me to meet him at three o'clock, as he had something of importance to say that concerned not me but those I loved. When he said *that*," says Mona, looking round upon them all with a large, soft, comprehensive glance, and a sweet smile, "I knew he meant *you*. So I went. I got into my coat and hat, and ran all the way to the spot he had appointed,—the big chestnut-tree near the millstream: you know it, Geoff, don't you?"

"Yes, I know it," says Geoffrey.

"He was there before me, and almost immediately he drew the will from his pocket, and said he would give it to me if—if—well, he gave it to me," says Mrs. Geoffrey, changing color as she remembers her merciful escape. "And he desired me to tell you, Nicholas, that he would never claim the title, as it was useless to him and it sits so sweetly on you. And then I clutched the will, and held it tightly, and ran all the way back with it, and—and that's all!"

She smiles again, and, with a sigh of rapture at her own success, turns to Geoffrey and presses her lips to his out of the very fulness of her heart.

"Why have you taken all this trouble about us?" says Lady Rodney, leaning forward to look at the girl anxiously, her voice low and trembling.

At this Mona, being a creature of impulse, grows once more pale and troubled.

"It was for you," she says, hanging her head. "I thought if I could do something to make you happier, you might learn to love me a little!"

"I have wronged you," says Lady Rodney, in a low tone, covering her face with her hands.

"Go to her," says Geoffrey, and Mona, slipping from his embrace, falls on her knees at his mother's feet. With one little frightened hand she tries to possess herself of the fingers that shield the elder woman's face.

"It is too late," says Lady Rodney, in a stifled tone. "I have said so many things about you, that—that——"

"I don't care what you have said," interrupts Mona, quickly. She has her arms round Lady Rodney's waist by this time, and is regarding her beseechingly.

"There is too much to forgive," says Lady Rodney, and as she speaks two tears roll down her cheeks. This evidence of emotion from her is worth a torrent from another.

"Let there be no talk of forgiveness between you and me," says Mona, very sweetly, after which Lady Rodney fairly gives way, and placing her arms round the kneeling girl, draws her to her bosom and kisses her tenderly.

Every one is delighted. Perhaps Nolly and Jack Rodney are conscious of a wild desire to laugh, but if so, they manfully suppress it, and behave as decorously as the rest.

"Now I am quite, quite happy," says Mona, and, rising from her knees, she goes back again to Geoffrey, and stands beside him. "Tell them all about last night," she says, looking up at him, "and the secret cupboard."

CHAPTER XXXIV.

HOW THE RODNEYS MAKE MERRY OVER THE SECRET PANEL—HOW GEOFFREY QUESTIONS MONA—AND HOW, WHEN JOY IS AT ITS HIGHEST EVIL TIDINGS SWEEP DOWN UPON THEM.

At the mention of the word "secret" every one grows very much alive at once. Even Lady Rodney dries her tears and looks up expectantly.

"Yes, Geoffrey and I have made a discovery,—a most important one,—and it has lain heavy on our breasts all day. Now tell them everything about last night, Geoff, from beginning to end."

Thus adjured,—though in truth he requires little pressing, having been devoured with a desire since early dawn to reveal the hidden knowledge that is in his bosom,—Geoffrey relates to them the adventure of the night before. Indeed, he gives such a brilliant coloring to the tale that every one is stricken dumb with astonishment, Mona herself perhaps being the most astonished of all. However, like a good wife, she makes no comments, and contradicts his statements not at all, so that (emboldened by her evident determination not to interfere with anything he may choose to say) he gives them such a story as absolutely brings down the house,—metaphorically speaking.

"A secret panel! Oh, how enchanting! do, *do* show it to me!" cries Doatie Darling, when this marvellous recital has come to an end. "If there is one thing I adore, it is a secret chamber, or a closet in a house, or a ghost."

"You may have the ghosts all to yourself. I sha'n't grudge them to you. I'll have the cupboards," says Nicholas, who has grown at least ten years younger during the last hour. "Mona, show us this one."

Mona, drawing a chair to the panelled wall, steps up on it, and, pressing her finger on the seventh panel, it slowly rolls back, betraying the vacuum behind.

They all examine it with interest, Nolly being specially voluble on the occasion.

"And to think we all sat pretty nearly every evening within a yard or two of that blessed will, and never knew anything about it!" he says, at last, in a tone of unmitigated disgust.

"Yes, that is just what occurred to me," says Mona, nodding her head sympathetically.

"No? did it?" says Nolly, sentimentally. "How—how awfully satisfactory it is to know we both thought alike on even one subject!"

Mona, after a stare of bewilderment that dies at its birth, gives way to laughter: she is still standing on the chair, and looking down on Nolly, who is adoring her in the calm and perfectly open manner that belongs to him.

Just then Dorothy says,—

"Shut it up tight again, Mona, and let *me* try to open it." And, Mona having closed the panel again and jumped down off the chair, Doatie takes her place, and, supported by Nicholas, opens and shuts the secret door again and again to her heart's content.

"It is quite simple: there is no deception," says Mr. Darling, addressing the room, with gracious encouragement in his tone, shrugging his shoulders and going through all the airs and graces that belong to the orthodox French showman.

"It is quite necessary you should know all about it," says Nicholas, in a low tone, to Dorothy, whom he is holding carefully, as though under the mistaken impression that young women if left on chairs without support invariably fall off them. "As the future mistress here, you ought to be up to every point connected with the old place."

Miss Darling blushes. It is so long since she has given way to this weakness that now she does it warmly and generously, as though to make up for other opportunities neglected. She scrambles down off the chair, and, going up to Mona, surprises that heroine of the hour by bestowing upon her a warm though dainty hug.

"It is all your doing. How wretched we should have been had we never seen you!" she says, with tears of gratitude in her eyes.

Altogether it is a very exciting and pleasurable moment.

The panel is as good as a toy to them. They all open it by turns, and wonder over it, and rejoice in it. But Geoffrey, taking Mona aside, says curiously, and a little gravely,—

"Tell me why you hesitated in your speech a while ago. Talking of Rodney's giving you the will, you said he offered to give it you if—if——What did the 'if' mean?"

"Come over to the window, and I will tell you," says Mrs. Geoffrey. "He—he—you must take no notice of it, Geoffrey, but he wanted to kiss me. He offered me the will for one kiss, and——"

"You didn't get possession of it in that way?" asks he, seizing her hands and trying to read her face.

"Oh, no! But listen to my story. When he saw how I hated his proposal, he very generously forgave the price, and let me have the document a free gift. That was rather good of him, was it not? because men like having their own way, you know."

"Very self-denying of him, indeed," says Geoffrey, with a slight sneer, and a sigh of relief.

"Had I given in, would you have been very angry?" asks she regarding him earnestly.

"Very."

"Then what a mercy it is I didn't do it!" says Mona, naively. "I was very near it, do you know? I had actually said 'Yes,' because I could not make up my mind to lose the deed, when he let me off the bargain. But, if he had persisted, I tell you honestly I am quite sure I should have let him kiss me."

"Mona, don't talk like that," says Geoffrey, biting his lips.

"Well, but, after all, one can't be much of a friend if one can't sacrifice one's self sometimes for those one loves," says Mrs. Geoffrey, reproachfully. "You would have done it yourself in my place!"

"What! kiss the Australian? I'd see him—very well—that is—ahem! I certainly would not, you know," says Mr. Rodney.

"Well, I suppose I am wrong," says Mona, with a sigh. "Are you very angry with me, Geoff? Would you ever have forgiven me if I had done it?"

"I should," says Geoffrey, pressing her hands. "You would always be to me the best and truest woman alive. But—but I shouldn't have liked it."

"Well, neither should I!" says Mrs. Geoffrey, with conviction. "I should perfectly have hated it. But I should never have forgiven myself if he had gone away with the will."

"It is quite a romance," says Jack Rodney: "I never heard anything like it before off the stage." He is speaking to the room generally. "I doubt if any one but you, Mona, would have got the will out of him. He hates the rest of us like poison."

"But—bless me!—how awfully he must be in love with you to resign the Towers for your sake!" says Nolly, suddenly giving words to the thought that has been tormenting him for some time.

As this is the idea that has haunted every one since the disclosure, and that they each and all have longed but feared to discuss, they now regard Nolly with admiration,—all save Lady Rodney, who, remembering her unpleasant insinuations of an hour ago, moves uneasily in her chair, and turns an uncomfortable crimson.

Mona is, however, by no means disconcerted; she lifts her calm eyes to Nolly's, and answers him without even a blush.

"Do you know it never occurred to me until this afternoon?" she says, simply; "but now I think—I may be mistaken, but I really do think he fancies himself in love with me. A very silly fancy, of course."

"He must adore you; and no wonder, too," says Mr. Darling, so emphatically that every one smiles, and Jack, clapping him on the back, says,—

"Well done, Nolly! Go it again, old chap!"

"Oh, Mona, what courage you showed! Just imagine staying in the library when you found yourself face to face with a person you never expected to see, and in the dead of night, with every one sound asleep! In your case I should either have fainted or rushed back to my bedroom again as fast as my feet could carry me; and I believe," says Dorothy, with conviction, "I should so far have forgotten myself as to scream every inch of the way."

"I don't believe you would," says Mona. "A great shock sobers one. I forgot to be frightened until it was all over. And then the dogs were a great support."

"When he held the pistol to your forehead, didn't you scream then?" asks Violet.

"To my forehead?" says Mona, puzzled; and then she glances at Geoffrey, remembering that this was one of the slight variations with which he adorned his tale.

"No, she didn't," interposes he, lightly. "She never funked it for a moment: she's got any amount of pluck. He didn't exactly press it against her forehead, you know; but," airily, "it is all the same thing."

"When you got the pistol so cleverly into your own possession, why on earth didn't you shoot him?" demands Mr. Darling, gloomily, who evidently feels bloodthirsty when he thinks of the Australian and his presumptuous admiration for the peerless Mona.

"Ah! sure you know I wouldn't do that, now," returns she, with a stronger touch of her native brogue than she has used for many a day; at which they all laugh heartily, even Lady Rodney chiming in as easily as though the day had never been when she had sneered contemptuously at that selfsame Irish tongue.

"Well, 'All's well that ends well,'" says Captain Rodney, thoughtlessly. "If that delectable cousin of ours would only sink into the calm and silent grave now, we might even have the title back without fear of dispute, and find ourselves just where we began."

It is at this very moment the library door is suddenly flung open, and Jenkins appears upon the threshold, with his face as white as nature will permit, and his usually perfect manner much disturbed. "Sir Nicholas, can I speak to you for a moment?" he says, with much excitement, growing positively apoplectic in his endeavor to be calm.

"What is it, Jenkins? Speak!" says Lady Rodney, rising from her chair, and staying him, as he would leave the room, by an imperious gesture.

"Oh, my lady, if I must speak," cries the old man, "but it is terrible news to tell without a word of warning. Mr. Paul Rodney is dying: he shot himself half an hour ago, and is lying now at Rawson's Lodge in the beech wood."

Mona grows livid, and takes a step forward.

"Shot himself! How?" she says, hoarsely, her bosom rising and falling tumultuously. "Jenkins, answer me."

"Tell us, Jenkins," says Nicholas, hastily.

"It appears he had a pocket-pistol with him, Sir Nicholas, and going home through the wood he stumbled over some roots, and it went off and injured him fatally. It is an internal wound, my lady. Dr. Bland, who is with him, says there is no hope."

"No hope!" says Mona, with terrible despair in her voice: "then I have killed him. It was I returned him that pistol this evening. It is my fault,—mine. It is I have caused his death."

This thought seems to overwhelm her. She raises her hands to her head, and an expression of keenest anguish creeps into her eyes. She sways a little, and would have fallen, but that Jack Rodney, who is nearest to her at this moment, catches her in his arms.

"Mona," says Nicholas, roughly, laying his hand on her shoulder, and shaking her slightly, "I forbid you talking like that. It is nobody's fault. It is the will of God. It is morbid and sinful of you to let such a thought enter your head."

"So it is really, Mrs. Geoffrey, you know," says Nolly, placing his hand on her other shoulder to give her a second shake. "Nick's quite right. Don't take it to heart; don't now. You might as well say the gunsmith who originally sold him the fatal weapon is responsible for this unhappy event, as—as that you are."

"Besides, it may be an exaggeration," suggests Geoffrey "he may not be so bad as they say."

"I fear there is no doubt of it, sir," says Jenkins, respectfully, who in his heart of hearts looks upon this timely accident as a direct interposition of Providence. "And the messenger who came (and who is now in the hall, Sir Nicholas, if you would wish to question him) says Dr. Bland sent him up to let you know at once of the unfortunate occurrence."

Having said all this without a break, Jenkins feels he has outdone himself, and retires on his laurels.

Nicholas, going into the outer hall, cross-examines the boy who has brought the melancholy tidings, and, having spoken to him for some time, goes back to the library with a face even graver than it was before.

"The poor fellow is calling for you, Mona, incessantly," he says. "It remains with you to decide whether you will go to him or not. Geoffrey, *you* should have a voice in this matter, and I think she ought to go."

"Oh, Mona, do go—do," entreats Doatie, who is in tears. "Poor, poor fellow! I wish now I had not been so rude to him."

"Geoffrey, will you take me to him?" says Mona, rousing herself.

"Yes. Hurry, darling. If you think you can bear it, you should lose no time. Minutes even, I fear, are precious in this case."

Then some one puts on her again the coat she had taken off such a short time since, and some one else puts on her sealskin cap and twists her black lace round her white throat, and then she turns to go on her sad mission. All their joy is turned to mourning, their laughter to tears.

Nicholas, who had left the room again, returns now, bringing with him a glass of wine, which he compels her to swallow, and then, pale and frightened, but calmer than she was before, she leaves the house, and starts with Geoffrey for the gamekeeper's lodge, where lies the man they had so dreaded, impotent in the arms of death.

Night is creeping up over the land. Already in the heavens the pale crescent moon just born rides silently,—

"Wi' the auld moon in hir arme,"

A deep hush has fallen upon everything. The air is cold and piercing. Mona shivers, and draws even closer to Geoffrey, as, mute, yet full of saddest thought, they move through the leafless wood.

As they get within view of the windows of Rawson's cottage, they are met by Dr. Bland, who has seen them coming, and has hurried out to receive them.

"Now, this is kind,—very kind," says the little man, approvingly, shaking both their hands. "And so soon, too; no time lost. Poor soul! he is calling incessantly for you, my dear Mrs. Geoffrey. It is a sad case,—very—very. Away from every one he knows. But come in; come in."

He draws Mrs. Geoffrey's hand through his arm, and goes towards the lodge.

"Is there no hope?" asks Geoffrey, gravely.

"None; none. It would be useless to say otherwise. Internal hemorrhage has set in. A few hours, perhaps less, must end it. He knows it himself, poor boy!"

"Oh! can nothing be done?" asks Mona, turning to him eyes full of entreaty.

"My dear, what I could do, I have done," says the little man, patting her hand in his kind fatherly fashion; "but he has gone beyond human skill. And now one thing: you have come here, I know, with the tender thought of soothing his last hours: therefore I entreat you to be calm and very quiet. Emotion will only distress him, and, if you feel too nervous, you know—perhaps—eh?"

"I shall not be too nervous," says Mona, but her face blanches afresh even as she speaks; and Geoffrey sees it.

"If it is too much for you, darling, say so," whispers he; "or shall I go with you?"

"It is better she should go alone," says Dr. Bland. "He would be quite unequal to two; and besides,—pardon me,—from what he has said to me I fear there were unpleasant passages between you and him."

"There were," confesses Geoffrey, reluctantly, and in a low tone. "I wish now from my soul it had been otherwise. I regret much that has taken place."

"We all have regrets at times, dear boy, the very best of us," says the little doctor, blowing his nose: "who among us is faultless? And really the circumstances were very trying for you,—very—eh? Yes, of course one understands, you know; but death heals all divisions, and he is hurrying to his last account, poor lad, all too soon."

They have entered the cottage by this time, and are standing in the tiny hall.

"Open that door, Mrs. Geoffrey," says the doctor pointing to his right hand. "I saw you coming, and have prepared him for the interview. I shall be just here, or in the next room, if you should want me. But I can do little for him more than I have done."

"You will be near too, Geoffrey?" murmurs Mona, falteringly.

"Yes, yes; I promise for him," says Dr. Bland. "In fact, I have something to say to your husband that must be told at once."

Then Mona, opening the door indicated to her by the doctor, goes into the chamber beyond, and is lost to their view for some time.

CHAPTER XXXV.

HOW MONA COMFORTS PAUL RODNEY—HOW NIGHT AND DEATH DESCEND TOGETHER—AND HOW PAUL RODNEY DISPOSES OF HIS PROPERTY.

On a low bed, with his eyes fastened eagerly upon the door, lies Paul Rodney, the dews of death already on his face.

There is no disfigurement about him to be seen, no stain of blood, no ugly mark; yet he is touched by the pale hand of the destroyer, and is sinking, dying, withering beneath it. He has aged at least ten years within the last fatal hour, while in his eyes lies an expression so full of hungry expectancy and keen longing as amounts almost to anguish.

As Mona advances to his side, through the gathering gloom of fast approaching night, pale almost as he is, and trembling in every limb, this miserable anxiety dies out of his face, leaving behind it a rest and peace unutterable.

To her it is an awful moment. Never before has she stood face to face with dissolution, to wait for the snapping of the chain,—the breaking of the bowl. "Neither the sun nor death," says La Rochefoucauld, "can be looked at steadily;" and now "Death's thousand doors stand open" to receive this man that but an hour agone was full of life as she is now. His pulses throbbed, his blood coursed lightly through his veins, the grave seemed a far-off destination; yet here he lies, smitten to the earth, beaten down and trodden under, with nothing further to anticipate but the last change of all.

"O Death! thou strange, mysterious power, seen every day yet never understood but by the incommunicative dead, what art thou?"

"You have come," he says, with a quick sigh that be speaks relief. "I knew you would. I felt it; yet I feared. Oh, what comfort to see you again!"

Mona tries to say something,—anything that will be kind and sympathetic,— but words fail her. Her lips part, but no sound escapes them. The terrible reality of the moment terrifies and overcomes her.

"Do not try to make me any commonplace speeches," says Rodney, marking her hesitation. He speaks hastily, yet with evident difficulty. "I am dying. Nothing, can alter that. But death has brought you to my side again, so I cannot repine."

"But to find you like this"—begins Mona. And then overcome by grief and agitation, she covers her face with her hands, and bursts into tears.

"Mona! Are you crying for me?" says Paul Rodney, as though surprised. "Do not. Your tears hurt me more than this wound that has done me to death."

"Oh, if I had not given you that pistol," sobs Mona, who cannot conquer the horror of the thought that she has helped him to his death, "you would be alive and strong now."

"Yes,—and miserable! you forget to add that. Now everything seems squared. In the grave neither grief nor revenge can find a place. And as for you, what have you to do with my fate?—nothing. What should you not return to me my own? and why should I not die by the weapon I had dared to level against yourself? There is a justice in it that smacks of Sadlers' Wells."

He actually laughs, though faintly, and Mona looks up. Perhaps he has forced himself to this vague touch of merriment (that is even sadder than tears) just to please and rouse her from her despondency,—because the laugh dies almost as it is born, and an additional pallor covers his lips in its stead.

"Listen to me," he goes on, in a lower key, and with some slight signs of exhaustion. "I am glad to die,—unfeignedly glad: therefore rejoice with me! Why should you waste a tear on such as I am? Do you remember how I told you (barely two hours ago) that my life had come to an end where other fellows hope to begin theirs? I hardly knew myself how prophetic my words would prove."

"It is terrible, terrible," says Mona, piteously sinking on her knees beside the bed. One of his hands is lying outside the coverlet, and, with a gesture full of tender regret, she lays her own upon it.

"Are you in pain?" she says, in a low, fearful tone. "Do you suffer much?"

"I suffer nothing: I have no pain now. I am inexpressibly, happy," replies he, with a smile radiant, though languid. Forgetful of his unfortunate state, he raises his other hand, and, bringing it across the bed, tries to place it on Mona's. But the action is too much for him. His face takes a leaden hue, more ghastly than its former pallor, and, in spite of an heroic effort to suppress it, a deep groan escapes him.

"Ah!" says Mona, springing to her feet, and turning to the door, as though to summon aid; but he stops her by a gesture.

"No, it is nothing. It will be over in a moment," gasps he. "Give me some brandy, and help me to cheat Death of his prey for a little time, if it be possible."

Seeing brandy, on a table near, she pours a little into a glass with a shaking hand, and passing her arm beneath his neck, holds it to his parched lips.

It revives him somewhat. And presently the intenser pallor dies away, and speech returns to him.

"Do not call for assistance," he whispers, imploringly. "They can do me no good. Stay with me. Do not forsake me. Swear you will remain with me to— to the end."

"I promise you faithfully," says Mona.

"It is too much to ask, but I dread being alone," he goes on, with a quick shudder of fear and repulsion. "It is a dark and terrible journey to take, with no one near who loves one, with no one to feel a single regret when one has departed."

"*I* shall feel regret," says, Mona, brokenly, the tears running down her cheeks.

"Give me your hand again," says Rodney, after a pause; and when she gives it to him he says, "Do you know this is the nearest approach to real happiness I have ever known in all my careless, useless life? What is it Shakspeare says about the folly of loving 'a bright particular star'? I always think of you when that line comes to my mind. You are the star; mine is the folly."

He smiles again, but Mona is too sad to smile in return.

"How did it happen?" she asks, presently.

"I don't know myself. I wandered in a desultory fashion through the wood on leaving you, not caring to return home just then, and I was thinking of— of you, of course—when I stumbled against something (they tell me it was a gnarled root that had thrust itself above ground), and then there was a report, and a sharp pang; and that was all. I remember nothing. The gamekeeper found me a few minutes later, and had me brought here."

"You are talking too much," says Mona, nervously.

"I may as well talk while I can: soon you will not be able to hear me, when the grass is growing over me," replies he, recklessly. "It was hardly worth my while to deliver you up that will, was it? Is not Fate ironical? Now it is all as it was before I came upon the scene, and Nicholas has the title without dispute. I wish we had been better friends,—he at least was civil to me,—but I was reared with hatred in my heart towards all the Rodneys; I was taught to despise and fear them as my natural enemies, from my cradle."

Then, after a pause, "Where will they bury me?" he asks, suddenly. "Do you think they will put me in the family vault?" He seems to feel some anxiety on this point.

"Whatever you wish shall be done," says Mona earnestly, knowing she can induce Nicholas to accede to any request of hers.

"Are you sure?" asks he, his face brightening. "Remember how they have drawn back from me. I was their own first-cousin,—the son of their father's brother,—yet they treated me as the veriest outcast."

Then Mona says, in a trembling voice and rather disconnectedly, because of her emotion, "Be quite sure you shall be—buried—where all the other baronets of Rodney lie at rest."

"Thank you," murmurs he, gratefully. There is evidently comfort in the thought. Then after a moment or two he goes on again, as though following out a pleasant idea: "Some day, perhaps, that vault will hold you too; and there at least we shall meet again, and be side by side."

"I wish you would not talk of being buried," says Mona, with a sob. "There is no comfort in the tomb: *there* our dust may mingle, but in *heaven* our souls shall meet, I trust,—I hope."

"Heaven," repeats he, with a sigh. "I have forgotten to think of heaven."

"Think of it now, Paul,—now before it is too late," entreats she, piteously. "Try to pray: there is always mercy."

"Pray for me!" says he, in a low tone, pressing her hand. So on her knees, in a subdued voice, sad but earnest, she repeats what prayers she can remember out of the grand Service that belongs to us. One or two sentences from the Litany come to her; and then some words rise from her own heart, and she puts up a passionate supplication to heaven that the passing soul beside her, however erring, may reach some haven where rest remaineth!

Some time elapses before he speaks again, and Mona is almost hoping he may have fallen into a quiet slumber, when he opens his eyes and says, regretfully,—

"What a different life mine might have been had I known you earlier!" Then, with a faint flush, that vanishes almost as it comes, as though without power to stay, he says, "Did your husband object to your coming here?"

"Geoffrey? Oh, no. It was he who brought me. He bade me hasten lest you should even imagine me careless about coming. And—and—he desired me to say how he regrets the harsh words he uttered and the harsher thoughts he may have entertained towards you. Forgive him, I implore you, and die in peace with him and all men."

"Forgive him!" says Rodney. "Surely, however unkind the thoughts he may have cherished for me, I must forget and forgive them now, seeing all he has done for me. Has he not made smooth my last hours? Has he not lent me you? Tell him I bear him no ill will."

"I will tell him," says Mona.

He is silent for a full minute; then he says,—

"I have given a paper to Dr. Bland for you: it will explain what I wish. And, Mona, there are some papers in my room: will you see to them for me and have them burned?"

"I will burn them with my own hands," says Mona.

"How comforting you are!—how you understand," he says, with a quick sigh. "There is something else: that fellow Ridgway, who opened the window for me, he must be seen to. Let him have the money mentioned in the paper, and send him to my mother: she will look after him for my sake. My poor mother!" he draws his breath quickly.

"Shall I write to her?" asks Mona, gently. "Say what you wish done."

"It would be kind of you," says he, gratefully. "She will want to know all, and you will do it more tenderly than the others. Do not dwell upon my sins; and say I died—happy. Let her too have a copy of the paper Dr. Bland has now."

"I shall remember," says Mona, not knowing what the paper contains. "And who am I, that I should dwell upon the sins of another? Are you tired, Paul? How fearfully pale you are looking!"

He is evidently quite exhausted. His brow is moist, his eyes are sunken, his lips more pallid, more death-like than they were before. In little painful gasps his breath comes fitfully. Then all at once it occurs to Mona that though he is looking at her he does not see her. His mind has wandered far away to those earlier days when England was unknown and when the free life of the colony was all he desired.

As Mona gazes at him half fearfully, he raises himself suddenly on his elbow, and says, in a tone far stronger than he has yet used,—

"How brilliant the moonlight is to-night! See—watch"—eagerly—"how the shadows chase each other down the Ranger's Hill!"

Mona looks up startled. The faint rays of the new-born moon are indeed rushing through the casement, and are flinging themselves languidly upon the opposite wall, but they are pale and wan, as moonlight is in its infancy, and anything but brilliant. Besides, Rodney's eyes are turned not on them, but on the door that can be seen just over Mona's head, where no beams disport themselves, however weakly.

"Lie down: you will hurt yourself again," she says, trying gently to induce him to return to his former recumbent position; but he resists her.

"Who has taken my orders about the sheep?" he says, in a loud voice, and in an imperious tone, his eyes growing bright but uncertain. "Tell Grainger to see to it. My father spoke about it again only yesterday. The upper pastures are fresher—greener——"

His voice breaks: with a groan he sinks back again upon his pillow.

"Mona, are you still there?" he says, with a return to consciousness: "did I dream, or did my father speak to me? How the night comes on!" He sighs wearily. "I am so tired,—so worn out: if I could only sleep!" he murmurs, faintly.

Alas! how soon will fall upon him that eternal sleep from which no man waketh!

His breath grows fainter, his eyelids close.

Some one comes in with a lamp, and places it on a distant table, where its rays cannot distress the dying man.

Dr. Bland, coming into the room, goes up to the bedside and feels his pulse, and tries to put something between his lips, but he refuses to take anything.

"It will strengthen you," he says, persuasively.

"No, it is of no use: it only wearies me. My best medicine, my only medicine, is here," returns Paul, feebly pressing Mona's hand. He is answering the doctor, but he does not look at him. As he speaks, his gaze is riveted upon Mona.

Dr. Bland, putting down the glass, forbears to torment him further, and moves away; Geoffrey, who has also come in, takes his place. Bending over the dying man, he touches him lightly on the shoulder.

Paul turns his head, and as he sees Geoffrey a quick spasm that betrays fear crosses his face.

"Do not take her away yet,—not yet," he says, in a faint whisper.

"No, no. She will stay," says Geoffrey, hurriedly: "I only want to tell you, my dear fellow, how grieved I am for you, and how gladly I would undo many things—if I could."

The other smiles faintly. He is evidently glad because of Geoffrey's words, but speech is now very nearly impossible to him. His attempt to rise, to point out the imaginary moonlight to Mona, has greatly wasted his small remaining stock of life, and now but a thin partition, frail and broken, lies between him and that inexorable Rubicon we all must one day pass.

Then he turns his head away again to let his eyes rest on Mona, as though nowhere else can peace or comfort be found.

Geoffrey, moving to one side, stands where he can no longer be seen, feeling instinctively that the ebbing life before him finds its sole consolation in the thought of Mona. She is all he desires. From her he gains courage to face the coming awful moment, when he shall have to clasp the hand of Death and go forth with him to meet the great unknown.

Presently he closes his fingers upon hers, and looking up, she sees his lips are moving, though no sound escapes them. Leaning over him, she bends her face to his and whispers softly,—

"What is it?"

"It is nearly over," he gasps, painfully. "Say good-by to me. Do not quite forget me, not utterly. Give me some small place in your memory, though— so unworthy."

"I shall not forget; I shall always remember," returns she, the tears running down her cheeks; and then, through divine pity, and perhaps because Geoffrey is here to see her, she stoops and lays her lips upon his forehead.

Never afterwards will she forget the glance of gratitude that meets hers, and that lights up all his face, even his dim eyes, as she grants him this gentle pitiful caress.

"Pray for me," he says.

And then she falls upon her knees again, and Geoffrey in the background, though unseen, kneels too; and Mona, in a broken voice, because she is crying very bitterly now, whispers some words of comfort for the dying.

The minutes go by slowly, slowly; a clock from some distant steeple chimes the hour. The soft pattering of rain upon the walk outside, and now upon the window-pane, is all the sound that can be heard.

In the death-chamber silence reigns. No one moves, their very breathing seems hushed. Paul Rodney's eyes are closed. No faintest movement disturbs the slumber into which he seems to have fallen.

Thus half an hour goes by. Then Geoffrey, growing uneasy, raises his head and looks at Mona. From where he sits the bed is hidden from him, but he can see that she is still kneeling beside it, her hand in Rodney's, her face hidden in the bedclothes.

The doctor at this instant returns to the room, and, going on tiptoe (as though fearful of disturbing the sleeper) to where Mona is kneeling, looks anxiously at Rodney. But, alas! no sound of earth will evermore disturb the slumber of the quiet figure upon which he gazes.

The doctor, after a short examination of the features (that are even now turning to marble), knits his brows, and, going over to Geoffrey, whispers something into his ear while pointing to Mona.

"At once," he says, with emphasis.

Geoffrey starts. He walks quickly up to Mona, and, stooping over her, very gently loosens her hand from the other hand she is holding. Passing his arm round her neck, he turns her face deliberately in his own direction—as though to keep her eyes from resting on the bed and lays it upon his own breast.

"Come," he says, gently.

"Oh, not yet!" entreats faithful Mona, in a miserable tone; "not *yet*. Remember what I said. I promised to remain with him until the very end."

"You have kept your promise," returns he, solemnly, pressing her face still closer against his chest.

A strong shudder runs through her frame; she grows a little heavier in his embrace. Seeing she has fainted, he lifts her in his arms and carries her out of the room.

Later on, when they open the paper that had been given by the dead man into the keeping of Dr. Bland, and which proves to be his will, duly signed and witnessed by the gamekeeper and his son, they find he has left to Mona all of which he died possessed. It amounts to about two thousand a year; of which one thousand is to come to her at once, the other on the death of his mother.

To Ridgway, the under-gardener, he willed three hundred pounds, "as some small compensation for the evil done to him," so runs the document, written in a distinct but trembling hand. And then follow one or two bequests to those friends he had left in Australia and some to the few from whom he had received kindness in colder England.

No one is forgotten by him; though once "he is dead and laid in grave" he is forgotten by most.

They put him to rest in the family vault, where his ancestors lie side by side,—as Mona promised him,—and write Sir Paul Rodney over his head, giving him in death the title they would gladly have withheld from him in life.

CHAPTER XXXVI.

HOW MONA DEFENDS THE DEAD—AND HOW LADY LILIAS EATON WAXES ELOQUENT.

As hour follows upon hour, even the most poignant griefs grow less. Nature sooner or later will come to the rescue, and hope "springing eternal" will cast despair into the background. Paul Rodney's death being rather more a shock than a grief to the inmates of the Towers, the remembrance of it fades from their minds with a rapidity that astonishes even themselves.

Mona, as is only natural, clings longest to the memory of that terrible day when grief and gladness had been so closely blended, when tragedy followed so fast upon their comedy that laughter and tears embraced each other and gloom overpowered their sunshine. Yet even she brightens up, and is quite herself again by the time the "merry month of May" comes showering down upon them all its wealth of blossom, and music of glad birds, as they chant in glade and dell.

Yet in her heart the erring cousin is not altogether forgotten. There are moments in every day when she recalls him to her mind, nor does she ever pass the huge tomb where his body lies at rest, awaiting the last trump, without a kindly thought of him and a hope that his soul is safe in heaven.

The county has behaved on the occasion somewhat disgracefully, and has declared itself to a man—without any reservation—unfeignedly glad of the chance that has restored Sir Nicholas to his own again. Perhaps what they just do *not* say is that they are delighted Paul Rodney shot himself: this might sound brutal, and one must draw the line somewhere, and a last remnant of decency compels them to draw it at this point. But it is the thinnest line possible, and easily stepped across.

Even the duchess refuses to see anything regrettable in the whole affair, and expresses herself to Lady Rodney on the subject of her nephew's death in terms that might almost be called congratulatory. She has been listened to in silence, of course, and with a deprecating shake of the head, but afterwards Lady Rodney is unable to declare to herself that the duchess has taken anything but a sound common-sense view of the matter.

In her own heart, and in the secret recesses of her chamber, Nicholas's mother blesses Mona for having returned the pistol that February afternoon to the troublesome young man (who is so well out of the way), and has entertained a positive affection for the roots of trees ever since the sad (?) accident.

But these unholy thoughts belong to her own breast alone, and are hidden carefully out of sight, lest any should guess at them.

The duke calling at the Towers about a month after Paul Rodney's death, so far forgets himself as to say to Mona, who is present,—

"Awful luck, your getting rid of that cousin, eh? Such an uncomfortable fellow, don't you know, and so uncommonly in the way."

At which Mona had turned her eyes upon him,—eyes that literally flashed rebuke, and had told him slowly, but with meaning, that he should remember the dead could not defend themselves, and that she, for one, had not as yet learned to regard the death of any man as "awful luck."

"Give you my word," said the duke afterwards to a select assembly, "when she looked at me then out of her wonderful Irish eyes, and said all that with her musical brogue, I never felt so small in all my life. Reg'lar went into my boots, you know, and stayed there. But she is, without chaff or that, she really *is* the most charming woman I ever met."

Lady Lilias Eaton, too, had been rather fine upon the Rodney ups and downs. The history of the Australian's devotion had been as a revelation to her. She had actually come out of herself, and had neglected the Ancient Britons for a full day and a half,—on the very highest authority,—merely to talk about Paul Rodney. Surely "nothing in his life became him like the leaving it:" of all those who would scarcely speak to him when living, not one but converses of him familiarly now he is dead.

"So very strange, so unparalleled in this degenerate age," says Lady Lilias to Lady Rodney speaking of the will episode generally, and with as near an approach to enthusiasm as it is possible to her to produce, "A secret panel? How interesting! We lack that at Anadale. Pray, dear Lady Rodney, do tell me all about it again."

Whereupon Lady Rodney, to whom the whole matter is "cakes and ale," does tell it all over again, relating every incident from the removal of the will from the library by Paul, to his surrender of it next day to Mona.

Lady Lilias is delighted.

"It is quite perfect, the whole story. It reminds me of the ballads about King Arthur's Knights of the Round Table."

"Which? the stealing of the will?" asks Lady Rodney, innocently. She knows nothing about the Ancient Britons, and abhors the very sound of their name, regarding them as indecent, immoral people, who went about insufficiently clothed. Of King Arthur and his round knights (as she *will* call them, having once got so hopelessly mixed on the subject as to disallow of her ever being disentangled again) she knows even less, beyond what Tennyson has taught her.

She understands, indeed, that Sir Launcelot was a very naughty young man, who should not have been received in respectable houses,—especially as he had no money to speak of,—and that Sir Modred and Sir Gawain, had they lived in this critical age, would undoubtedly have been pronounced bad form and expelled from decent clubs. And, knowing this much, she takes it for granted that the stealing of a will or more would be quite in their line: hence her speech.

"Dear Lady Rodney, no," cries the horrified Æsthetic, rather losing faith in her hostess. "I mean about his resigning lands and heritage, position, title, everything—all that a man holds most dear, for a mere sentiment. And then it was so nice of him to shoot himself, and leave her all his money. Surely you must see that?"

She has actually forgotten to pose, and is leaning forward quite comfortably with her arms crossed on her knees. I am convinced she has not been so happy for years.

Lady Rodney is somewhat shocked, at this view of the case.

"You must understand," she says emphatically, "he did not shoot himself purposely. It was an accident,—a pure accident."

"Well, yes, so they say," returns her visitor, airily who is plainly determined not to be done out of a good thing, and insists on bringing in deliberate suicide as a fit ending to this enthralling tale. "And of course it is very nice of every one, and quite right too. But there is no doubt, I think, that he loved her. You will pardon me, Lady Rodney, but I am convinced he adored Mrs. Geoffrey."

"Well, he may have," admits Lady Rodney, reluctantly, who has grown strangely jealous of Mona's reputation of late. As she speaks she colors faintly. "I must beg you to believe," she says, "that Mona up to the very last was utterly unaware of his infatuation."

"Why, of course; of course. One can see that at a glance. And if it were otherwise the whole story would be ruined,—would instantly become tame and commonplace,—would be, indeed," says Lady Lilias, with a massive wave of her large white hand, "I regret to say, an occurrence of everyday life. The singular beauty that now attaches to it would disappear. It is the fact that his passion was unrequited, unacknowledged, and that yet he was content to sacrifice his life for it, that creates its charm."

"Yes, I dare say," says Lady Rodney, who is now wondering when this high-flown visitor will take her departure.

"It is like a romaunt of the earlier and purer days of chivalry," goes on Lady Lilias, in her most prosy tone. "Alas! where are they now?" She pauses for an answer to this difficult question, being in her very loftiest strain of high art depression.

"Eh?" says Lady Rodney, rousing from a day-dream. "I don't know, I'm sure; but I'll see about it; I'll make inquiries."

In thought she had been miles away, and has just come back to the present with a start of guilt at her own neglect of her guest. She honestly believes, in her confusion, that Lady Lilias has been making some inquiries about the secret panel, and therefore makes her extraordinary remark with the utmost *bonhommie* and cheerfulness.

It is quite too much for the Æsthetic.

"I don't think you *can* make an inquiry about the bygone days of chivalry," she says, somewhat stiffly, and, having shaken the hand of her bewildered friend, and pecked gently at her cheek, she sails out of the room, disheartened, and wounded in spirit.

CHAPTER XXXVII.

HOW MONA REFUSES A GALLANT OFFER—AND HOW NOLLY VIEWS LIFE THROUGH THE BRANCHES OF A PORTUGAL LAUREL.

Once again they are all at the Towers. Doatie and her brother—who had returned to their own home during March and April—have now come back again to Lady Rodney, who is ever anxious to welcome these two with open arms. It is to be a last visit from Doatie as a "graceful maiden with a gentle brow," as Mary Howitt would certainly have called her, next month having been decided upon as the most fitting for transforming Dorothy Darling into Dorothy Lady Rodney. In this thought both she and her betrothed are perfectly happy.

Mona and Geoffrey have gone to their own pretty house, and are happy there as they deserve to be,—Mona proving the most charming of chatelaines, so naive, so gracious, so utterly unaffected, as to win all hearts. Indeed, there is not in the county a more popular woman than Mrs. Geoffrey Rodney.

Yet much of their time is spent at the Towers. Lady Rodney can hardly do without Mona now, the pretty sympathetic manner and comprehensive glance and gentle smile having worked their way at last, and found a home in the heart that had so determinedly hardened itself against her.

As to Jack and Violet, they have grown of late into a sort of moral puzzle that nobody can solve. For months they have been gazing at and talking to each other, have apparently seen nothing but each other, no matter how many others may be present; and yet it is evident that no understanding exists between them, and that no formal engagement has been arrived at.

"Why on earth," says Nolly, "can't they tell each other, what they have told the world long ago, that they adore each other? It is so jolly senseless, don't you know?"

"I wonder when you will adore any one, Nolly," says Geoffrey, idly.

"I do adore somebody," returns that ingenuous youth, staring openly at Mona, who is taking up the last stitch dropped by Lady Rodney in the little scarlet silk sock she is knitting for Phyllis Carrington's boy.

"That's me," says Mona, glancing at him archly from under her long lashes.

"Now, how did you find it out? who told you?" asks Mr. Darling, with careful surprise. "Yes, it is true; I don't seek to deny it. The hopeless passion I entertain for you is dearer to me than any other more successful affection can ever be. I worship a dream,—an idea,—and am happier in my maddest moments than others when most same.

"Bless me, Nolly, you are not going to be ill, are you?" says Geoffrey. "Such a burst of eloquence is rare."

"There are times, I confess," goes on Mr. Darling, disposing of Geoffrey's mundane interruption by a contemptuous wave of the hand, "when light breaks in upon me, and a joyful, a thrice-blessed termination to my dream presents itself. For instance, if Geoffrey could only be brought to see things as they are, and have the grace to quit this mortal globe and soar to worlds unknown, I should then fling myself at your feet, and——"

"Oh—well—don't," interrupts Mrs. Geoffrey, hastily.

"Eh! you don't mean to say that after all my devotion you would then refuse me?" asks Mr. Darling, with some disgust.

"Yes, you, and every other man," says Mona, smiling, and raising her loving eyes to her husband.

"I think, sir, after that you may consider yourself flattened," says Geoffrey, with a laugh.

"I shall go away," declares Nolly; "I shall go aboard,—at least as far as the orchard;" then, with a complete change of tone, "By the by, Mrs. Geoffrey, will you come for a walk? Do: the day is 'heavenly fair.'"

"Well, not just now, I think," says Mona, evasively.

"Why not?" persuasively: "it will do you a world of good."

"Perhaps then a little later on I shall go," returns Mona, who, like all her countrywomen, detests giving a direct answer, and can never bring herself to say a decided "no" to any one.

"As you evidently need support, I'll go with you as far as the stables," says Geoffrey, compassionately, and together they leave the room, keeping company until they gain the yard, when Geoffrey turns to the right and makes for the stables, leaving Nolly to wend his solitary way to the flowery orchard.

———

It is an hour later. Afternoon draws towards evening, yet one scarcely feels the change. It is sultry, drowsy, warm, and full of a "slow luxurious calm."

"Earth putteth on the borrow'd robes of heaven,And sitteth in a Sabbath of still rest;And silence swells into a dreamy sound,That sinks again to silence.The runnel hathIts tune beneath the trees,And through the woodlands swellThe tender trembles of the ringdove's dole."

The Rodneys are, for the most part, in the library, the room dearest to them. Mona is telling Doatie's fortune on cards, Geoffrey and Nicholas are discussing the merits and demerits of a new mare, Lady Rodney in still struggling with the crimson sock,—when the door is opened, and Nolly entering adds himself to the group.

His face is slightly flushed, his whole manner full of importance. He advances to where the two girls are sitting, and stops opposite Mona.

"I'll tell you all something," he says, "though I hardly think I ought, if you will swear not to betray me."

This speech has the effect of electricity. They all start; with one consent they give the desired oath. The cards fall to the ground, the fortune forgotten; the mare becomes of very secondary importance; another stitch drops in the fated sock.

"They've done it at last," says Mr. Darling, in a low, compressed voice. "It is an accomplished fact. I heard 'em myself!"

As he makes this last extraordinary remark he looks over his left shoulder, as though fearful of being overheard.

"Who?" "What?" say Mona and Dorothy, in one breath.

"Why, Jack and Violet, of course. They've had it out. They are engaged!"

"No!" says Nicholas; meaning, "How very delightful!"

"And you heard them? Nolly, explain yourself," says his sister, severely.

"I'm going to," says Nolly, "if you will just give me time. Oh, what a day I've been havin', and how dear! You know I told you I was going to the orchard for a stroll and with a view to profitable meditation. Well, I went. At the upper end of the garden there are, as you know, some Portugal laurels, from which one can get a splendid survey of the country, and in an evil moment it occurred to me that I should like to climb one of them and look at the Chetwoode Hills. I had never got higher than a horse's back since my boyhood, and visions of my earlier days, when I was young and innocent, overcame me at that——"

"Oh, never mind your young and innocent days: we never heard of them," says Dorothy, impatiently. "Do get on to it."

"I did get on to it, if you mean the laurel," says Nolly with calm dignity. "I climbed most manfully, and, beyond slipping all down the trunk of the tree twice, and severely barking my shins, I sustained no actual injury."

"What on earth is a shin?" puts in Geoffrey, *sotto voce*.

"Part of your leg, just below your knee," returns Mr. Darling, undaunted. "Well, when I got up at last, I found a capital place to sit in, with a good branch to my back, and I was so pleased with myself and my exploit that I really think—the day is warm, you know—I fell asleep. At least I can remember nothing until voices broke upon my ear right below me."

Here Mona and Dorothy grow suddenly deeply interested, and lean forward.

"I parted the leaves of the laurel with cautious hand and looked down. At my very feet were Jack and Violet, and"—mysteriously—"she was pinning a flower into his coat!"

"Is that all?" says Mona, with quick contempt, seeing him pause. "Why, there is nothing in that! I pinned a flower into *your* coat only yesterday."

The *naivete* of this speech is not to be surpassed.

Nolly regards her mournfully.

"I think you needn't be unkinder to me than you can help!" he says, reproachfully. "However, to continue. There's a way of doing things, you know, and the time Violet took to arrange that flower is worthy of mention; and when at last it was settled to her satisfaction, Jack suddenly took her hands in his, just like this, Mrs. Geoffrey," going on his knees before Mona, and possessing himself of both her hands, "and pressed them against his heart, like this and said he——"

Nolly pauses.

"Oh, Nolly, what?" says Mona; "do tell us." She fixes her eyes on his.

"'What darling little hands you have!'" begins Nolly, quite innocently.

"Well, really!" says Mona, mistaking him. She moves back with a heightened color, disengages her hands from his and frowns slightly.

"I wasn't alluding to your hands; though I might," says Nolly, pathetically. "I was only going to tell you what Jack said to Violet. 'What darling little hands you have!' he whispered, with the very silliest expression on his face I ever saw in my life; 'the prettiest hands in the world. I wish they were mine.' 'Gracious powers!' said I to myself, 'I'm in for it;' and I was as near falling off the branch of the tree right into their arms as I could be. The shock was too great. I suppressed a groan with a manful determination to 'suffer and be strong,' and——"

"Never mind all that," says Doatie: "what did she say?"

By this time both Nicholas and Geoffrey are quite convulsed with delight.

"Yes, go on, Noll: what did she say?" repeats Geoffrey, the most generous encouragement in his tone. They have all, with a determination worthy of a better cause, made up their minds to forget that they are listening to what was certainly never meant for them to hear. Or perhaps consideration for Nolly compels them to keep their ears open, as that young man is so overcome by the thought of what he has unwillingly gone through, and the weight of the secret that is so disagreeably his, that it has become a necessity with him to speak or die; but I believe myself it is more curiosity than pity prompts their desire for information on the subject in hand.

"I didn't listen," says Nolly, indignantly. "What do you take me for? I crammed my fingers into my ears, and shut my eyes tight, and wished with all my heart I had never been born. If you wish very hard for anything, they say you will get it. So I thought if I threw my whole soul into that wish just then I might get it, and find presently I never *had* been born. So I threw in my whole soul; but it didn't come off. I was as lively as possible after ten minutes' hard wishing. Then I opened my eyes again and looked,—simply to see if I oughtn't to look,—and there they were still; and he had his arm round her, and her head was on his shoulder, and——"

"Oh, Nolly!" says Dorothy, hastily.

"Well, it wasn't my fault, was it? *I* had nothing to do with it. She hadn't her head on *my* shoulder, had she? and it wasn't *my* arm was round her," says Mr. Darling losing patience a little.

"I don't mean that; but how could you look?"

"Well, I like that!" says her brother. "And pray what was to happen if I didn't? I gave 'em ten minutes; quite sufficient law, I think. If they couldn't get it over in that time, they must have forgotten their native tongue. Besides, I wanted to get down; the forked seat in the laurel was not all my fancy had painted it in the beginning, and how was I to know when they were gone unless I looked? Why, otherwise I might be there now. I might be there until next week," winds up Mr. Darling, with increasing wrath.

"It is true," puts in Mona. "How could he tell when the coast was clear for his escape, unless he took a little peep?"

"Go on, Nolly," says Nicholas.

"Well, Violet was crying (not loudly, you know, but quite comfortably): so then I thought I had been mistaken, and that probably she had a toothache, or a headache, or something, and that the foregoing speech was mere spooning; and I rather lost faith in the situation, when suddenly he said, 'Why do you cry?' And what do you think was her answer? 'Because I am so happy.' Now, fancy any one crying because she was happy!" says Mr. Darling, with fine disgust. "I always laugh when I'm happy. And I think it rather a poor thing to dissolve into tears because a man asks you to marry him: don't you, Mrs. Geoffrey?"

"I don't know, I'm sure. I have never thought about it. Did I cry, Geoffrey, when——" hesitates Mrs. Geoffrey, with a laugh, and a faint sweet blush.

"N—o. As far as I can remember," says Geoffrey, thoughtfully, pulling his moustache, "you were so overcome with delight at the unexpected honor I did you, that——"

"Oh, I dare say," Nicholas, ironically. "You get out!"

"What else did they say, Nolly?" asks Dorothy, in a wheedling tone.

"If they could only hear us now!" murmurs Geoffrey, addressing no one in particular.

"Go on, Nolly," says Doatie.

"You see, I was so filled with the novelty of the idea that it is the correct thing to weep when seated on your highest pinnacle of bliss, that I forgot to put my fingers in my ears again for a few moments, so I heard him say, 'Are you sure you love me?' whereupon she said, 'Are *you* quite sure you love *me*?' with lots of emphasis. That finished me! Did you ever hear such stuff in your life?" demands Mr. Darling, feeling justly incensed. "When they have been gazing into each other's eyes and boring us all to death with their sentimentality for the last three months, they coolly turn round and ask each other if they are sure they are in love!"

"Nolly, you have no romance in your nature," says Nicholas, severely.

"No, I haven't, if that's romance. Of course there was nothing for it but to shut my eyes again and resign myself to my fate. I wonder I'm not dead," says Nolly, pathetically. "I never put in such a time in my life. Well, another quarter of an hour went by, and then I cautiously opened my eyes and looked again, and—would you believe it?"—indignantly,—"there they were still!"

"It is my opinion that you looked and listened all the time; and it was shamefully mean of you," says Dorothy.

"I give you my honor I didn't. I neither saw nor heard but what I tell you. Why, if I had listened I could fill a volume with their nonsense. Three-quarters of an hour it lasted. How a fellow can take forty-five minutes to say, 'Will you marry me?' passes my comprehension. Whenever *I* am going to do that sort of thing, which of course," looking at Mona, "will be never now, on account of what you said to me some time since,—but if ever I should be tempted, I shall get it over in twenty seconds precisely: that will even give me time to take her hand and get through the orthodox embrace."

"But perhaps she will refuse you," says Mona, demurely.

"No such luck. But look here, I never suffered such agony as I did in that laurel. It's the last tree I'll ever climb. I knew if I got down they would never forgive me to their dying day, and as I was I felt like a condemned criminal."

"Or like the 'sweet little cherub that sits up aloft.' There *is* something cherubic about you, do you know Nolly, when one comes to think of it. But finish your tale."

"There isn't much more; but yet the cream of the joke remains," says Nolly, laughing heartily. "They seemed pretty jolly by that time, and he was speaking. 'I was afraid you would refuse me,' he said, in an imbecile tone. 'I always thought you liked Geoffrey best.' 'Geoffrey!' said Violet. (Oh, Mrs. Geoffrey, if you could have heard her voice!) 'How could you think so! Geoffrey is all very well in his way, and of course I like him very much, but he is not to be compared with you.' 'He is very handsome,' said Jack, fishing for compliments in the most indecent manner. 'Handsome! Oh, no,' said Violet. (You really *should* have heard her, Mrs. Geoffrey!) 'I don't think so. Passably good-looking, I allow, but not—not like *you*!' Ha, ha, ha!"

"Nolly, you are inventing," says Mrs. Geoffrey, sternly.

"No; on my word, no," says Nolly, choking with laughter, in which he is joined by all but Mona. "She said all that, and lots more!"

"Then she doesn't know what she is talking about," says Mrs. Geoffrey, indignantly. "The idea of comparing Geoffrey with Jack!"

At this the laughter grows universal, Geoffrey and Nicholas positively distinguishing themselves in this line, when just at the very height of their mirth the door opens, and Violet enters, followed by Captain Rodney.

CHAPTER XXXVIII.

HOW NOLLY DECLINES TO REPEAT HIS STORY—HOW JACK RODNEY TELLS ONE INSTEAD—AND HOW THEY ALL SHOW THEIR SURPRISE ABOUT WHAT THEY KNEW BEFORE.

As they enter, mirth ceases. A remarkable silence falls upon the group. Everybody looks at anything but Violet and her companion.

These last advance in a leisurely manner up the room, yet with somewhat of the sneaking air of those who are in the possession of embarrassing news that must be told before much time goes by. The thought of this perhaps deadens their perception and makes them blind to the fact that the others are unnaturally quiet.

"It has been such a charming day," says Violet, at last, in a rather mechanical tone. Yet, in spite of its stiltedness, it breaks the spell of consternation and confusion that has bound the others in its chains, and restores them to speech.

They all smile, and say, "Yes, indeed," or "Oh, yes, indeed," or plain "Yes," in a breath. They all feel intensely obliged to Violet for her very ordinary little remark.

Then it is enchanting to watch the *petit soins*, the delicate little attentions that the women in a carefully suppressed fashion lavish upon the bride-elect,— as she already is to them. There is nothing under heaven so dear to a woman's heart as a happy love-affair,—except, indeed, it be an unhappy one. Just get a woman to understand you have broken or are breaking (the last is the best) your heart about any one, and she will be your friend on the spot. It is so unutterably sweet to her to be a *confidante* in any secret where Dan Cupid holds first place.

Mona, rising, pushes Violet gently into her own chair, a little black-and-gold wicker thing, gaudily cushioned.

"Yes, sit there," she says, a new note of tender sympathy in her tone, keeping her hand on Violet's shoulder as the latter makes some faint polite effort to rise again. "You must indeed. It is such a dear, cosey, comfortable little chair."

Why it has become suddenly necessary that Violet should be made cosey and comfortable she omits to explain.

Then Dorothy, going up to the new-comer, removes her hat from her head, and pats her cheeks, and tells her with one of her loveliest smiles that she has "such a delicious color, dearest! just like a wee bit of fresh apple-blossom!"

Apple-blossom suggests the orchard, whereon Violet reddens perceptibly, and Nolly grows cold with fright, and feels a little more will make him faint.

Lastly, Lady Rodney comes to the front with,—

"You have not tired yourself, dear, I hope. The day has been so oppressively warm, more like July than May. Would you like your tea now, Violet? We can have it half an hour earner if you wish."

All these evidences of affection Violet notices in a dreamy, far-off fashion: she is the happier because of them; yet she only appreciates them languidly, being filled with one absorbing thought, that dulls all others. She accepts the chair, the compliment, and the tea with grace, but with somewhat vague gratitude.

To Jack his brothers are behaving with the utmost *bonhommie*. They have called him "old fellow" twice, and once Geoffrey has slapped him on the back with a heartiness well meant, and no doubt encouraging, but trying.

And Jack is greatly pleased with them, and, seeing everything just now through a rose-colored veil, tells him self he is specially blessed in his own people, and that Geoffrey and old Nick are two of the decentest old men alive. Yet he too is a little *distrait*, being lost in an endeavor to catch Violet's eyes,—which eyes refuse persistently to be so caught.

Nolly alone of all the group stands aloof, joining not at all in the unspoken congratulations, and feeling indeed like nothing but the guilty culprit that he is.

"How you were all laughing when we came in!" says Violet, presently: "we could hear you all along the corridor. What was it about?"

Everybody at this smiles involuntarily,—everybody, that is, except Nolly, who feels faint again, and turns a rich and lively crimson.

"It was some joke, of course?" goes on Violet, not having received any answer to her first question.

"It was," says Nicholas, feeling a reply can no longer be shirked. Then he says, "Ahem!" and turns his glance confidingly upon the carpet.

But Geoffrey to whom the situation has its charm, takes up the broken thread.

"It was one of Nolly's good things," he says, genially. "And you know what he is capable of when he likes! It was funny to the last degree,—calculated to set any 'table in a roar.'—Give it to us again, Nolly—it bears repeating.—Ask him to tell it to you, Violet."

"Yes, do, Nolly," says Violet.

"Go on, Noll," exclaims Dorothy, in her most encouraging tone. "Let Violet hear it. *She* will understand it."

"I would, of course, with pleasure," stammers the unfortunate Nolly,—"only perhaps Violet heard it before!"

"Well, really, do you know, I think she did!" says Mona, so demurely that they all smile again.

"I call this beastly mean," says Mr. Darling to Geoffrey in an indignant aside. "You all gave your oaths to secrecy before I began, and now you are determined to betray me, I call it right-down shabby. And I sha'n't forget it to any of you, let me tell you that."

"My dear fellow, you can't have forgotten it so soon," says Geoffrey, pretending to misunderstand this vehement whisper. "Don't be shy! or shall I refresh your memory? It was, you remember, about——"

"Oh, yes—yes—I know; it doesn't matter; (I'll pay you out for this"), says Nolly, savagely, in an aside.

"Well, I do like a good story," says Violet, carelessly.

"Then Nolly's last will suit you down to the ground," says Nicholas. "Besides its wit, it possesses the rare quality of being strictly true. It really occurred. It is founded on fact. He himself vouches for the truth of it."

"Oh, go on; do," says Mr. Darling, in a second aside, who is by this time a brilliant purple from fear and indignation.

"Let's have it," says Jack, waking up from his reverie, having found it impossible to compel Violet's eyes to meet his.

"It is really nothing," says Nolly, feverishly. "You have all heard it before."

"I said so," murmurs Mona, meekly.

"It is quite an old story," goes on Nolly.

"It is, in fact, the real and original 'old, old story," says Geoffrey, innocently, smiling mildly at the leg of a distant table.

"If you are bent on telling 'em, do it all at once," whispers Nolly, casting a withering glance at the smiling Geoffrey. "It will save time and trouble."

"I never saw any one feel the heat so much as our Oliver," says Geoffrey, pleasantly. "His complexion waxeth warm."

"Would you like a fan, Nolly?" says Mona, with a laugh, yet really with a kindly view to rescuing him from his present dilemma. "Do you think you could find me mine? I fancy I left it in the morning-room."

"I am sure I could," says Nolly, bestowing upon her a grateful glance, after which he starts upon his errand with suspicious alacrity.

"How odd Nolly is at times!" says Violet, yet without any very great show of surprise. She is still wrapped in her own dream of delight, and is rather indifferent to objects in which but yesterday she would have felt an immediate interest. "But, Nicholas, what was his story about? He seems quite determined not to impart it to me."

"A mere nothing," says Nicholas, airily; "we were merely chaffing him a little, because you know what a mess he makes of anything of that sort he takes in hand."

"But what was the subject of it?"

"Oh—well—those thirty-five charming compatriots of Mona's who are now in the House of Commons, or, rather, out of it. It was a little tale that related to their expulsion the other night by the Speaker—and—er—other things."

"If it was a political quip," says Violet, "I shouldn't care about it."

This is fortunate. Every one feels that Nicholas is not only clever, but singularly lucky.

"It wasn't *all* politics, of course," he says carefully.

Whereupon every one thinks he is a bold and daring man thus to risk fortune again.

It is at this particular moment that Violet, inadvertently raising her head, lets her eyes meet Jack Rodney's. On which that young man—being prompt in action—goes quickly up to her, and in sight of the assembled multitude takes her hand in his.

"Violet, you may as well tell them all now as at any other time," he says, persuasively.

"Oh, no, not now," pleads Violet, hastily. She rises hurriedly from her seat, and lays her disengaged hand on his lips. For once in her life she loses sight of her self-possession, and a blush, warm and rich as carmine, mantles on her cheek.

This fond coloring, suiting the exigencies of the moment suits her likewise. Never before has she looked so entirely pretty. Her lips tremble, her eyes grow pathetic. And Captain Rodney, already deeply in love, grows one degree more impressed with the fact of his own good fortune in having secured so enviable a bride.

Passing his arm round her, he draws her closer to him.

"Mother, Violet has promised to marry me," he says abruptly. "Haven't you, Violet?"

And Violet says, "Yes," obediently, and then the tears come into her eyes, and a smile is born upon her lips, so sweet, so new, as compels Doatie to whisper to Mona, a little later on, that she "didn't think it was in Violet to look like that."

Here of course everybody says the most charming thing he or she can think of at a moment's notice; and then they all kiss Violet, and Nolly, coming back at this auspicious instant with the fan and recovered temper, joins in the general congratulations, and actually kisses her too, though Geoffrey whispers "traitor" to him in an awful tone, as he goes forward to do it.

"It is the sweetest thing that could have happened," says Dorothy, enthusiastically. "Now Mona and you and I will be real sisters."

"What a surprise it all is!" says Geoffrey, hypocritically.

"Yes, isn't it?" says Dorothy, quite in good faith; "though I don't know after all why it should be; we could see for ourselves; we knew all about it long ago!"

"Yes, *long* ago," says Geoffrey, with animation. "Quite an hour ago."

"Oh! hardly!" says Violet with a soft laugh and another blush. "How could you?"

"A little bird whispered it to us," explains Geoffrey, lightly. Then, taking pity on Nolly's evident agony, he goes on "that is, you know, we guessed it; you were so long absent, and—and that."

There is something deplorably lame about this exposition, when you take into consideration the fact that the new lovers have been, during the past two months, *always* absent from the rest of the family, as a rule.

But Violet is content.

"It is like a fairy-tale, and quite as pretty," says little Dorothy, who is quite safe to turn out an inveterate matchmaker when a few more years have rolled over her sunny head.

"Or like Nolly's story that he declines telling me," says Violet, with a laugh.

"Well, really, now you say it," says Geoffrey, as though suddenly struck with a satisfactory idea, "it is uncommonly like Nolly's tale: when you come to compare one with the other they sound almost similar."

"What! How could Jack or I resemble an Irish member?" asks she, with a little grimace.

"Everything has its romantic side," says Geoffrey, "even an Irish member, I dare say. And when you do induce Nolly to favor you with his last joke, you will see that it is positively bristling with romance."

CHAPTER XXXIX.

HOW WEDDING-BELLS CAN BE HEARD IN THE DISTANCE—HOW LOVE ENCOMPASSES MONA—AND HOW AT LAST FAREWELL IS SPOKEN.

And now what remains to be told? But little, I think! For my gentle Mona has reached that haven where she would be!

Violet and Dorothy are to be married next month, both on the same day, at the same hour, in the same church,—St. George's Hanover Square, without telling. From old Lord Steyne's house in Mayfair, by Dorothy's special desire, both marriages are to take place, Violet's father being somewhat erratic in his tastes, and in fact at this moment wandering aimlessly among the Himalayas.

Mona is happier than words can say. She is up to her eyes in the business, that business sweetest to a woman's soul, the ordering and directing and general management of a trousseau. In her case she is doubly blessed, because she has the supervizing of two!

Her sympathy is unbounded, her temper equal to the most trying occasion, her heart open to the most petty grievances; she is to the two girls an unfailing source of comfort, a refuge where they may unrebuked pour out the indignation against their dressmakers that seems to rage unceasingly within their breasts.

Indeed, as Dorothy says one day, out of the plenitude of her heart, "How we should possibly have got on without you, Mona, I shudder to contemplate."

Geoffrey happening to be present when this flattering remark is made, Violet turns to him and says impulsively,—

"Oh, Geoffrey, wasn't it well you went to Ireland and met Mona? Because if you had stayed on here last autumn we might have been induced to marry each other, and then what would have become of poor Jack?"

"What, indeed?" says Geoffrey, tragically. "Worse still, what would have become of poor Mona?"

"What is it you would say?" exclaims Mona, threatingly, turning towards him a lovely face she vainly tries to clothe with anger.

"It is insupportable such an insinuation," says the lively Doatie. "Violet, Mona's cause is ours: what shall we do with him?"

"'Brain him with his lady's fan!'" quotes Violet, gayly, snatching up Mona's fan that lies on a *prie-dieu* near, and going up to Geoffrey.

So determined is her aspect that Geoffrey shows the white feather, and, crying "*mea culpa*," beats a hasty retreat.

From morn to dewy eve, nothing is discussed in bower or boudoir but flounces, frills, and furbelows,—three *f*'s that are considered at the Towers of far more vital importance than those other three of Mr. Parnell's forming. And Mona, having proved herself quite in good taste in the matter of her own gowns, and almost an artist where coloring is concerned, is appealed to by both girls on all occasions about such things as must be had in readiness "Against their brydale day, which is not long."—As, for instance:—

"Mona, do you think Elise is right? she is so very positive; are you sure heliotrope is the correct shade to go with this?" Or—

"Dearest Mona, I must interrupt you again. Are you very busy? No? Oh, then do come and look at the last bonnet Madame Verot has just sent. She says there will be nothing to equal it this season. But," in a heart-broken voice, "I cannot bring myself to think it becoming."

Lady Rodney, too, is quite happy. Everything has come right; all is smooth again; there is no longer cause for chagrin and never-ending fear. With Paul Rodney's death the latter feeling ceased, and Mona's greatness of heart has subdued the former. She has conquered and laid her enemy low: without the use of any murderous force the walls have fallen down before her, and she has marched into the citadel with colors flying.

Yet does she not triumph over her beaten foe; nay, so different is it with her that she reaches forth her hand to raise her again, and strives by every tender means in her power to obliterate all memory of the unpleasant past.

And Lady Rodney is very willing that it should be obliterated. Just now, indeed, it is a favorite theory of hers that she could never have been really uncivil to dear Mona (she is always "dear Mona" of late days) but for the terrible anxiety that lay upon her, caused by the Australian and the missing will, and the cruel belief that soon Nicholas would be banished from the home where he had reigned so long as master. Had things gone happily with her, her mind would not have been so warped, and she would have learned at once to understand and appreciate the sweetness of the dear girl's character! And so on.

Mona accepts this excuse for bygone injustice, and even encourages her mother-in-law to enlarge upon it,—seeing how comfortable it is to her so to do,—and furthermore tries hard in her own kind heart to believe in it also.

She is perhaps as near being angry with Geoffrey as she can be when one day he pooh-poohs this charitable thought and gives it as his belief that worry had nothing to do with it, and that his mother behaved uncommonly badly all through, and that sheer obstinacy and bad temper was the cause of the whole matter.

"She had made up her mind that you would be insupportable, and she couldn't forgive you because you weren't," says that astute young man, with calm conviction. "Don't you be taken in, Mona."

But Mona in such a case as this prefers being "taken in" (though she may object to the phrase), and in process of time grows positively fond of Lady Rodney.

"In company with so divine a face, no rancorous thoughts could live," said the duke on one memorable occasion, alluding to Mona, which speech was rather a lofty soat for His Grace, he being for the most part of the earth, earthy.

Yet in this he spoke the truth, echoing Spenser (though unconsciously), where he says,——

"So every spirit, as it is most pureAnd hath in it the more of heavenly light.So it the fairer bodie doth procureTo habit in.For of the soule the bodie forme doth take,For soule is forme and doth the bodie make."

With Lady Rodney she will, I think, be always the favorite daughter. She is quite her right hand now. She can hardly get on without her, and tells herself her blankest days are those when Mona and Geoffrey return to their own home, and the Towers no longer echoes to the musical laugh of old Brian Scully's niece, or to the light footfall of her pretty feet. Violet and Dorothy will no doubt be dear; but Mona, having won it against much odds, will ever hold first place in her affections.

After all, she has proved a great success. She has fought her fight, and gained her victory; but the conquered has deep reason to be grateful to her victor.

Where would they all be now but for her timely entry into the library on that night never to be forgotten, and her influence over the poor dead and gone cousin? Even in the matter of fortune she has not been behindhand, Paul Rodney's death having enriched her beyond all expectation. Without doubt, therefore, there is good reason to rejoice over Mrs. Geoffrey.

To this name, given to her in such an unkindly spirit, Mona clings with singular pertinacity. Once when Nolly has called her by it in Lady Rodney's hearing, the latter raises her head, and a remorseful light kindles in her eyes; and when Mr. Darling has taken himself away she turns entreatingly to Mona, and, with a warm accession of coloring, says, earnestly,—

"My dear, I behaved badly to you in that matter. Let me tell Oliver to call you Mrs. Rodney for the future. It is your proper name."

But Mona will not be entreated; sweetly, but firmly, she declines to alter the *sobriquet* given her so long ago now. With much gentleness she tells Lady Rodney that she loves the name; that it is dearer to her than any other could ever be; that to be Mrs. Geoffrey is the utmost height of her very heighest ambition; and to change it now would only cause her pain and a vague sense of loss.

So after this earnest protest no more is ever said to her apon the subject, and Mrs. Geoffrey she is now to her mends, and Mrs. Geoffrey, I think, she will remain to the end of the chapter.

THE END.

9 789357 95928